Daylight Come

ALSO BY JOSHUA JELLY-SCHAPIRO

Names of New York

Island People

Nonstop Metropolis
(with Rebecca Solnit)

Cuba Then, Cuba Now

Chris Ofili:
Paradise LostPòtoprens: The Urban Artists
of Port-au-Prince (contributing editor)

SIGNIFICATIONS

Series editor
Henry Louis Gates, Jr.

Daylight Come

Harry Belafonte
and the World
He Made

JOSHUA JELLY-SCHAPIRO

PENGUIN PRESS   NEW YORK   2026

PENGUIN PRESS
An imprint of Penguin Random House LLC
1745 Broadway, New York, NY 10019
penguinrandomhouse.com

[TK; If applicable, insert the photo/text credits or the page reference to the credits here.]

LIBRARY OF CONGRESS CATALOGING-IN-PUBLICATION DATA
INSERT CIP DATA [TK]

Printed in the United States of America
$PrintCode

The authorized representative in the EU for product safety and compliance is Penguin
Random House Ireland, Morrison Chambers, 32 Nassau Street, Dublin D02 YH68,
Ireland, https://eu-contact.penguin.ie.

[ded tk]

Daylight Come

1

Harry was the first. You have to start with that. In 1956, a Harlem-bred son of Caribbean immigrants released the first million-selling LP in history. Belafonte was bigger than Elvis. And that's not the only first to which he laid claim in his triumphant march across American media in the years that followed. He was the first Black movie star, thanks to a star turn in *Island in the Sun* (in 1957), to become a matinee idol, and the first Black person to produce a prime-time special on network TV and to win an Emmy (for *Tonight with Belafonte* in 1959). He was America's first Black pop star to be as desired for his body as his music, and the first to cause a major scandal for having his elbow touched by a white lady (Petula Clark) on television. His performance-cum-translation of the Caribbean for the masses—white

Americans for whom his music felt playful, foreign, and thereby racially and sexually safe—allowed him to straddle racial, sexual, and political taboos unthinkable to his Black contemporaries.

Calypso, the historic LP that helped him do so, was a suite of Caribbean folk tunes that won the top spot on *Billboard*'s charts in June 1956—and stayed there for an unprecedented thirty-one weeks (before being knocked from its perch by—who else—Elvis Presley). Belafonte's name-making record didn't just cement his stature as a new kind of American celebrity. It launched a putative "calypso craze," which convinced not a few commentators that calypso was poised to upend rock 'n' roll as the dominant fad among American teens. ("Warning: Calypso Next New Beat; R.I.P. for R'n'R?," trumpeted *Variety* in December 1957.) In retrospect, such predictions seem to have had less to do with the music's actual popularity than with the wishful thinking of parents who found Belafonte's open-collared-but-still-dignified eroticism less scandalous than the louche gyrations of Elvis's pelvis. Nonetheless: it is hard to oversell the significance of the record that heralded the curious genre of world music; inspired the name of the most popular vocal group in America prior to the Beatles—the Kingston Trio; and perhaps most important, as Belafonte himself later put it, "proved that Americans were more ready than had been assumed to hear the voices of others or the culture of other people."

That last potent fact was, and remains, a crucial achievement. But what's perhaps most remarkable about it, and all those firsts that followed, is that his early success was a mere forerunner and spark for his larger public life. He used the cash he earned from scaling pop's heights not to build mansions but to bankroll, in the late 1950s, a still-speculative movement for civil rights—and then to assume an indispensable role, as that movement picked up steam, as the crucial bridge between its protest marches and Hollywood's stars; between Black preachers who led the movement and white liberals who backed it; between Martin Luther King Jr., the minister who became Harry's best friend, and the federal government. As the movement reached its most intense phase in the early 1960s, he was the only person to speak, on a near-daily basis, with both Dr. King and Robert F. Kennedy, the attorney general who was at first a tricky foil for King's aims but became a crucial ally.

But those also-remarkable facts, and all the firsts that marked his career's opening acts, are only part of how his story at once resonated with, and has shaped, the story of his age. When in 1968 he accepted a historic invitation from Johnny Carson to serve as a guest host of *The Tonight Show* for an entire week, he invited his august friends from politics and showbiz—from Lena Horne and Bobby Kennedy to Marlon Brando, Sidney Poitier, and Buffy Sainte-Marie—to speak with unvarnished candor about America's ills and the disastrous war in Vietnam. He used an interview with Dr. King, not two months before King was killed, to ask if he feared for his life. It was an encounter on national TV, seen by millions, that only one man—Harry Belafonte—could have made happen. But it bears new weight when you consider that Harry had for years by then footed the bill for his friend's health care and supported his family. Far more than a celebrity fundraiser or spokesman, he was an integral part of this movement that changed the country forever.

America had seen Black celebrities before Belafonte. And in the postwar years, others also won mass-market appeal. Sammy Davis Jr. did so as the Rat Pack's self-deprecating mascot. Sidney Poitier became one of Hollywood's biggest stars by enacting, with gracious manners and un-American charm, a Black man who anyone but the most dire racist would be glad to bring home to dinner. The persona that Harry cultivated wasn't dissimilar to the one his close friend Sidney, a fellow West Indian who was from the Bahamas, used to scale Hollywood's heights: as a "Caribbean gentleman"— foreign and charming, proper and safe—whose image was far more palatable to whites than were Black entertainers descended from America's slaves. But behind Harry's easeful smile, there was also a dose of sexuality and rage that left him allergic to playing roles meant to make whites comfortable. He turned down a few of those that made Poitier famous.

Decades later, talking to me at a restaurant near his home on Manhattan's Upper West Side, he said, "When me and Sidney were coming up, people took the way we carried ourselves as proud, imperial." That's how Harry broke it down, over a plate of littleneck clams the first time we met. "But that's every fucking Jamaican I know! And a lot of them are a pain in the ass!"

Harry, to those closest to him, could be a pain in the ass himself. His outlook was shaped from boyhood by extended sojourns in a Black-majority society—Jamaica—whose history and culture were shaped by its slaves' rebellions against the island's colonial owners, and where mixed-race families like his were commonplace. His Caribbean roots were inseparable from his American success. "I think people perceive him as a nice person," said Johnny Carson, "and if people seem to like you, that's half the game in the entertainment business." Yet part of his magnetism also derived from the anger that drove him—anger at America's racism; anger at himself and his dyslexia; anger at the demons he spent decades unpacking on his therapist's couch. "Perhaps in the end," he said of what he learned there, "where your anger comes from is less important than what you do with it." What he did with his, in alchemizing his ire into his art and activism, changed the world.

Just as remarkable was the more personal journey he undertook to wrestle with his demons and with his country by evolving its culture—a journey that saw him, in ensuing decades, produce a film *(Beat Street)* that helped introduce hip-hop to the world; turn the world's eyes to modern Africa's urgent needs by convening stars ranging from Michael Jackson to Bruce Springsteen and Cyndi Lauper, to record "We Are the World"; and move from being a genial fixture on *The Muppet Show* and *Sesame Street,* in the 1970s and '80s, to later become an elder radical and sometimes moral scold. Harry's life's third and fourth and fifth acts were as remarkable as those preceding them.

What forces conspired, back when it all began, to help him become America's "first Negro matinée idol"? How did he become the dominant figure in American pop right before the emergence of Elvis? What made him a kind of Representative Man capable of meaning all things to all people? In his life's last decades, he became a totem of black pride known for his intemperate radicalism (calling fellow son of the Caribbean Colin Powell "a house slave"). But once he was our first post-racial pop star. He was also a hero to immigrants, a sex symbol who was also a wholesome folkie, a teen idol who even your parents could love. How did Belafonte—not only brown-skinned but an avowed leftist, and an actor of unexceptional talent who got over as a singer—achieve his astonishingly wide appeal in Eisenhower's America? One obvious answer is the one his fellow folk singer Odetta supplied to that question: "Have you *seen* the man?"

Quite apart from his looks, though, were Belafonte's innovations as a performer. He took folk music off its stool to make the presentation of dusty old songs an occasion for dynamic modern theater, and he used Caribbean music to forge his image as an erotic symbol and romantic lead. A decade before interracial marriage became fully legal in the United States, Belafonte's evocation of the islands got Americans to confront their history and try to change their present. As a struggling young actor in New York, he began singing in jazz clubs to make rent. But then he found his musical métier in the "folk revival" that took root among urban sophisticates in Greenwich Village and beyond, drawn to the musical traditions of common people. He reveled in learning to perform Irish ballads and Israeli reels and folk tunes from Mexico and Mississippi. But his act also departed, in the pop polish and verve he lent that repertoire, from the folkies' fetish for authenticity—a mysterious quality whose strictures seemed to eschew any Black singer who hadn't done time on a chain gang or sold his soul at some crossroads down south.

A 1962 cover story on folk's rise in *Time* magazine, focusing on Joan Baez, went so far as to dub him "Belaphony." An appraisal that's aged better came from Baez's ex, Bob Dylan, who also transcended the scene that nurtured them all by plugging in at Newport to become an icon of uncompromising art. "Everything about him was gigantic," Dylan wrote. "The folk purists had a problem with him, but Harry—who could have kicked the shit out of all of them—couldn't be bothered, said that all folksingers were interpreters."

Unlike Dylan, he didn't write his own songs; he mediated others'. And it was as a mediator of culture and enactor of songs—carried by his gorgeous voice, lent the beauty of his person—that he brought the stories of his people to the world. His brilliance as a performer was as a translator of folk histories, and the lives of working people, into the idiom of pop. By performing these stories, he created his own—and insisted, as he would his whole career, on telling his story on his terms. On the eve of the civil rights movement, he used his canny charisma to turn Americans' minds toward the legacies of slavery by singing of the Caribbean—a region that abounded in lilting melodies, but to whose islands were also trafficked the majority of the more than ten million enslaved Africans who, between the sixteenth and nineteenth centuries, survived the Middle Passage to this hemisphere.

The fact and legacies of that history have suffused this republic's culture and politics since its founding. Ongoing battles over iniquities that endure, and resentment at attempts to redress them, powered the ascent to the White House of a president who has suffused our public sphere with venality and hate, and with edicts proclaiming English the "official" tongue of the most polyglot society the world has ever seen. In Trump's America, "the voices of others or the culture of other people," upon which Harry built his career, are verboten. About these developments, Harry had much to say before he passed. Criticizing presidents, notwithstanding his old friendship with the Kennedys, was a lifelong vocation (and extended to his often-fierce frustration with the moderate policies, from 2008 to 2016, of America's first Black one). Before he was a friend to the establishment, he was a man of the left and of the streets. His heroes and pals were political radicals like Paul Robeson, his mentor in stage-craft and Marxism; Dr. King and Nelson Mandela; prison abolitionists and trade unionists and advocates for #Black-LivesMatter whose comradeship he cherished later on—these were his people. One way to understand how his devotion to the edges shifted the mainstream is to see how his history entwined with that of the American president before Trump—and not merely because Harry used his juice, in 1961 and with JFK, to help arrange an airlift that brought hundreds of African students, including one from Kenya who became Barack Obama's dad, to the United States.

In Obama's memoir *Dreams from My Father*, there's a passage in which Obama describes a moment with his mother in a Manhattan movie house watching the Marcel Camus film *Black Orpheus*. He observes, with growing discomfort, the delight his white mother takes in the images of brown-skinned bodies dancing their way through a Brazilian slum. He realizes then how much of his cherished mom's life and politics—and indeed her attraction to his Kenyan father—had been born of her curiosity about difference—or perhaps her erotic attachment to it. This curiosity was first instilled, she'd often tell her son, when she'd fallen in love as a Kansas schoolgirl with the music and person of Harry Belafonte. For Obama, this moment arrives as a subtle lesson about the intimate registers on which race can act in our lives. But what it suggests as well is Belafonte's larger significance to post-war U.S. culture—as a figure Obama's mother was hardly alone in regarding as "the best-looking man on the planet."

In his stage shows from those years, it was that very universal appeal out of which he liked to make a famous spectacle. "Women over forty!" he'd entreat during the chorus to "Matilda," as captured on his famous *Belafonte at Carnegie Hall* record. "Now the intellectuals!" Decades before Barack Obama won the White House and Beyoncé became American culture's queen, Belafonte forged a blackness safe enough for the masses not by kowtowing to whites, or occluding his ethnicity and pride, but by making both essential to his glamour and grace. The story of his extraordinary rise, and of the ends to which he leveraged his affinities and fame, is not solely about his personal gifts and the anger that drove him. Nor is it one about the talents and acumen, not only onstage but also for business, that helped him succeed. It is also a story about the larger shifts in postwar America's economy and culture that shaped his sensibility and afforded his success—the advent of stereo sound and the long-playing record; the flourishing of a folk revival whose ethos and sounds would long reverberate; the rise of television as the prime medium and maker of celebrity in American life.

And it's a story, too, about political history: the ending of colonial rule across the Third World and the admittance of one hundred new member-nations to the UN; the mass migration, during the Cold War, of thousands of immigrants from the Caribbean to New York; the birth and rise, in the United States, of a mass movement for racial justice.

All of us, of course, are products of our age. But Belafonte was that rare popular figure who also both exemplified and influenced the larger cultural and political history of his. His pop heyday is now seven decades past, but few Americans haven't heard "Day O" echoing around a ballpark, smiled at its rendition in *Beetlejuice*, or tapped their feet to "Jamaica Farewell" during a cruise vacation. Many baby boomers recall Belafonte as a pleasant if disposable part of their youth, but by the time he died in 2023, at age ninety-six, he was venerated by a new generation of activists and entertainers for connecting dots between popular culture and politics and grassroots movements for justice. In the century since he was born, in March 1927, to a young woman who'd just landed in New York from an impoverished corner of the British West Indies, Harry's voice has resounded across America and around the globe to help create the culture we inhabit today.

2

Melvine Love, known as Millie to her friends, was twenty-one when she boarded a steamer in Jamaica bound for jazz-age New York. She arrived at Ellis Island with fifty dollars of "show money" (a sum then required of all migrants there) furnished by a sister who'd preceded her to Harlem. She became one of the 300,000 West Indians who left the British Caribbean in the first decades of the twentieth century, and whose growing presence in New York was, as the Barbadian American novelist Paule Marshall wrote in her novel *Brown Girl, Brownstones*, "like a dark sea nudging its way onto a white beach and staining the sand."

Around the same time Marshall released that book in the fifties, another child of the same migration—Millie

Love's son—scored an American hit with his version of a song from Trinidad, the island where calypso was born, called "Man Smart (Woman Smarter)." The tune had been penned there in the 1930s by a calypsonian called King Radio. It was later covered by everyone from Joan Baez to the Grateful Dead: its pop feminist sentiment may have been timeless. But its original context was an era when large numbers of King Radio's countrywomen, like women across the West Indies, were decamping for New York to "work some money" in the United States. Most of the West Indian women who joined this migration were unmarried. Many of them, upon arriving in Harlem or Brooklyn, took rooms in apartments or boarding houses run by other women from their home islands. Millie Love wasn't so lucky. Her big sister Liz promptly told her, when Millie landed at her flat in Harlem, that she'd need to find another place to stay and a man to help her.

Liz had found her way in New York by running her own "bank" in the illegal numbers game by which Harlem's denizens, placing bets on which three digits would end the day's Treasury yield or total purse at Belmont Park, played the lottery. She knew that Millie, who'd been a fine student in Jamaica, was determined to thrive by other means in what Paule Marshall called "this man country." Before Millie left her flat, Liz succeeded in introducing her sister to a handsome fellow Jamaican who shared her light-brown complexion—Harold Bellanfanti said his father was a Dutch Jew from Martinique—and who was also commended by the fact that he had a steady job. He was a shipboard cook on United Fruit Company vessels steaming between the Caribbean and New York Harbor. Millie's big sister, approving of their union, offered her a room to consummate it. The next year, on March 1, Millie had a son. She named him Harold Bellanfanti Jr.

Her new husband's surname, now bequeathed to her son, sounded French. But its syllables meant something like "beautiful child" in Portuguese, and its roots are commonly traced to the era of the Spanish Inquisition, when Iberia's Jews, known as *conversos,* were forced to hide their heritage and adopt Catholic-sounding monikers. The alchemy by which "Bellanfanti" became "Belanfonte" and finally "Belafonte," in New York in the thirties, derived from a new era's needs for concealment. Harold's bride, Millie, wasn't a legal resident of the U.S., and nor was he. For this reason, and because she was poor, she moved her family often. Changing her married name's spelling, when she moved apartments or registered her sons for school (Harry's little brother, Dennis, arrived when he was five), was about staying out of sight. So was her determination, as Harry later said of why he had no family photos from boyhood, that they never be photographed. She wanted, at least until she got her papers, to stay invisible.

———

Jamaica, the island from which Millie Love hailed, and where she'd soon return with her son to leave him with her own mum for "safekeeping," was still a British crown colony: a Black-majority and patois-speaking society whose official language was the Queen's English and whose head of state, until it finally won independence in 1962, was a white regent in far-off London. Its demography and culture were molded by its longtime stature as the most lucrative and brutal of England's plantation colonies—an island to which nearly two million enslaved Africans, among them Belafonte's Black forebears, were trafficked to cut sugarcane during the Triangle Trade, which began in earnest about 150 years after Christopher Columbus bumped into what he called the "Indies."

It was on the island of Barbados that an enterprising Englishman first realized, in the 1600s, there were fortunes to be made in America's tropics from growing a crop whose refined form, as a white powder called sucrose, soon hooked Europe's plebes and nobles alike. The Caribbean's other colonial powers, French and Spanish and otherwise, followed the English lead. Needful of workers for their fields, they spent the next two-plus centuries importing enslaved Black ones from across the sea. The trade's ships joined the Old World's ports to West Africa and the Americas in an ignoble circuit that built its owners châteaus and factories in Europe. It also brought no fewer than six million enslaved Africans, from the ancient kingdoms of Congo and Calabar and Dahomey, to the ports of the Caribbean and turned Jamaica—where fully a third of those Africans who reached the region disembarked—into one of the Triangle Trade's most vital nodes.

The Caribbean wasn't the only corner of this hemisphere where enslaved Africans landed, of course. Of the 12.5 million people who began the Middle Passage, and the 10.7 million who survived it, more than four million landed in Brazil. The North American colonies that became the United States also received some—but less than 400,000. Picking cotton in Dixie, while awful work, wasn't so brutal an industry as not to allow people to survive more than a few harvests, as was the case among many sugar workers in the West Indies. By the start of the Civil War, that 400,000 had grown into an African American populace of over four million. But the stark fact of the far larger number of enslaved Africans who landed in the Caribbean, where tens of millions of their descendants live today, suggests a larger historical truth about this region that's long been viewed as marginal.

The Caribbean islands were and remain the Americas' foremost beachhead, alongside Brazil, for the arrival and evolution of African cultures in this hemisphere. The wealth that those cultures' bearers created, for its islands' colonial owners, was vital to the forging of a global economy. The raw materials they harvested and the money they made them also afforded the factories that spawned the industrial revolution in Europe and the rise of capitalism worldwide. The Caribbean was, in a sense, where globalization began. Its islands have been central to the making of our modern world. And this is largely why one of the region's leading historians, C. L. R. James, also argued that its islands' enslaved peoples and their descendants have had a unique role to play in shaping modern world culture.

For James, who hailed from Trinidad, the progeny of the Caribbean's slaves were unique among the world's formerly colonized people because even the islands' poorest denizens, as he put it in 1963, had for centuries "lived what was in its essence a modern life." They'd crossed the ocean to toil at industry; they'd learned European languages and made them their own; they'd lived on islands where "even the cloth they wore and [what] they ate was imported." Caribbean societies were defined by long-distance trade, and cultural mixing, from the start. And now their daughters and sons, in C. L. R. James's view, were unique. "Of all the world's formerly colonial coloured peoples," he wrote, "the West Indian masses are the most highly experienced in the ways of Western civilization and most receptive to its requirements in the twentieth century."

In the latter half of that century, as a hundred old colonies of Europe joined the UN as newly sovereign nations, exponents of the Caribbean did their best to prove James right. Many leading intellectuals from what came to be called the Third World—figures with names like Fanon and Garvey and Castro and Césaire—hailed from here. So did fashioners of its islands' music, from reggae and salsa to reggaeton and hip-hop, which became the rhythms to which the globe danced. The daughters and sons of the Caribbean, steeped equally in the cultures of Africa and the languages and ideas of Europe for centuries, have shaped "the ways of Western civilization" indeed. One reason is how Caribbean sugar slavery differed from its counterpart in the cotton kingdom of the U.S. south. Slave regimes varied—in Spanish Cuba and Puerto Rico, for example, the enslaved were allowed to play drums and assemble in ways the English, in Jamaica and Antigua and Nevis, wholly proscribed. But across an archipelago whose ties to Africa were constantly replenished by new arrivals from the continent, sugar slavery bore some common traits. One was its sheer brutality. Another, not unrelated, was the vigor with which it was resisted by enslaved Africans who fled coastal plantations to join fugitive "Maroons" in their islands' mountains and launched armed revolts on many of them.

The most famous of these occurred in France's prize plantation colony of Saint-Domingue, a sugar juggernaut where a million enslaved Africans rose up, in 1791, to burn their master's fields and proclaim the constitution, with rhetoric borrowed from Rousseau and Voltaire, of a new Black nation on the world stage. How universal, really, the Black followers of Toussaint L'Ouverture asked the *Lumières* in Paris, were universal rights? The Haitian Revolution inspired slave revolts across the islands. In nearby Jamaica, England's own sugar juggernaut, Haiti's model inspired folk songs hailing the deaths of white masters— "buckra buckra, he be die!" goes one. The Maroons who'd settled Jamaica's forbidding interior had waged guerrilla war on the English, by then, for decades; Maroon leaders like Queen Nanny and Cudjoe were folk heroes. So were the leaders of rebellions against the British like one in the 1760s known as Tacky's Revolt, and a later one launched by a Baptist deacon called Samuel Sharpe that compelled them, in the early 1830s, to move toward abolishing slavery throughout their empire.

When Harry told me that the West Indians with whom he was raised in New York "were constantly in a state of rebellion," he wasn't just referring to his mother's cohort of immigrants. In Jamaica, the fact and memory of rebellions launched by the island's enslaved has long been key to the nation's identity. And it remained so when Jamaicans left their island, alongside emigrants from across the Caribbean, for world cities in Europe and North America where they were destined, per C. L. R. James, to leave their mark on the world.

This out-migration from the British West Indies didn't commence immediately upon slavery's end. For several decades after 1838, most descendants of the enslaved stayed put. On some English islands—notably Trinidad—they were replaced by indentured workers from India. On others, like Barbados and Jamaica, some ex-slaves briefly became "apprentices" whose lives differed little from their forebears'. The sugar trade's center moved to places—notably Cuba and Brazil—where slavery lasted nearly until the age of the automobile. In Jamaica, the owners and overseers of old plantations began planting other crops for export—coffee and cacao, and bananas later on—to wrest profits from their acreage by the island's edges. Many of their old fieldhands headed for its interior. They gained communal title to sloping plots where they grew food—sweet potatoes and yams, ackee and okra—that's still peddled in the market towns dotting Jamaica's hills by women, known as "higglers," who drive a peasant economy that's never been rich in cash.

For Jamaicans, winning access to money and to a life not lived in a zinc-roofed shack has long meant leaving the countryside—whether for the island's capital of Kingston, or, beginning in the early 1900s, leaving altogether. The first large spur to do so arrived in the form of recruiters from the Panama Canal project: U.S.-based contractors who, between 1904 and 1914, recruited thousands of men from across the West Indies to dig their canal across Panama's isthmus. In that era when the United States—whose troops had just expelled Spain from Cuba and Puerto Rico— was asserting itself as the Caribbean basin's de facto imperial minder, the second spur to emigration was less discreet. It was dominated not by men but by women who, in many cases, were staked by "Panama money" from their brothers or uncles. They headed not for Central America but to the U.S., where the "great migration" of Blacks from the southern U.S., who were fleeing Jim Crow for new lives in northern cities, was in full flood. These pioneering West Indians set their sights especially to New York, decades before many of their peers headed for England. And they settled there in new Black enclaves where their sisters and kin—in Brooklyn neighborhoods like Bedford Stuyvesant and Crown Heights;

the part of Manhattan's west side once known as San Juan Hill; and uptown, too—were setting up shop.

In Harlem, where Millie Love settled and set out to raise her son, the Black American paragons of the Harlem Renaissance—Langston Hughes and Duke Ellington, Countee Cullen and Zora Neale Hurston—were joined by eminences from the Caribbean whose creativity and drive, in political activism as much as the arts and business, also molded its culture. Among these were Claude McKay, the Jamaica-born writer who published proud poems in island patois and whose novels, from *Banana Bottom* to *Home to Harlem*, evinced love for both his natal and adopted homes and excoriated the idiocy of American racism; Arturo Schomburg, the Puerto Rican bibliophile and scholar whose grand home, on 135th Street, became a branch of the New York Public Library that Harry frequented in his youth (and where he had his papers sent before he died); and, most especially, Marcus Garvey—a fellow child of Jamaica's Saint Ann Parish who in 1914 founded an organization there, the Universal Negro Improvement Association, whose cause he then brought to Harlem and trumpeted to the world.

Garvey first engaged with politics as a trade unionist while working as a printer in Kingston, but after traveling to Costa Rica and then to England as a young man, he hatched his dream of uniting persons of African descent, around the world, into a single political community. "Africa for the Africans, those at home and those abroad": that was the slogan he touted in an admiral's hat befitting the founder of the shipping company—the Black Star Line—by which he proposed to return the continent's children to her. That scheme, like Garvey's larger sojourn in America, came to grief when he was indicted on charges of mail fraud and deported. But that didn't stop Millie, like many of her contemporaries in jazz-age and Depression-era Harlem, from joining his ardent followers, becoming a "Garveyite," and impressing on her son that their people's identity, and prospects for uplift, were inseparable from belonging to a larger diaspora.

In his boyhood, Harry was less interested in these ideas than in getting into fights on Harlem's streets. Notwithstanding the wealth of role models to choose from in the neighborhood, his first hero was another one of Millie's streetwise siblings who ran its numbers games. His uncle Lenny was a charismatic crook around town who took his nephew to see Joe Louis fight and helped his mum buy groceries each week. Once, young Harry saw Lenny knock out a cop with one punch for quibbling over his protection money from the numbers racket. That was one strong childhood memory. Another was accompanying his mum, on weekday mornings, to the stone archways under the elevated train lines on upper Park Avenue where domestics like her, lining 96th Street where Harlem met the Upper East Side, went to hunt work. Picked up by society women and housewives, whether WASPs from the East Side or Jews from across Central Park, she often brought her young son to the tony apartments where she cooked or washed clothes for pay. At night, they'd return to Harlem and one or other of the cramped rooms Millie rented, usually in a flat shared with other women and only sporadically with her husband, Harold. He would turn up, after weeks away at sea, to listen to Millie decry his failings as a husband, and then, after the pair downed a bottle of rum to salve their pain, to make drunken love behind a thin curtain that did little to hide what was happening from their young son a few feet away.

Thus did young Harry learn, as he'd later recall in his memoir, *My Song*, that "sex was a powerful thing [that] changed people. But not completely, and not for long." From his parents, this future carnival king learned, he said, "that sex wasn't about two people with real feelings communicating; it was a strange and rather alarming exercise in unreality in which both participants were drunk: a bacchanal." But Harry's strongest memories of his father, from those years, were more painful. They involved a tricycle his hardworking mum bought him for his fourth birthday; an outing with his father to try it out; a mischievous ride, defying his father's orders to stop, down a hill near Harlem's Polo Grounds; a stand of bushes and a switch that Harold Sr. used to beat the boy once he caught up to him; and his false promise, as he walked his bloodied son home, to buy him a toy boat if he repeated his lie, to Millie, that his wounds derived not from his father's hand but some bullies who'd tried to steal his trike.

These are the aspects of Harold Sr.'s involvement in Harry's boyhood, and lack thereof, that he spent years unpacking in therapy. But there was another way, at once more prosaic and more germane to the art he made later on, that Harold Sr. shaped the course of his young son's life. For it was Harold Sr.'s vocation aboard a freighter that ferried tropical fruit that enabled Millie to send Harry to her own mum there, more than once in his boyhood, for "safekeeping." I don't know whether Harry ever spoke to his analyst about how, or if, his relationship with his dad played into his feelings about the tune—"The Banana Boat Song"—that became his biggest hit. But it's only apt that these ships, which for a big span of the twentieth century tied America to the tropics, so colored his boyhood.

3

The cultivation of sweet-tasting foodstuffs has shaped Caribbean history for five hundred years. And in the late 1800s, after slavery's end in the British islands, sugar was joined by another cash crop for which a market was fast emerging up north. At the 1876 Centennial Exposition in Philadelphia, some inspired mind seized on the idea of selling pieces of brown-speckled yellow fruit from the island, wrapped in foil, for a dime. Bananas were a hit. Within a few decades, big *Gros Michel* bananas—picked green in the Caribbean, and allowed to ripen en route to New Orleans or New York—became the first tropical fruit to be a part of Americans' daily diet. The silly yellow fruit became a part of their culture that was freighted, from the start, with suggestive meaning.

In 1923, the United States' most popular song was called "Yes! We Have No Bananas," a ditty first penned for Broadway that Louis Prima, a son of Italian immigrants in New Orleans who grew up alongside the booming banana trade there, later scored a hit with. Josephine Baker, also in the twenties, thrilled audiences from Stockholm to San Francisco with her "banana dance," performed nude save for a skirt of bananas dangling from her waist, suggesting the members of her conquests. A couple of decades later, the United Fruit Company introduced their ubiquitous mascot: a comely singing piece of fruit, Miss Chiquita Banana, who was at least partly modeled on Carmen Miranda, the Brazilian bombshell whose banana-bedecked headdress, in movies like *The Gang's All Here* (1943), helped make her a symbol of tropical sex. In the fifties, when Belafonte was a symbol of tropical and other kinds of sex, too, he recorded the most famous banana song of all. But already by his Depression-era boyhood, Americans had made bananas their favorite fruit—we still eat more of them than apples and oranges combined. The banana trade's leading companies maintained fleets of freighters to ferry fruit north from Central America and the Antilles. In the 1920s and '30s, the United Fruit Company's "great white fleet" steamed between the U.S. and ports across the Caribbean basin to herald the modern cruise industry: booking passage in its ships' staterooms was a way for adventuresome Americans to visit the tropics—and for emigrants from the islands to head in the other direction.

It was on one such boat that Millie Love made her way from Jamaica to Manhattan. And it was on another that she deposited her son—in care of his dad after he got into too many fistfights in first grade and had his leg broken by a car on Harlem's streets—to go home again to the Jamaican village where her mum lived.

"I still have the impression of an environment that sang." That's how, later on, Harry described what he found in Jamaica in 1934. "Nature sang, and the people sang, too." That may have been so: Belafonte the singer always made his island boyhood—his stay in Jamaica lasted, off and on, until his teens—a staple of his onstage patter. The affection his grandmother Jane Love offered, which matched her name and was less complicated than his troubled mum's, afforded him happiness during his time in her humble home. It also granted him the ease he felt, later on, moving between races and classes as an adult: in his memoir, he credits that trait "to the fact that Jane, who was as white and blue-eyed as a person can be, so enveloped me with love." Since the 1700s, Jamaica's populace has been dominated by the descendants of African slaves. But the island was also a haven for outcasts and pirates and merchants, from across Europe and the Levant and beyond, who came to the Caribbean to seek their fortunes or, more commonly, to help grow the fortunes of others.

The Love family's forebears, as evinced by his grandmother's white skin, belonged to a latter group: the class of impoverished Scots, known as "red legs," who came to the West Indies as indentured workers or to work as overseers on English-owned plantations. Those owners named the hamlet near Jamaica's north coast where Jane Love lived Aboukir, after another corner of their empire: the town in Egypt where Horatio Nelson famously bested Napoleon, in 1798, in the Battle of the Nile. Pronounced "Ah-boo-ka" by locals, Aboukir is in the island's "garden parish" of Saint Ann—a corner of Jamaica best known for being where Columbus alighted in 1494, on a beach called Discovery Bay, and for a pair of native sons who became world-famous later on.

Marcus Garvey, born in Saint Ann's Bay in 1887, grew up there before he left for New York. So did Bob Marley, who was born in 1945 and later laid to rest in a hamlet a few hilltops from Aboukir, where sandal-wearing tourists now come to hail the reggae superstar's music and memory. Marley's own family history, as a mixed-race son of Saint Ann's hills, resembled Belafonte's. His mother was a dark-skinned granddaughter of Saint Ann's enslaved; her peasant kin, farming its sloping plots, grew dasheen and yams. His white father was the ne'er-do-well son of an imperial merchant in Kingston, employed as a surveyor of crown lands in the area. This pair's son, Nesta Robert Marley, moved to the island's capital with his mum and grew up alongside a new homegrown record business whose signature rhythms— ska, rocksteady, reggae—made Jamaica famous. After heading to London in the early 1970s, he joined reggae to a rock star's mien and wrote brilliant songs that would make him, before the decade was out, the first "Third World Superstar." Many of those songs evoked the afterlives of the TriangleTrade that formed the Jamaican countryside where he—and Belafonte and Garvey—grew up.

On "Slave Driver," the second track on Marley's breakout LP in 1973, he addressed himself to the enforcers of old iniquities ("Slave driver / the tables have turned . . .") and then to his people who, whether dwelling back in Jamaica or in the ghettos of northern cities, were still suffering its legacies: "Today they say that we are free," he sang, "only to be chained in poverty." His worldview, on that record and every one that followed, was deeply shaped by the ideas of Marcus Garvey. If one of Garvey's legacies was the conception of a Black diaspora, another was a supposed prophecy that helped found the religion—Rastafari—that Marley and many of his cohort embraced, a couple generations later, to confront history's scars. (It was Garvey's urging, "Look to the east, for the crowning of a Black king," that led Rastafari's founders to adopt Emperor Haile Selassie of Ethiopia as their savior.) Belafonte, sandwiched between them at the century's middle, was raised by a Garveyite and led a peripatetic youth that fed his determination, later on and in the stories he collected and the songs he sung, to illuminate what bound Harlem's tenements to Jamaica's fields, and the poverty he grew up amidst in both.

When he was nine, after another ill-starred stab at school in Harlem, Millie brought Harry and his younger brother, Dennis, back to Jamaica once more. She looked for but didn't find work in Kingston, and installed her boys in what became a series of boarding homes, including one owned by some cousins who were far less loving than their grandmother, but who Millie paid to house Harry—poor Dennis, only four years old, was placed elsewhere—while she went back to Harlem. In Kingston, he was no less given to the strict British curricula at the schools he attended—Morris Knibb, Wolmer's, Half Way Tree—than he was to the lessons on offer at PS 186 on 145th Street. He attributed his struggles learning to read to an injury he'd sustained to his left eye while playing with scissors at his grandmother's in Aboukir; in fact, he was dyslexic. When decades later he was awarded an honorary doctorate by the University of the West Indies, he joked to Jamaica's former prime minister, Michael Manley, that he'd attended every school in Kingston. More memorable than his time in any of them were the hours he spent, after dismissal, wandering a town whose jangling streets echoed with song.

"*Guava jelly, guava cheese . . . yellow yam, yellow yam, come get your yellow yam,*" the higglers cried, as he described in his memoir, along with the streets' other songs:

> The fishmongers were the best; they had a new song for whatever their catch of the day was. At the wharf, mento bands would sing to the endless stream of tourists disembarking from cruise ships. Even politicians sang to gather crowds before delivering their speeches. A politician named Simpson had an artificial leg made of cork that buffered the stump against the wooden peg. "*Cork foot Simpson, the Vagabon' / If I catch you I chop off the other one*" was the verse written and sung by the opposition candidate. Simpson won the contest, and on the night of his victory he responded by singing his victory rebuttal.

Among the instruments those mento bands played, alongside their guitars and shakers, was a wood-and-iron thumb piano that's known in Jamaica as a "rumba box," which closely resembles the instrument, from Central Africa, best known as an mbira.

In Harlem, Harry's favorite radio show was *Amos 'n' Andy*. His mother, who worshipped Franklin and Eleanor Roosevelt, never missed one of FDR's fireside chats. In Kingston, Harry's colonial kin spent evenings glued to a wood-paneled radio tuned to the BBC. Listening to the London Philharmonic play Beethoven, conducted by Sir Thomas Beecham, left an impression. So did the stentorian diction of the BBC's presenters. Jamaica's official language and civilizational ideal was the Queen's English, but the island's lingua franca was the marvelous variant of that tongue called patois. Its tuneful lilt joined England's lexicon to African syntax; Jamaicans approach consonants and diphthongs by removing "h" sounds from some English words and adding it to others ("eggs" are "heggs"), while eschewing the "th" sound altogether. It's the tongue Harry's Scots Jamaican grandmother used when she cried, as he'd lovingly recall, "Where me 'arry? Where me sweet boy 'arry?"

Years later, Belafonte and his marketers would claim that his biggest hits were songs he'd first learned in Jamaica as a boy. It wasn't true: his repertoire was adopted, in the main, from tunes he first heard or learned not in Jane Love's hamlet, but Greenwich Village. But in the hills of Saint Ann, where he spent breaks from school in Kingston, he absorbed the language and sounds that inspired them. And seventy years after he did so, in a rum shop by the dusty soccer field in Aboukir, it didn't take me long to find one of his maternal cousins, a brown-skinned man who recalled Jane Love's old home, by a nearby knoll called Old Bethany. When I asked if I could see it, he told me that the place was knocked down after Harry's uncle Callbeck, the last of the Loves to live there, sold it off to take a job, down in Saint Ann's Bay, working for Kaiser Aluminum.

Back in New York, I wrote Belafonte a letter about this encounter. He replied warmly and arranged to meet for lunch near his home on the Upper West Side. I brought him a book that I thought he'd enjoy: a first edition of Katherine Dunham's *Journey to Accompong*—a landmark portrait of Jamaica's Maroons that Dunham, the pioneering choreographer of Afro-American dance, penned from fieldwork she conducted there as a PhD student in anthropology in the 1930s. Harry thanked me kindly. And then he reflected, in the gravelly voice for which he became known in old age, on how his Caribbean identity aided his success in Eisenhower's America. Harry's white fans, who embraced his sunny songs of the West Indies, he agreed, were responding to the same "unthreatening" quality they projected onto his pal Sidney—and to that imperious pride, not unrelated, with which they carried themselves. "People from the Caribbean," he said, "did not respond to America's oppressions in the same way that Black Americans did. We were constantly in a state of rebellion, constantly in a state of thinking way above that which we were given." He explained further, over his littleneck clams and cranberry juice: "I had no particular crisis with white people. Because I never really saw them as in any way superior. Americans—Black Americans—had crises, because not only were they forced to believe that white people were superior, but in many instances they bought it. And they made peace with it. We didn't."

4

They made peace with it. We didn't." Those are fighting words. And words that distill much about why, in the United States, West Indians and U.S.-born Blacks, despite being placed in the same category by America's racial mores, haven't always gotten along. But race, like beauty, is in the eye of the beholder. And Harry's boyhood travels between Jamaica and New York influenced his understanding of both. He was darker-skinned than his brother and his mum, whose olive complexion helped her talk her way into more than one Manhattan apartment verboten to Negroes by claiming to be "Spanish." Meanwhile, in Kingston, the light skin of the family who housed Harry signaled their membership in the island's Creole elite. Harry's own au-lait aspect may have been browner than theirs. But in a still-colonial society, that higher "mulatto" status distinguished him from the island's African masses—even if he and his adoring Scots Jamaican grandmother shared their poverty.

But that was Jamaica. In 1940, he returned to New York. Race, as a nonsensical idea, is confusing everywhere. But in the United States, social hierarchies have been a matter not of gradation but of stark divides, still drawn according to the "one-drop rule." And at his new junior high school in Upper Manhattan, Harry's Irish and Greek classmates reminded him as much. They appraised his kinky hair and not-white skin, and told him: "You're a nigger."

He denied it by insisting, with force backed up by his fists, that his family from Martinique was French. Bemused, they called him "Frenchy"—but still didn't invite them to their parties. In the fifties, he was profiled by *The Saturday Evening Post* and recounted how jarring this was, after having spent his pubescence absorbing the contradictions of caste and color in Jamaica. "Those class distinctions," he said, "seemed a peculiar set of values. Then at thirteen I came back to New York, and ran smack into racial discrimination. This was not only very painful, but something I could not reason out. It sort of shut me up inside myself." He was lonely and friendless, and still struggling to read. Halfway through the ninth grade, he dropped out.

By then his parents had moved on from their stormy

marriage and found new mates. Millie had taken up with the kindly super in her building; she'd soon have two more kids to care for. Her ex, Harold, now the head chef at a restaurant in Union Square, married a German woman with whom he lived in the Bronx and plainly enjoyed, to the wonder of a fourteen-year-old Harry, a far more pacific relationship than he'd had with Millie. His parents' union was molded by poverty and youth and drink; it was perhaps doomed from the start. But now Harry, visiting his father at his restaurant or up in the Bronx, got to know a softer side of Harold. Harry was also now contending, in new ways, with Millie's berate-ments. His leaving school had crushed her immigrant's dreams. He saw with new eyes how her "deeply rooted cer-tainty that men were feckless creatures destined to fail her," as he put it, may have played a role in his dad doing so. And he worried, as he absorbed her disapproval into his own ad-olescent torpor, if he might himself fulfill her prophecy.

He delivered groceries and worked as a tailor's assis-tant. He pushed racks of clothes in Manhattan's garment district. And then, as he neared his seventeenth birthday, a better way to get further from Millie than midtown became clear. This was late 1943; World War II was in full swing. One day, Harry went to the movies and caught *Sahara*, a Humphrey Bogart vehicle that left him transfixed not by Bogie's presence but by that of a Black American actor named Rex Ingram. In the film, Ingram plays a Sudanese soldier who aids a motley crew of Allied soldiers on the run, in the Libyan desert, from a German regiment. He meets his heroic end by chasing down a German soldier and strangling him in the desert's sands to save Bogie and his friends, before dying under a hail of bullets. Harry had never witnessed Black heroism in a Hollywood movie. Doing so left its mark. So did *Sahara*'s depiction of the role that Blacks might play in the righteous fight against the Nazis.

By early 1944, the Allies were beginning, in North Africa and Europe, to turn the tide against Hitler. Uncle Sam needed recruits; seventeen-year olds could join the fight, with a letter from a parent. March 1 of that year, his birthday, was the first day Harry could sign up. He knew he liked being at sea, from his voyages to and from Jamaica. With a letter from Millie, he enlisted in the Navy. He shipped out for basic training to a naval base by Lake Michigan.

"Diaspora": the word derives from the Greek—to sow over, or scatter. Its first use to refer to people rather than seeds was Thucydides's; in the fifth century BC, he described a diaspora of Greeks, scattered across the Aegean by war. Later on, "diaspora" showed up in the Greek translation of the Hebrew Bible: in Deuteronomy, the dispersal of Jews from

Babylon was a diaspora, too. The Jewish diaspora, for a couple of millennia thereafter and well into the twentieth century, was the one people knew: its scattered members' dream of return to an ancestral home shaped modern Zionism. Marcus Garvey, and the generation of Pan-Africanists who followed, were inspired by Zionists' aims. They applied similar ideas, as proponents of a diaspora whose own existence and name became common knowledge only in the mid-twentieth century, to Black people around the globe.

For Belafonte, the son of a Garveyite who'd spent his youth moving between the Black mecca of Harlem and Jamaica's fields, the African diaspora was life. His time among Black midshipmen and draftees from across the country gave him a greater sense of its diversity and reach. In New York he had passed for a time, or tried to, as "Frenchy." In the military there would be none of that. The Navy, like all the Pentagon's forces' in 1944, was segregated: Uncle Sam, it became clear, saw Seaman Belafonte just as his white classmates had in junior high: as a "nigger," only fit to serve America's cause as a munitions loader or clerk. At Naval Station Great Lakes, outside Chicago, he was placed in an all-Black camp.

His time among his fellow Black servicemen was eye-opening. It also supplied him, as a high school dropout who became a proud autodidact, with his essential political education. He met impoverished Alabamans and Texans who spoke in thick drawls he could barely understand; educated dentists and CPAs who spoke proudly of their families and nice houses on the Black sides of Pittsburgh or Kansas City; attitudinal draftees, from Chicago and New Orleans, who ridiculed any Negro dumb enough to have volunteered—Harry stayed quiet—for an army led by crackers. It was, as he later told an interviewer, "diaspora in the flesh." And his company also included, among its more sophisticated members, proud "race men" to whose bull sessions he listened with fascination. They gave him pamphlets published by the NAACP and books by W. E. B. Du Bois—revelatory accounts of the larger history of Black people in America that suggested a program for advancing their lot in American society, not boarding a flotilla of steamers for Africa, as Marcus Garvey advocated.

Reading Du Bois's *Dusk of Dawn,* as he worked to conquer his dyslexia at last, wasn't easy. But he came away intrigued by Du Bois's learning—and by his advocacy for a brand of advancement that didn't involve separating from American institutions but integrating them. He was also eager to impress the men who'd handed this book to him, and hungry to know more. He rode the train into Chicago from the base and, having worked out that the footnotes to

Du Bois's text contained a skeleton key to a larger body of learning, visited the public library. Several of the titles he asked for were available. His requests for others didn't bear fruit—but did yield an anecdote that this proud autodidact loved to repeat: in those footnotes he pored through, there was one source that Professor Du Bois cited more than any other. Belafonte insisted, to a librarian, that he wanted every book she had by the writer "Ibid." To her confused protests that there was no such author, he replied with rage. It was only when he returned to base and recounted what had happened to his intellectual mentors, that he understood. The poor volunteer librarian he'd berated at Chicago's public library also hadn't known, as they explained with laughter, that "Ibid." was mere scholarly shorthand for the Latin term, *ibidem*, used to cite a source previously listed.

At the end of basic training, Harry took an exam: it revealed an aptitude for organizing spreadsheets. He was sent, with a portion of his Great Lakes cohort, to the Navy's new school for shopkeepers in Hampton Roads, Virginia. Doling out skivvies and toothpaste to sailors seemed a better way to serve than humping bombs onto boats. And the shopkeepers' school had also been set up on the grounds of the Hampton Institute—a historically Black university that was founded after the Civil War on the grounds of an old plantation by the Chesapeake to train freed slaves to be teachers. The proximity of his new barracks to Hampton's library, and the new pool and gym the Navy built for its "gobs" there, was a bonus. The proximity to Hampton's coeds, and to one of them in particular, even more so.

Marguerite Byrd was a senior at Hampton studying to be a child psychologist. She first caught Harry's eye when he glimpsed her giving prospective students a tour of campus. She caught it again when, at a Hampton football game, he saw her ride across the field, gorgeous and poised atop a Chevrolet ragtop: the homecoming queen. He convinced her, after weeks of pestering her outside her dorm, to go out with him on a date. He vowed, recalling his mother's proviso that he had to marry a girl with "good hair" (which Marguerite had: it wasn't kinky, and fell to her shoulders), to wed her. Marguerite was a daughter of Washington, D.C.'s Black bourgeoisie—her father was an accountant—who exemplified another side of Black America that was new to her odd immigrant suitor from New York: the segregated middle class, content to live and strive in a Black American world, and who had as little interest in integrating white society as in boarding a steamer for Africa. The pair's dates quickly became debates, in ways that agreed with them both, about whether racism was best confronted by battling second-class citizenship head-on, as Harry's temper led him to do, or by seeking more gradual upliftment, as Marguerite was doing, by pursuing a profession via Black institutions like Hampton.

―――

Harry's hot head, and his tendency toward fisticuffs, didn't depart him in the Navy. One night while on guard duty, he was reprimanded by a white officer for falling asleep. Harry went to punch him, but landed in the brig instead. He was sentenced to two weeks at the Portsmouth Naval Prison, up in Maine. There he was shocked to find that a coterie of German prisoners of war—captured U-boat captains in fur-lined jackets—were treated far better, by its guards, than the prison's Black inmates.

At another point during Harry's eighteen-month stint in the service, Harry and a trainload of fellow Black seamen were deposited to a part of the Navy's vast "fleet city," on the northern edge of the Bay above San Francisco and Oakland, called Port Chicago. Its docks had just been the site of a disaster whose remnants were still visible: bent steel and debris were everywhere. On July 17, 1944, munitions being loaded onto a ship at Port Chicago by Black servicemen ignited, causing a chain reaction and huge explosion that shook the port and sent a fireball skyward that was visible for miles. Three hundred twenty sailors died and three hundred ninety more were wounded. Most of them were Black.

Hundreds of their fellow seamen, in the blast's aftermath, had refused to return to work. Fifty of these had been court-martialed and were standing trial for mutiny as Harry and his company arrived in Port Chicago.

His company had been summoned here, it seemed, to replace these men in a role—munitions loaders—that the Navy had long assigned its most expendable men. During the trial of Port Chicago's court-martialed rebels, who were quickly convicted and sentenced to prison terms that ranged from eight to fifteen years, this practice wasn't mentioned. But it would become central to the appeal that the NAACP, and the head of its Legal Defense Fund, Thurgood Marshall, launched on their behalf. Marshall, pleading their case in Washington, noted that the Navy contained 100,000 Black servicemen and not a single Black officer. His cause, and the imprisoned mutineers', was joined by prominent allies like Eleanor Roosevelt—and led the Navy, a couple of years later, to begin desegregating its forces. The "Port Chicago mutiny" came to be seen as a watershed in a larger reckoning in which President Harry Truman, in 1948, desegregated every branch of the service. But what happened at Port Chicago, for many Black Americans, had more expansive implications. It became key to the Double V Campaign that was launched by *The Pittsburgh Courier* and advanced by the Black press nationwide, and which urged that victory over fascism abroad be joined by victories for equality at home for Black servicemen and their families. And it galvanized the determination of many, after the war and in ways that would soon feed a larger movement for civil rights, to stop being treated as second-class citizens.

In the event, and while the war was still going on, Harry was spared the ignominy of replacing deceased or mutinous sailors: Port Chicago's brass filled their ranks of torpedo handlers before his name was called. He was shipped back east. At Weapons Station Earle in New Jersey, where he was stationed for the rest of the war, he was close to home. Happily, he was also in range of Washington, D.C., where Marguerite had returned after graduating from Hampton. He traveled there by train to continue their halting courtship. When Harry's eighteen months in the service were up, he didn't reenlist. He moved back to Harlem, and to the apartment his mother now shared with her new husband, Bill, and their kids, Raymond and Shirley. Harry's stepfather hired him as an assistant janitor. There wasn't much on his horizon beyond cleaning buildings and doing odd jobs for their tenants. But then one of those tenants, in the winter of 1946 and after he helped hang her venetian blinds, gave him a life-changing tip: she handed him a ticket to a play she was appearing in, put on by the American Negro Theatre, at an Elks Lodge on 126th Street.

5

The American Negro Theatre had been founded six years before by an actor named Frederick O'Neal and the playwright Abram Hill, who'd spent the Depression seeking to build a company in Harlem, with support from the Federal Theatre Project, that hewed to W. E. B. Du Bois's vision for a new kind of theater "by, about, for, and near [African Americans]." In 1940, they'd created the ANT. O'Neal and Hill had come of age at a time when good work for Black actors was limited to a few shopworn roles in *The Emperor Jones* and *Porgy and Bess*. Their company became a vital partner for Black dramatists—among them Owen Dodson and Abram Hill—who were writing different ones. The ANT also staged plays by white playwrights—Sean O'Casey, Eugene O'Neill— whose works' aims resonated with its own. It was headquartered in the basement of the Schomburg Library on 135th Street, but staged plays in community venues across Harlem. The ANT would fold a few years later, in 1955 but during its short but impactful life, the company launched the careers of not a few of America's best-known Black actors—and of many others who, if less well-known than ANT alums like Ossie Davis and Ruby Dee, enjoyed decades-long careers. The woman who got Harry to his first-ever play, Clarice Taylor, worked into her dotage in the 1990s: if you grew up on *The Cosby Show*, you know her as Heathcliff Huxtable's mother.

The play that Taylor and her colleagues performed, that January night in 1946, was called *Home Is the Hunter*. It was by Samuel Kootz, a Jewish art dealer better known for peddling abstract canvases than for writing realist dramas. But his play's timely subject matter—it engaged the daily struggles and lives of Black soldiers home from the war—was a revelation. Harry was mesmerized by the play's dramatization of worlds and characters he knew. He didn't have the impulse, right away, to try to get on stage himself. But he sensed that this was a world, the world of the theater, that he wanted to be a part of. After the show, he lingered to help the company's stagehands strike the set. He asked Clarice Taylor, the next day, if the ANT might like a new volunteer.

He became one—and quickly met a brooding young man with a West Indian accent who'd also just landed in Harlem, also after a stint in the service. Harry and Sidney Poitier were near exact contemporaries—born nine days apart in 1927—who shared island roots, an outlook as angry misfits, and a hunger to leave their mark on the world by means that ran, they both sensed in an inchoate way, through the theater. Poitier had been raised by tomato-farming peasants on remote Cat Island in the Bahamas, and grown up between there and Miami. He'd failed an initial audition with the ANT but had taken work as a janitor in hopes of joining the company onstage. To this end, Poitier had been trying hard to lose his accent. It wasn't his only hurdle. He couldn't sing or dance. When he spoke, which wasn't often, it was in monosyllables. But the kinship Harry felt for him, from the start, was deep. Poitier became, Belafonte would recall, "my first friend—my first friend in life."

It's a remarkable fact: the two performers most responsible for integrating postwar American culture met in a dingy basement in Harlem at the age of nineteen. That early meeting and the bond they formed as friends would prove essential to their success. And their relationship, bordering on twinship, would remain fundamental to them both for seventy years.

Like Harry, Sidney was born in the United States but spent most of his boyhood offshore—he was only born in

Miami because his mother was bringing tomatoes to market from the island where they lived as peasants, and went into labor early. His youth was marked by moving back and forth between these worlds—and then, when he emigrated permanently to the U.S. at sixteen, by a formative dose of American racism. "I couldn't understand it," Poitier said of landing in Jim Crow Florida during the war. "Every sign in Miami. 'White' and 'Colored,' every rebuff, was like saying to me, 'You're not a human being.'" Folk wisdom and social scientists have long concurred that West Indian immigrants enjoy advantages over American-born blacks in the U.S. labor market. The factors helping them do so no doubt contributed to their pathbreaking success. If distinct in their image—the one darker and a picture of quiet decorum; the other light-skinned and quick-to-anger—the two men also shared in their diction and heritage a "foreign" allure that helped them connect with all kinds of Americans—and allowed them, too, not to blink at their success in doing so. "I firmly believe," as Poitier bluntly put it, "that we both had the opportunity to arrive at the formation of a sense of ourselves without having it fucked with by racism as it existed in the United States."

But before any of the success, they bonded as restless young men drawn to the theater and determined not to live out their days as janitors in Harlem. They ventured downtown to Broadway and to off-Broadway shows, too. They would share a single ticket: Poitier would attend the first act and then hand off his stub, along with a summary of the first act's plot, so that Harry, after pulling a shift pushing carts in the garment district or cleaning tenements uptown, could take in the second. They also hatched schemes to get rich quick. Among these was a plan to peddle an aphrodisiac made from queen conch extract. That venture failed. But soon enough, one of them—Harry—won an opportunity that became a break for them both.

When Belafonte was asked by the head of the ANT's drama school, Osceola Archer, if he'd like to read for a part in Abram Hill's *On Striver's Row*, he was surprised. Unlike Poitier, his attraction to drama hadn't yet become an ambition to act. Poitier, by contrast, had been angling for a part in the play and practicing a distinctive new speech pattern, modeled on the radio broadcaster Norman Brokenshire's, that became his trademark. He blamed Harry's getting the call on colorism: he felt that Osceola Archer, whose copper skin and hair evinced her given name's "Indian" aspect, preferred lighter-skinned actors to dark ones. It wasn't the last time the two would vie for similar roles or see their contrasting priorities, and complexions, shade who landed them. In later years, Poitier became Hollywood's most bankable star with the help of roles he made iconic after they were turned down, in at least a couple of instances, by Belafonte. And when they were first starting out, as Harry never tired of reminding him, it was as a stand-in for his friend that Sidney first got over.

Harry, after handling his bit part in Hill's Harlem drama, was given a larger role in ANT's next production. *Days of Our Youth* was a slight college drama by Frank Gabrielson. Poitier again was made Harry's understudy—only to get his turn on a fateful night when a big Broadway producer came by to see the show. Belafonte had arranged, on nights he was meant to be onstage, to have someone cover his janitorial shift. But on this night, his sub called to tell him he couldn't make it. Harry spent the evening despondent, hauling garbage. Thus did his understudy take the stage—and promptly win a role, from the watching producer James Light, in a new staging of *Lysistrata*, with an all-Black cast, that Light was mounting on Broadway. *Lysistrata* bombed, but Poitier's luck didn't end with its run. Among those who caught the show before it closed was a Hollywood agent who would cast him, in a new film directed by Joseph L. Mankiewicz, as a hospital resident dealing with two racist brothers who've landed in his care after a bank robbery. *No Way Out* was a hit, and launched him in Hollywood.

Harry's own big break, thanks to the demands of garbage, would have to wait. But after a performance of his next play at the ANT, in which he was cast as one of the leads in Sean O'Casey's *Juno and the Paycock*, he had an encounter that marked him deeply. It was easy for this son of another island colony to connect with O'Casey's play about Irish peasants resisting their British oppressors. The brogue the play required him to speak—he riffed on a Jamaican accent to conjure a faux-Irish lilt—was another story. But what made *Juno* most memorable for him was the night that the eminence of art and activism who would become his hero, Paul Robeson, dropped by the ANT's basement stage to see it. Since the 1920s, Robeson had been America's foremost Black thespian: a towering figure who lent his basso profundo voice and presence to hallowed roles in *Othello* and *Show Boat*, the musical in which his showstopping rendition of "Ol' Man River" became a trademark. Belafonte admired equally the gravitas with which Robeson devoted himself, with news-making elan, to backing causes he believed in.

Robeson's presence at *Juno*, in the ANT's basement theater under the Schomburg Library, would prove, for Belafonte, a life-changing affirmation. He was nineteen. He'd just experienced, after he'd nailed his lines and taken a bow on *Juno*'s opening night, a new feeling: the sensation, for the first time in his life, of "being part of something grand and wonderful." Now his and his company's hero had come to see them in the flesh—and lingered, after their curtain call, to offer encouragement and praise.

Juno, Robeson said, was a fine production: all its players, who gathered around him in the emptying theater, should be proud. But as exciting, he said, was their willingness to take on O'Casey's work at all. Producing plays by Black playwrights was a worthy and important goal. But it was also vital, in an era when their artform's leaders included dramatists with names like O'Neill and Odets and George Bernard Shaw, not to limit themselves. Robeson's own activism and artistic identity was always based, whether in advocating for civil rights or performing "Ol' Man River," in his blackness. But his political awakening had occurred when, after a concert in Wales in the 1930s, he'd met a group of impoverished miners for whose strike and cause, he realized, his voice could be a potent weapon. During the Spanish Civil War, he had famously turned up in Madrid to assert, as Hitler's bombs pummeled the city, that defeating Franco's fascism was vital to humans everywhere. He used his stature in the culture to espouse his political ideals of internationalism, communism, and a devout belief, which also became Belafonte's, in "the family of man."

Belafonte had found, in a stage role as an Irish peasant, the joy of performing before a crowd. He now sensed that doing so might furnish a way to transcend his circumstances and inhabit a wider world. He also had, in Robeson, a role model for how to turn his inchoate love for the theater into a platform for fighting injustice. The stage would be his ticket from Harlem to that wider world. But to get there, first he had to take the subway downtown.

6

To reach Greenwich Village from Harlem, some seven miles to the south along Manhattan's spine, there are a few ways you can go. One of these, if you're standing on 135th Street by the Schomburg Center for Research in Black Culture, is to hop a 2 or 3 subway train outside. Identifiable by its red signage, the line's modern steel cars run down a track first opened in 1904, as the Lenox Avenue line of the IRT, or Interborough Rapid Transit system: after hitting the top of Central Park at 110th Street, its route bends westward to Broadway and down to where, a hundred blocks downtown, the Village's crooked streets huddle around the base of the city's numbered grid (before thence hurtling onwards to Brooklyn). Another way downtown is to ride the A train, a few blocks to the west, which has shuttled up and down Eighth Avenue since it opened in 1932 as the Independent Subway Line, or IND.

Since its opening, the New York subway system has been an engine not merely of the city's economy but of its culture. One way it served that role was hymned by Duke Ellington's big band on "Take the 'A' Train"—an injunction to denizens of downtown, seeking excitement, to take the train up to where Harlem's nightspots thrummed. But New York's culture industries, and attendant cultural circuitry, have long thrived on pulling the lifeways of the city's margins to where, in Manhattan's core or further downtown, the worlds of theater and music and publishing and art were based. Jewish songwriters and Italian crooners from Brooklyn and Queens made their way to Tin Pan Alley by subway. The rappers and graffiti writers who invented hip-hop in the Bronx, too, voyaged by subway to the galleries and nightclubs where their subculture was embraced by hipsters downtown. Decades later, Belafonte would produce a seminal film—*Beat Street* (1984)—about that story. But the crucial foray down to 14th Street, in Harry's own questing youth, was to the vaunted Dramatic Workshop at the New School for Social Research where ANT colleagues had said that a legendary German director was enrolling students.

Founded in 1919, the New School had earned its reputation as a haven for European intellectuals in exile even before the rise to power in Germany, in 1933, of the Third Reich. But once that happened, the New School welcomed a new influx of leading Jewish artists and left-wing thinkers in flight from the Nazis. Erwin Piscator, who founded his Dramatic Workshop there in 1939, was chased from Berlin on account not of his ethnicity (Piscator was of Prussian stock) but his politics. A giant of the rich theater world of Germany's Weimar years, Piscator was also a committed Communist who'd spent time in Moscow, as an acolyte of Maxim Gorky, and was a close colleague of the era's foremost left-wing dramatist, Bertolt Brecht. In launching the Dramatic Workshop, Piscator enlisted an august faculty, including the legendary acting instructor Stella Adler, and set out to build an American beachhead for "the political theater"— his vision of the artform as an arena for class struggle with power to address defining tensions in society via inventive stagecraft and direct engagement with audiences.

The arrival of many of Europe's foremost intellects was one silver lining to the horrors of World War II, at least for American culture. Another was the GI Bill. Signed into law by Franklin Roosevelt in 1944, its largesse enabled millions of veterans to attend college and join America's middle class. It enabled Harry and his pal Poitier, following the advice of their mentors uptown, to enroll in Piscator's Workshop. When Belafonte told his mother that he was going to spend his veterans' benefits on acting classes, she was only slightly more aghast than his love Marguerite, who had by now moved to New York herself and enrolled in a graduate program in child psychology. The frivolities to which her suitor gave his time, in her eyes, didn't help his cause. "He reminded me of a big kid," she'd later say of their reuniting in New York after the war, "who was about to get into trouble if somebody didn't watch and help him. I had to keep him from becoming a delinquent." Their romance wouldn't blossom again in earnest until the next year. But that was perhaps for the best for Harry, who thrilled to Erwin Piscator's lectures, and also embraced his Workshop's insistence that acting students also learn other skills—set-dressing and lighting, script-writing and directing—needed to produce theater. Harry also fell in, thanks to his move downtown and his studies, with a remarkable cohort of new friends.

Those classmates who became friends were all, like Harry, young products of New York's working class or of provincial places further afield, who nurtured dreams of becoming actors—and had the great fortune, in landing at Piscator's Workshop, of being mentored by teachers whose techniques would soon revolutionize Broadway and Hollywood. Apart from Poitier and Belafonte, their class included Marlon Brando, recently arrived in New York from the Midwest; Walter Matthau and Bea Arthur; Elaine Stritch and

Rod Steiger and Wally Cox. Bernie Schwartz, a pretty-eyed Jewish kid from the Bronx, would win fame a few years later as Tony Curtis. Harry grew close with them all. But he grew closest of all, apart from Poitier, with Brando, whose intensely emotive presence, and the depth with which he absorbed the methods of their acting teacher Stella Adler, made him a model for them all.

Belafonte and Brando bonded over having grown up in alcoholic families, and their shared love for conga drums and for the dancers, in Katherine Dunham's pioneering company, who liked dancing to them. They rode motorcycles around the Village and frequented jazz clubs in midtown where their hero of Afro-Cuban percussion, Chano Pozo, held forth with the makers of bebop. By the fall of 1947, Brando was in rehearsals on Broadway for the show—*A Streetcar Named Desire*—that would make him a star. He stopped coming to many classes at the Workshop. But their friendship only grew. Where Belafonte helped furnish Brando access to the Black social spaces, Black music, and Black women he loved, Brando's prowess as an actor, and his intuitive interest in how music and dance might feed his craft, left a large impression on Belafonte—who was as drawn as Brando was, from the other side of the color line, to forms of expression and social milieus born of interracial exchange. And their pastimes and bond shaped how Belafonte decided, as he toiled on productions with the Workshop without catching a larger break, to earn money between rehearsals.

For productions staged by its students, the Workshop used two theaters. One was a small space leased from an old Yiddish theater on Houston Street downtown. The other was a larger venue, up on 48th Street in Hell's Kitchen, where Harry often volunteered to rig lights or dress sets, even when he didn't have a part in the production. One reason he loved doing so was that the theater was just a couple blocks from his favorite after-hours jazz spot. The Royal Roost's bandstand was home to bebop's leading lights. Charlie Parker, Lester Young, Max Roach—he watched them all strip old harmonies to their essence and add exultant dissonance and jive. Entranced, Harry looked up especially to Young, the mighty saxophonist whom Billie Holiday dubbed "Prez" and with whose sly mien and personal lexicon—it was Young who taught hipsters everywhere to call money "bread"—Belafonte was especially taken. Young's standard greeting, when he saw the young actor who'd become a fixture at the Roost, was this: "How are your feelings?"

One night, Harry's reply to that query led Young and a few other musicians, along with the Roost's promoter and booking agent Monte Kay, to wander over to where Harry was appearing in a Dramatic Workshop production of John Steinbeck's *Of Mice and Men.* Harry's role in the show wasn't a character from Steinbeck's novel. He played the Troubadour—a figure the play's director had added, per the ethos of Piscator's "epic" approach, to function as a kind of au courant chorus and commentator, appearing onstage between scenes, and as the stagehands changed sets, to add musical color and resonance by singing excerpts from songs by Lead Belly and Woody Guthrie. Harry had never considered himself a singer—but he'd been cast as the Troubadour because he could, unlike many of his peers at the Workshop, carry a tune. And singing in character, not as himself but an actor in a play, freed him to do so. What he sang was miles from bebop, but his musician pals saw something in his delivery and presence.

By this time, many of his cohort in the Workshop had ascended to professional roles, while Harry was still making rent by pushing carts in the garment district. He was also spending increasing amounts of time, as his funding from the GI Bill ran out, engaged in agitprop theater and helping lead sing-alongs at union halls and rallies organized by backers of the Progressive Party's candidate for President, Henry Wallace. Where many of his Workshop colleagues cared more about learning acting than politics from Erwin

Piscator, Harry—whose hero, after all, was Paul Robeson—was an increasingly impassioned lefty himself. His political hectoring of his Workshop peers, which he'd admit was also tinged with professional envy, led some of those youthful friendships to dissolve. But in the spring of 1948, he finally won his first role in an off-Broadway production not put on by the Workshop.

Harry's old mentor at the ANT, Osceola Archer, was directing *Sojourner Truth*—a play about the famed abolitionist that would star Muriel Smith, a rising star on Broadway who'd just come off a fourteen-month run as the title character in *Carmen Jones*, Oscar Hammerstein's adaptation of Bizet's *Carmen* to backwoods Black America. When Archer asked Harry if he'd like to appear opposite Smith in *Sojourner Truth* at the 92nd Street Y, he was thrilled. His role in the production didn't lead to more work straightaway, but it proved important to him for other reasons. One was that the great Eleanor Roosevelt, his mother's hero and also one of his own, came one night to see the show and wrote, in her syndicated My Day column, about what a fine actress Muriel Smith was, and—in a vague aside that was nonetheless thrilling to Harry—also how "many of the men impressed me also." Even more significant than Roosevelt's approval, at the time, was that of his old sweetheart Marguerite. Since moving to New York, she'd dismissed Harry's acting as a lark; seeing him in this show, excelling onstage in this serious endeavor, changed her view. After his performance in *Sojourner Truth*, she agreed to a new proposal of marriage.

Her acceptance made Harry happy, but didn't help him make ends meet—and by early 1949, they would have a baby on the way. He was still a habitué of the Royal Roost, and it was Lester Young who suggested, one night after he confessed that his feelings and his bank balance were both running low, that he ask the club's booker, Monte Kay, for a gig. Kay recalled having seen Harry sing in that play—and Kay liked the kid. Harry worked up a few songs with Charlie Parker's pianist, Al Haig. Kay let him sing them. And then— aided by the fact that his star friends like Max Roach and Parker also deigned to back him up—he landed a regular gig. Singing wasn't his passion. But it was better than pushing carts: Monte Kay paid him seventy dollars a week. Belafonte enjoyed modest success as a jazz singer, and Symphony Sid, the jazz-loving radio DJ who broadcast his syndicated show from a booth at the Roost—he was soon to reach listeners in thirty states, on the ABC radio network—loved extolling Harry as their scene's "Cinderella Man." Harry won positive notices in *DownBeat*. Sharing a bandstand with the likes of Roach and Parker, he also gained a first-rate musical education. But he enjoyed listening to their music, as it turned out, more than singing it.

"I became subservient, tonally and musically, to what those cats were playing," he'd recall of gigging with bebop's gods. "I had to think exclusively in terms of vocal gymnastics. It was a valuable experiment, but I knew it wasn't my style." Monte Kay, who'd now also become his manager, helped him adopt a more pop-oriented vibe. He grew a pencil mustache and took to crooning ballads in a tuxedo. Beloved of the ladies in his crowds, he headlined in other nightclubs and recorded standards like "Close Your Eyes" for Capitol Records, which released a series of unheralded sides by the young singer. But his heart wasn't in it. Where the bebop gigs were all about melodic invention, he felt that pop crooning, his manager recalled, was "about exploiting the feelings of immature women." Neither idiom was about inhabiting the lyrics of the song, which is what excited Belafonte the actor about performing.

After a disheartening nightclub stint during the 1950 Christmas season in Miami, Harry doffed his tux and rang his manager Monte to say he was through. Back in New York he used his modest savings from his singing act to open a burger joint down in the Village. The initial aim of the Sage, where Belafonte manned the grill while his friend and business partner, the novelist Bill Attaway, waited tables, was to succeed as a business venture. But it became important for other reasons—not least because it was just up Seventh Avenue from the Village Vanguard, the basement club where the area's burgeoning folk music scene was centered in those days.

When Belafonte and his friends opened the Sage, the so-called folk revival had been bubbling up in the Village since the war; it was just then reaching an apex. When he wasn't flipping burgers, Harry caught sets at the Vanguard from Burl Ives and Josh White and other talismans of the scene. At the restaurant his future bandleader, the jazz clarinetist Tony Scott, was a regular; a local cantor taught Harry "Hava Nageela." "The restaurant," he'd recall, "was getting progressively more difficult to sustain." But "The folksingers would come in, and we [ran] tabs on people . . . they came in from all parts of America. White and black. They chatted, talked politics. It was a world that absolutely seduced me. I began to see my place in it. I could be an actor: a guy from the badlands, a chain gang singer. . . . I could sing Jewish folk songs. I could juggle emotions." Belafonte, in other words, could make the folkies' authenticity fetish an occasion for performance, applying to music the techniques of the method he'd studied at the Dramatic Workshop.

The Village of the postwar years—with its bohemian and interracial élan, its leftist politics and "open mics"—was crucial not just to shaping Belafonte's outlook as a performer, but American culture at large over ensuing decades. The area was a magnet for seekers, drawn by its cheap rent and bookshops, its buskers and soapbox socialists and weed dealers circling Washington Square. It was the hub of the folk revival that found young urbanites seeking new ways to live by looking toward what the writer Greil Marcus described as "old, weird America." That scene would not only foster the emergence of Belafonte, but also, a decade later, that of Bob Dylan (whose first recording gig was as a session harmonica-player on an album of Belafonte's called *Midnight Special*, shortly after Dylan landed in New York in 1962). The Sage, Belafonte's restaurant, soon folded: running tabs for broke musicians isn't how to succeed at business. But it helped give him his new act, which he would debut at the Village Vanguard in the fall of 1951—and take to the top.

7

The age of recording, it's been said, is necessarily an age of nostalgia. If that's true, it's perhaps inevitable that the rise of "field recording," a breed of phonography enabled by new technology from the 1920s on, shaped an American genre of recorded music—folk—that's predicated on nostalgia above all: on evoking and longing for a rural, premodern past wherein people worked not with machines but with their hands, often singing as they did, and traded laments and love songs on their porches at night. The same images and energy attended "country" and "blues", marketed to white and Black Americans, respectively (never mind that the closely linked songs of, say, the Carter Family and Bessie Smith were known simply as "music" where they came from). What distinguished the idiom that became known as "folk" was its creation as a genre by urban intellectuals with a yen for America's backwoods—and an inchoate sense that the music they found there might be key to advancing causes like fighting racism and advancing workers' rights. Its ur-scene involves John Lomax and his son Alan, Depression-era ethnomusicologists extraordinaire, lugging their Garwick disc recorder into Louisiana's Angola State Penitentiary in 1933 to aim its microphone at a Black inmate named Huddie Ledbetter, better known as Lead Belly, as he sang and strummed now-classic songs on a twelve-string guitar in the prison yard.

The modern concept of "folklore" reaches back to nearly a century earlier, when the English writer William Thoms coined the term. A fellow of London's Society of Antiquaries, Thoms was describing cultural forms—stories and sayings, customs and jokes, dances and songs—that are shared and passed on, via oral means, by common people (and sometimes collected for consumption by all, in compendiums by the likes of Thoms's German hero Jacob Grimm, whose *Grimms' Fairy Tales* was a bestseller in Victorian England). In English, Thoms's compound neologism was soon joined by several others—folk culture, folk life, folk dancing. Each of these, by the early twentieth century, was established at universities and among scholars of culture as legitimate objects of study, across the Anglo world and in

Germany, too (where the folk were *Volk* and folklore was *Volkskunde*). Other enthusiasts—activists and agitators, politicos and entrepreneurs—were quick to follow: plenty of societal actors have a stake in avowing the hopes and habits of "the common man," and in hailing the lifeways and balladry of working people.

There was nothing inherently left-wing about this impulse. After all, the Nazis' keen interest in *Volk*-ish culture—a national patrimony they saw as being sullied by foreign elements—was intrinsic to their ideology of hate. But after the Nazis' defeat and in the United States after World War II, a surge of interest in America's own folk heritage was fomented by a generation of musicians whose political sympathies lay squarely on the left.

Woody Guthrie, the patron saint of this movement, was a son of Oklahoma's Dust Bowl who settled in Brooklyn after the war and loved busking with Lead Belly, who also landed in New York in those years, in Harlem. Both were close to Pete Seeger, the figure most essential to their music's rise to prominence. Seeger was the privileged son of a prominent musicologist; he had joined the Young Communist League in 1936 and dropped out of Harvard and became a founding member, alongside Guthrie, of the Almanac Singers—a troupe of singing folkies whose sensibility was influenced by the Depression-era anti-fascism of the Popular Front, and whose great subject and muse was the indomitable rise, in the form of the Congress of Industrial Organizations, of the American labor movement. The Almanacs stood out for encouraging members of their crowds to sing along to their tunes and for performing, whether at rural hootenannies or before 20,000 union men in Madison Square Garden, not in slick suits but rather in the flannel shirts and dungarees of working people. Their repertoire and elastic lineup—which often featured Black fellow travelers like Josh White—was also distinguished by presenting string music and folk songs, born of commingled African and European roots in Appalachia and beyond, as part of a single tradition.

After a stint in the Army, Pete Seeger would form another ensemble of folkie harmonizers—the Weavers—whose approach proved more pop-friendly. Seeger also founded People's Songs, an organization devoted to collecting and disseminating folk tunes that became staples of the singalongs and rallies that accompanied Henry Wallace's Progressive campaign for president in 1948. Belafonte had volunteered for Wallace's campaign and encountered Seeger and his friends at rallies where Paul Robeson, a staunch Wallace ally, inveighed against the Ku Klux Klan and advocated for an American rapprochement with the USSR. And now, thanks to Harry's involvements with the Dramatic Workshop and the Sage, he was

also a denizen of the part of New York—Greenwich Village—
where the folk revival's foremost venues, backers, and record
labels were all located.

These included both Seeger's People's Songs and the
Folkways label run by Moe Asch. Asch was the Yiddish-
speaking son of a Polish immigrant called Sholem Asch, a
noted dramatist and writer for *The Jewish Daily Forward*.
The younger Asch got his start in the music business broad-
casting Yiddish-language concerts for the *Forward*'s radio
show, and producing 78-rpm discs, of the same music, for an
outfit called Asch Records. But then in 1948, when he
launched a new label that was devoted to producing not
heavy 78s but newfangled 33 1/3 long-playing records, he
also broadened his repertoire to release compendiums of
folk songs and field recordings ranging from *Negro Folk
Music of Alabama* to *Mormon Folk Songs, Songs and Dances
of Haiti, Folk Music of Ethiopia,* and *Folksongs of Vermont.* In
1952, Asch would release Harry Smith's seminal *Anthology
of American Folk Music,* whose sonic panorama of old, weird
America became a touchstone for the Woodstock generation
of folk-rockers who would define the counterculture. But in
the early years of Folkways Asch's other contributions to the
folk canon included recordings of Woody Guthrie's "This
Land Is Your Land" and Lead Belly's "Irene Goodnight"—
which would become, in the hands of the Weavers, an un-

likely pop hit: Seeger and company's 1950 cover of the Lead Belly classic sold two million copies, becoming the year's top song.

If the Weavers were like the Almanac Singers except they actually rehearsed, as Pete Seeger remarked, then Belafonte the showman would seek to go one better. He was a performer for whom artifice, and the power of acting, were intrinsic to moving a crowd—and to how he would seek to bring folk music up off its stool and make performing those dusty old songs a form of "people's theater" itself.

By the time Belafonte set about trying to do so, in the summer of 1951, he also had acquired a new manager. Jack Rollins was a regular at the Sage who'd later find success as a film producer with Woody Allen. But when he met Belafonte, he was a small-time booking agent. After he heard the Sage's proprietors singing some sea chanteys and field hollers around their counter after hours, with Belafonte always taking lead, he told Harry he could get him a gig singing the same music at the Village Vanguard. Harry loved nothing more than belting odes to John Henry, he replied with enthusiasm. And then he repaired, with Rollins, to a rehearsal space in midtown where the pair honed his act. They determined first how he'd carry himself onstage (always standing up and never carrying an instrument). They then worked out a costume meant to evoke the informal, thrift-store elegance of the Village scene, which he would wear onstage for the next decade: tight black pants; an unbuttoned shirt; a belt cinched together with a signature sailor's buckle of interlocking rings.

This was the look he trotted onto the Vanguard's small stage for his first bow there, in October 1951. His repertoire was another story. At the Sage, where the guitarist who accompanied him at the Vanguard, Craig Work, was also a regular, he learned several folk standards that became part of his set. From Moe Asch's Folkways records and Pete Seeger's magazine, *Sing Out!*, he picked up others. Another key resource, and lasting inspiration, was Asch's associate Tony Schwartz. An agoraphobic connoisseur of what came to be known as world music, Schwartz was a savant of audio culture who obsessively recorded the sounds and songs of his home zip code in Manhattan. His lasting contributions to culture included introducing Seeger, in the late 1940s, to a Zulu-derived song from South Africa—"Wimoweh"— which the Weavers turned into an unlikely pop hit that's been loved and covered by generations since. Belafonte, like all the folkies he consorted with, also made several pilgrimages to the Library of Congress, where Alan Lomax had deposited all his field recordings and corresponding sheet music for tunes he'd "collected" (with many now granted a dubious copyright shared by Lomax, but that's another story).

The result of all this, in the set that Belafonte crafted with Jack Rollins for his first shows at the Vanguard, was a mix of favorite field hollers and chain gang songs from the Black South ("John Henry," "Jerry"), Irish and Appalachian ballads ("Mo Mary," "Shenandoah"), and a couple of folk tunes in foreign tongues ("Hava Nageela," "Merci Bon Dieu"), that evinced his internationalism and belief in what his mentor Paul Robeson, who dropped by to catch Belafonte's Vanguard set and offer his approval, had taught him to call the human family.

The Vanguard set was a hit. Initial notices, in the Goings on About Town section of *The New Yorker*, were skeptical about the jazz crooner's shift ("Harry Belafonte, now a folk minstrel..."). But his crowds' enthusiasm was real. A week-long booking became two, and then six. His press followed suit. "It moves many to tears, this presentation of our international folk heritage," wrote *Metronome*'s reviewer. His bookings, to Jack Rollins's delight, grew apace.

From the Vanguard, Belafonte moved directly up to the Blue Angel, a club in midtown, for a monthlong stay that became two—and springboarded him, with his act that won over New York (opined *The New Yorker* that winter: "One of the season's catches—Harry Belafonte!") to a national tour of nightspots and hotel cabarets from coast to coast. He was also invited, out in Los Angeles, to do a screen test for MGM and was subsequently cast, in a low-budget film, opposite another young singer in LA—Dorothy Dandridge—who'd been hunting for a break in Hollywood. *Bright Road* made history as the first such studio film to feature two Black leads, but it was a trite drama that flopped at the box office. It laid down an important marker, however, for its two stars, who would soon enough share top billing on a much bigger film. The three-week shoot in LA in 1952 also saw Belafonte's on-screen chemistry with Dandridge extend to a halting off-screen affair. Their flirtation presaged difficulties, as he spent more and more time away from Marguerite and their toddler, Adrienne, back home in New York, that would soon test his young marriage. And from there, he landed on the Las Vegas strip.

In Vegas, Jack Rollins had booked him at the just-opened Thunderbird Hotel. The twenty-five-year-old Harry's residency there inaugurated what would become, for this child of numbers runners who loved to gamble, a life-long relationship with Sin City. But the refinements it offered his act, in a mob-run town whose high rollers and

Stetson-wearing patrons were a world away from Manhattan, were just as significant.

Years later, Belafonte would recall in *My Song* what touring the country at a time when the edicts and ideas of Jim Crow adhered far beyond the South was like. When he and his touring guitarist Millard Thomas arrived at the Thunderbird's southwestern-themed front desk, they weren't checked into rooms there but instead driven over to a flea-bitten "colored" motel across town, as was then the custom for Black entertainers in Vegas. Belafonte, who a week before had been detained by racist LA cops for taking a walk in Hollywood, was having none of it. He was able, with the help of his uncle Lenny back in New York, who put in a call to some friends in the Jewish mob, to be booked into a nice room at the Thunderbird instead. If Vegas's color bar with regards to accommodation was thusly jumped, the skepticism of the high rollers in the Thunderbird's theater, when he took the stage there, was harder to crack. The old English ballad with which he started his Vanguard set ("On yonder hill there stands a maiden . . .") left the Stetson-wearers cold. They cared less for delicacy than for oomph. Luckily for Belafonte, another member of his crowd that night was on hand to offer some advice.

Pete Kameron, the Weavers manager, had come up from LA to catch Belafonte's set and see, he told him, "where folk music was heading." A downhearted Harry, after his set fell flat, wasn't sure it was heading anywhere good—or that it could land in Vegas anyway. But Kameron's suggestion, as he and Harry looked over his set list and discussed a new way to pull this crowd's attention from their cocktails and dates, was a winner. The next time he took the stage, Harry didn't start with any mellow patter or balladry. He began, rather, by gripping the mic and belting, at the top of his lungs, a single elongated word.

"Timmmbbberrrrrrrr!"

He held the last "r" until every Stetson in the room turned his way. It was the opening line to "Jerry," a chain-gang song from Georgia whose verse, addressed to the tune's namesake mule, he now delivered to a crowd that was rapt: "Lord this timber gotta roll / Gotta get it down this dusty road . . ." Their attention thus won, he did another intense number next, and offered nary a smile or pleasantry until, a few songs into the set, he broke the tension by greeting these new fans and, having won their ears, going on to sing whatever he liked. It was a lesson in stagecraft, and a tactic for vesting a song's opening with dramatic heft, that he wouldn't forget.

His folk act had now triumphed at the Vanguard and in Vegas, but it wasn't in a club or cabaret or Hollywood where he caught his blooming career's key break. That break, fit-

DAYLIGHT COME

tingly, came on the theatrical stage after the producers of a new musical revue, on Broadway, caught his folk act. Belafonte's role in *John Murray Anderson's Almanac*, which opened in December 1953, was not a speaking but a singing one. The production had a disappointing run. But it was a triumph for Belafonte, who sang three songs, among them a showstopping rendition of the Jamaican folk tune "Hold 'Em Joe." With Harry shouting the tune's suggestive chorus ("Me donkey want water! / Hold 'em Joe!"), the song evinced many of the fruitful juxtapositions—a pastoral theme set against urbane orchestration; a simple workman-protagonist with unsubtle vocality—that would become hallmarks. For his trouble, he was awarded a Tony. "He was an actor," as the showbiz writer Maurice Zolotow later put it, "playing the best role he was ever to get: the role of a singer."

79

8

When Harry won that Tony for his singing turn in *Al-manac*, he already had a new record contract: he'd signed with RCA Victor as a folk act in 1952. Immediately after doing so, he'd recorded a series of singles for the label— a few of his folk favorites backed by full orchestras with strings—that sold little, and one—a novelty cover of the Japanese love song "Gomen Nasai (Forgive Me)" that sold a bit. But now his minders at RCA sought to leverage Harry's Broadway success with the help of a still-new technology— the 33 1/3 long-playing record—that revolutionized the record business. The LP, which was introduced in 1948, allowed for upward of twenty minutes of music per side and would eventually supplant 45- and 78-rpm singles as the culture's dominant tool for purveying music as commodity and art. In

1953, though, this hadn't yet occurred. RCA and its competitors were still experimenting with how best to exploit a format on which Harry made his debut with a slate of tunes called *"Mark Twain" and Other Folk Favorites*. His first LP found him singing his top numbers from *Almanac* accompanied not by a full orchestra, in the style of a cast recording, but a stripped-down ensemble matching the folkie affect of his club act. It sold better than his singles.

Harry and his label would build on this modest success, before long, to a spectacular degree. But what allowed him to do so, beyond seizing on some inspired ideas for how to win with vinyl, was another opportunity born of his star turn in *Almanac*. One night after the show, he was approached backstage by Otto Preminger. The hard-charging Austrian-born director and producer, who landed in America in 1936, had become a go-to helmsman, for Hollywood's leading studios and magnates, of lean B-movies and blockbusters alike. He also evidently concurred with Odetta about Harry's charms ("Have you *seen* the man?") after seeing him stride the boards in *Almanac* and coming backstage to meet him. Preminger informed him that he wanted him for the male lead in his new film.

Preminger's *Carmen Jones* was an adaptation of Oscar Hammerstein II's hit musical from a few years before, which was itself an adaptation of Georges Bizet's *Carmen* to a U.S.

South where backwoods Blacks stood in for Bizet's gypsies. The bald-headed Preminger was notorious in Hollywood for his temper—as an actor, he was best known for playing Nazis—who also became famous as an independent producer for bucking both the blacklist and the studio system later in the fifties. Such was Preminger's passion for *Carmen Jones*, and his belief that America was ready for a blockbuster with an all-Black cast to turn a profit, that he at first planned to finance it himself. But then Darryl F. Zanuck, his longtime patron at Twentieth Century–Fox, an executive enamored of Preminger's earned reputation for finishing his projects on time and under budget, agreed to fund the project. It would prove a good bet.

Preminger, having picked his leading man, proceeded to secure Harry's old crush Dorothy Dandridge to be his Carmen. A visit to the troubled actress at her LA apartment did the trick—and launched a yearslong affair that would see Dandridge, who made a habit of attaching herself to powerful and controlling white men to advance her fortunes, grow increasingly despondent when, with Preminger and others, those fortunes didn't improve. (She would die of sadness or an overdose or both in 1965.) But before all that, she hit her mark for her then-Svengali as a ravishing Carmen whose performance as an opera-singing parachute sewer during World War II, hell-bent on seducing a GI played by Belafonte, would make her the first Black woman to be nominated for an Oscar for Best Actress. That was one benchmark for *Carmen Jones*'s success. Another, more important to Zanuck's studio, was that it eventually did $10 million at the box office against a budget of $800,000—humongous numbers in 1954.

As a film and as art, *Carmen Jones* was a mixed bag—more a reflection of Hollywood's racial neuroses, which is to say of America's racial neuroses, than a real attempt to engage them. Belafonte's previous workout with Dandridge, *Bright Road*, was distinguished by a script that didn't mention or dwell on race at all. *Carmen Jones*, by contrast, was all about its characters' blackness—albeit through an exoticizing lens that had more to do with white fantasies of Black life than Black life itself. Dandridge played the untethered Negress as licentious hussy, her every line accompanied by a thrown hip; her love-quarry was a GI named Joe who was presented—perhaps with a nod to the threat Black male sexuality still posed to the mainstream American mind—as essentially passive. To make things even stranger, the film found them communicating in a strange mix of spoken Ebonics (every "the" is "de") and operatic vocals: despite Belafonte and Dandridge both being more-than-serviceable singers, they lip-synched along to Bizet's arias carried by operatic vocalists on the film's final score, whose classical-sounding trills bounced incongruously off the film's world of juke joints and canteens in the Carolina woods.

Which is all to say that it was precisely the kind of project that Harry would have turned down later in his career for being based less in actual Black culture than white ideas of it. But at the time, it was vital to getting that career underway—and represented, too, a big step for Hollywood. *Carmen Jones* wasn't the first all-Black film to be produced by a major studio. Among its predecessors, from Zanuck's Twentieth Century–Fox, was *Stormy Weather* in 1943, which helped launched the career of another au lait–complected actress with showgirl looks, Lena Horne. But Preminger's film was the first such picture to command a blockbuster's budget and publicity. When it landed in theaters, *Variety* praised the "taste and imagination [of] an opulent production." Other reviewers, like *The New York Times*'s Bosley Crowther, were more measured. Crowther commended "a big musical shenanigan and theatrical tour-de-force," but also observed that Preminger's interest in southern Black life was "not so much poignant as lurid and lightly farcical, with the African-American characters presented . . . as serio-comic devotees of sex." James Baldwin, for his part, eviscerated the film as a retrograde disaster. For him, its most interesting feature was Pearl Bailey: he noted how Bailey, as the film's voice of dark-skinned realness as against the milquetoast mien of its light-skinned stars, gave the whole enterprise side-eye even as she performed in it. "More than any movie I can recall seeing," Baldwin wrote in his cutting review, "it cannot afford, dare not risk, imagination."

But *Carmen Jones*, with its elaborate song-and-dance numbers and two gorgeous leads necking in Technicolor splendor, was also a commercial hit—the first all-Black picture to do such business. This was a big deal—not least for Black audiences who thrilled to see people who looked like them, in a Hollywood spectacle like this one, on the silver screen. The film also introduced Belafonte's visage and vibe, if not his actual voice, to a broader new public just as he was trying to translate his victories on stage and screen into even greater success as a recording artist for RCA.

On the October night in 1954 when *Carmen Jones* opened in cinemas nationwide, Belafonte was debuting a new revue-style show in Los Angeles. In *3 for Tonight*, he shared the stage with fellow singers Marge and Gower Champion, and performed a slate of his best-loved folk songs and spirituals. The show toured the country—except the South, where presenters couldn't countenance its mixed bill of headliners—and established him as a top national draw who would spend the next several years selling out weeks-long engagements at top nightspots, from the Cocoanut Grove in LA to the Venetian Room in San Francisco to the Copacabana and the Waldorf's Empire Room in New York. *3 for Tonight* also let him hone the songs that, back in Manhattan in the summer of 1955, he brought to the studio to record his second LP for RCA, in the same tile-walled room on 24th Street where a soulful young white kid from Mississippi—Elvis Presley—would soon record his first.

That second album, called *Belafonte*, had a photo on its cover of its eponymous star looking supremely handsome in a pink shirt—and featured an eclectic mix of tunes including "Scarlet Ribbons," "In That Great Gettin' Up Mornin'," and, perhaps most notably, a calypso called "Matilda." The tune's lyric, about an unfaithful woman who "take me money / and run' Venezuela," was composed in the thirties by King Radio in Trinidad. Now it was registered with ASCAP in New York as being by "Harry Thomas"—a portmanteau of Harry's name and his guitarist Millard Thomas's. Their role in penning its call-and-response chorus was nil; but they made it, that year, a beloved part of his stage show.

That stage show's success hadn't translated into record sales before *Belafonte*. Now that changed. His second album sold so well that in March 1956, when *Billboard* published its first-ever chart of the nation's top-selling LPs, *Belafonte* occupied the top spot. It was soon supplanted by his labelmate Presley—the first instance of a pas de deux the pair would play out atop the charts during an era best-recalled as America's birth years of rock 'n' roll, but during which Belafonte would ultimately sell more records than anyone. Presley's popularity, as a white singer of Black rhythm and blues, was famously tied—both for the shrieking girls at his concerts, and the sixty million Americans who tuned in to watch his first appearance on *The Ed Sullivan Show*—to his louche charm and circling pelvis. But sex appeal of a slightly different kind, tamer but no less transgressive in pre–Civil Rights America, was also key to the appeal that Belafonte cultivated for the mostly white crowds at his concerts.

The acclaim he received made him wonder as to its source. His friend Bill Attaway pointed to one such. "Although he is brown-skinned and unmistakably Negro," Attaway observed in the late fifties, "he is acceptable in terms of white standards of beauty. Brown up Tab Hunter and you could hardly tell him from Harry Belafonte." These aesthetic factors, for Attaway as for Harry soon enough, allied to political ones. "At the present stage of the struggle for human freedom, the need is for a bridge Negro—one who serves to connect white and Negro. Harry fills that need remarkably." Harry had only recently come to terms, after a hard-knock youth during which he'd felt attractive to no one, with the fact that he was easy on the eyes. Now he well saw how those looks could help him succeed, not least with white audiences for whom he carried a reassuring presence. He was "Black, but . . . not *too* black . . . ," as he reflected in his memoir. "[But] just as important, perhaps more so, I was a black entertainer who engaged the crowd without reference to color at all. . . . Everything about the way I comported myself onstage made clear that I assumed my audience and I were equals. So they reacted in kind. Which freed the women to regard me the way they did their white matinee idols, as a singer they could fantasize about getting to know—at least on their island vacations."

Some of those women, during his monthslong stints on the road, did more than fantasize; they found him backstage or at his hotel, and he returned their affections. By now his marriage to Marguerite was on the rocks. She'd never been given to the limelight, or much liked Harry's show business friends. In the house in Queens his success had bought the family, she was raising their first daughter, Adrienne—who in 1954 was joined by a second, Shari—with her husband's support but largely on her own. She was proud of his success, and happy to pose for family pictures when *Ebony* and *The Saturday Evening Post* ran profiles of the star at home.

But the two weren't happy. He was now inhabiting a world far from Queens. Dalliances on the road were also joined to a burgeoning affair with a dancer, Julie Robinson, whom he'd met through Marlon Brando and whose comfort with the bohemian worlds they shared, and passion for left-wing politics and Afro-Caribbean culture—Julie was the first white member of Katherine Dunham's company—accorded with his own. She wrote Harry a sheaf of love letters that Marguerite found.

Alongside that personal tumult, Belafonte entered psychotherapy. Analysis would see him grapple with fame's confusions and his boyhood's wounds, and have other fateful effects. He was also preoccupied with how best to leverage his stardom—and the juice he now had with his record label—to best effect. He grew convinced that he needed to put out a series of thematic LPs showcasing songs from around the world. He landed, perhaps with an eye toward the role he'd nurtured in his fans' fantasies about "island vacations," on a full album of songs from—or at least evoking—the Caribbean.

9

The idea arose suddenly. Harry had just wrapped recording *Belafonte* when he received an invitation: would he
like to produce and perform in a special guest segment on
NBC's *Colgate Comedy Hour*? Belafonte's first idea for how
to fill his twenty-minute segment was with a folk-blues story
built around John Henry, the rail-splitting giant of Negro
folklore. But in discussing his plans for the show with Bill
Attaway—who was now employed as a staff writer at NBC
with a portfolio, that fall, which included *The Colgate Comedy Hour*—another thought emerged: why not present a musical theme with Caribbean flavor? Attaway enlisted a New
York–based calypso composer called Lord Burgess (né Irving Burgie), and they worked with Belafonte to conceive a
segment called "Holiday in Trinidad." The show aired on

October 2, 1955. The host, Jack Carson, played the role of an island-hopping tourist who stops off in Trinidad to see Belafonte perform some tunes. Among those numbers, which Irving Burgie adapted from Jamaican and Trinidadian folk sources, were "Hosanna," "Come Back Liza," and "The Banana Boat Song" (or "Day O," as it was then known)—Belafonte's first public performance of his most famous number. The show didn't get great ratings, but it gave its star the template and material for his next LP.

The A and R men at RCA were dubious. But Belafonte, who'd added these tunes to his stage set alongside "Matilda," was adamant. And one night at dinner, he won the support of the label's boss. George Marek's call was in some ways a bold one. But the record companies were still figuring out how best to exploit the LP format at a time when other advances in recording and playback fidelity—including the incipient rise of multitrack recording and stereophonic sound—were making listening to records at home an ever-more more pleasurable experience.

In an era whose booming consumer economy joined with new technologies to change fundamentally how sounds circulated in the culture, the LP allowed for capturing and playing back longer songs and symphonies, and extended solos on jazz records. It also forged the modern concept of the "album" with which we're familiar today: as a linked suite of songs offering a coherent artistic statement by their creator. In the 1960s, college kids would become the great consumers of long-playing rock albums; in the LP's early days, young people stuck to feeding dimes into jukeboxes and buying 45s. The new format's primary consumers were the parents of sixties hippies: those "greatest generation" denizens of new postwar suburbs who, possessed of new-fangled hi-fi equipment for their Levittown living rooms, were newly in the market for recorded accompaniment to their cocktail parties or romantic evenings by the fire. At first this market was dominated by Broadway cast recordings like *South Pacific*—a hit that remained the top-selling album in America throughout 1949, 1950, and 1951. Soon enough, though, cast recordings were joined by records explicitly aimed at providing sonic wallpaper for those suburban "dens." Crooners like Perry Como and Johnny Mathis ruled the roost; Paul Weston launched an eponymous genre with his hit *Mood Music* LP in 1953; and the television comic Jackie Gleason scored that year's top album with *Music for Lovers Only*. With mood music's emergence also came that of "exotica." If the aim of mood music was to forge a particular atmosphere in its listeners' homes—cozy, nostalgic, sexy—its close cousin aimed to bring distant parts of the world into those same spaces.

Exotica's great purveyor, the Hollywood bandleader Les

Baxter, scored 1951's #3 seller with *Voice of the Ixtabay*, recorded with Yma Sumac's Inca orchestra. "Do the mysteries of native rituals intrigue you?" asked the liner notes to his other 1951 effort, *Ritual of the Savage.* "Does the haunting beat of savage drums fascinate you? . . . This original and exotic music by Les Baxter was conceived by blending his creative ideas with the ritualistic melodies and seductive rhythms of the natives of distant jungles and tropical ports to capture all the color and fervor so expressive of the emotions of these people." Belafonte's political and artistic aims may have diverged radically from Baxter's. But by the time he made *Calypso,* the idea of evoking a foreign, exotic world over the course of a whole LP wasn't new. What was novel was perhaps Belafonte's essential advantage—that he didn't need to hire Inca princesses to lend his albums their "exotic" tinge: he could embody it himself. As a folksinger, Harry had sung material from around the world from the start: his first RCA single to chart, in 1953, was "Gomen Nasai." What was new was the idea of recording a full album of songs from the foreign region he knew best.

The RCA honcho who embraced his pitch, George Marek, was a Vienna-born Jew who'd emigrated to New York in his teens. He'd gotten his start in the record business seeking to popularize Old World art music for U.S. listeners. First as music editor at *Good Housekeeping* and later as chief of Artists and Repertory at RCA, he'd released such records as *Classical Music for People Who Hate Classical Music* and penned books like *A Front Seat at the Opera*. Classical music was his passion, but Marek was a proselytizer for the sonic arts in general, with a keen marketer's mind. He'd overseen RCA's mood music series and initiated the label's shift to packaging its records in colorful dust jackets and offering them for sale in drugstores and supermarkets. Getting customers hooked on "music, any kind of music" was to be the record man's aim. "As the cigarette people believe," he said, "the habit is everything." Marek's ambit at corporate RCA was far different from that of famously uncommercial folk music impresarios like Moe Asch of Folkways, but his interest in what Belafonte had to say about Caribbean music went much deeper than the profit motive. "He was very much an intellectual," as Belafonte would later recall of that dinner with a professional colleague he came to cherish, "hugely sensitive to oppression. He loved culture, and he was very open toward all kinds of music."

Marek's openness, in the event, enabled Belafonte to release his most historic and popular record—and augured what became its signal triumph. *Calypso* would prove that Americans were themselves more open to absorbing a foreign musical idiom as American pop than common wisdom—and Marek's fellow executives at RCA—had previously assumed.

No one knows how to make a hit record. That's an industry truism with which pop savants like Taylor Swift and Ed Sheeran may now disagree. So might purveyors, nowadays, of dance hits and boy-band bait concocted with algorithmic precision to inflame the dopamine receptors of preteen girls. But every record business veteran has had the experience of seeing a record they thought to be brilliant flop in the marketplace—and of being surprised by what takes flight. As Quincy Jones said of producing Michael Jackson's *Thriller* in the 1980s, "If anyone tells you they know how to sell sixty million copies, they don't. You do something that you love and that gives you goose bumps. It works out or it doesn't." No one, in other words, can legislate for the kind of supernova success enjoyed by an album like *Thriller*—and its historic forebear, in the annals of LPs that became cultural touchstones, that Belafonte set out to record, in October 1955, at a storied concert hall and event space on East 11th Street—Webster Hall—that RCA's engineers had recently outfitted as a capacious studio for recording their biggest projects and stars.

Calypso, as Harry's new album was called, was recorded the same fall that his Colgate segment aired on NBC. It was released the following May, while *Belafonte* was also still riding high on the charts. The new album, buoyed by its breakout singles "Banana Boat (Day-O)" and "Jamaica Farewell," sold fast. By summer's end, it had bested Elvis's own sophomore album to top the charts—and would retain that spot, on its way to becoming the first LP by a solo artist to sell a million copies, for no fewer than thirty-one weeks. It would remain on the charts for 137 weeks—a mark not surpassed until *Thriller* came along three decades later. But it got its start in Manhattan's East Village, near the clubs where Harry's musical career had taken flight a few years before, and in a vaunted space that RCA acquired, in 1953, as a kind of acoustical annex to the company's main recording studio in the city on 24th Street.

Webster Hall's story began in 1886, when a Polish-born German Jew opened a grand new "hall for hire" near the northern end of *Kleindeutschland*—the sprawling enclave of German speakers that thrived across what's now Manhattan's Lower East Side. Charles Goldstein's place was built in a Renaissance Revival style, with an ornate mansard roof and brick facade accented with terra-cotta cherubs and was intended, reported *The New York Times*, "for balls, receptions, Hebrew weddings, and sociables." It also hosted working-class members of new immigrant groups, and revelers and radicals of all stripes. In one historic gathering in 1914, three years after the tragic Triangle Shirtwaist Factory fire a few blocks away, the Amalgamated Clothing Workers of America was founded. Webster Hall is where Emma Goldman propounded anarchism and birth control to insist that women had "the right to beautiful, radiant things," and where the socialist magazine *The Masses* staged masquerade balls. During Prohibition, drag fetes and *outré* bacchanals filled this "Devil's Playhouse," which also played host, at Prohibition's end and for a more upmarket set, to an epic party called The Return of John Barleycorn.

After World War II, the place became home to heroes of Latin music like Tito Puente and Tito Rodriguez, who turned its dance floor into a vital seedbed for New York's mania for mambo. Woody Guthrie and Pete Seeger hosted hootenannies that became integral to the founding of *Sing Out!* magazine, in 1950, and to the folk revival *in toto*. But what most drew RCA's engineers to the high-ceilinged space were acoustics at once reverberant and clear, which helped anything recorded at Webster Hall feel like sitting mid-orchestra at a Broadway show. Among the original cast recordings, made between 1953 and when RCA sold the place to open a new suite of studios at its uptown offices in 1969, were favorites including *Fiddler on the Roof* and Carol Channing's *Hello, Dolly!* Elvis Presley also came, in July 1956, a day after performing "Hound Dog" on *The Steve Allen Show* on NBC, to record his breakout hit. And any one lucky enough to happen into the place the fall before, on the afternoon of October 20, 1955, would have witnessed one of the most beloved vocal performances in the history of pop.

Harry, riffing on the lyric to a Jamaican work song around which he and Bill Attaway had also built his *Colgate Comedy Hour* segment, stepped back from the mic's metal grille to let his voice travel a little ways, through Webster Hall's echoing air, before hitting its diaphragm. He began this new record—the first seconds of what became *Calypso*'s first track—with the trick he'd picked up in Vegas of grabbing a crowd's attention with an a cappella cry: "Daaaaay O!" The words voiced the relief with which island stevedores, who loaded banana boats at night to avoid the sun's heat, met the arrival of daylight that let them go home. They might have been addressed to the unionists who'd once packed Webster Hall or the flappers who danced there until dawn, resounding as they did with a sense of a greater workers' history. Seven decades later, they still echo across our sports arenas and in the culture at large:

"Daaaaay O! Day-ay-ay O! Daylight come and me wan' go home. . . ."

Audiophiles and casual fans alike have marveled at this record's quality and wondered at the vibrating clarity of

Harry's voice. In truth its reverb was simply in the effects of Webster Hall, as captured by RCA's engineers with the help of what the company touted as a "New Orthophonic High Fidelity Recording." RCA had been using this mode of electronic recording ever since acquiring the Victor Talking Machine Company in 1929 but now had augmented it with state-of-the-art microphones and precision cutting heads that allowed its engineers, with newfound fidelity, to transfer what those microphones captured to lacquer grooves. Such was the alchemical technology by which the sounds aired here would reach peoples' hi-fis at home. But as with all creative projects that grow bigger than the sum of their parts, the ideas and forces that gathered in Webster Hall for the *Calypso* sessions (the October date was preceded by an earlier one on August 18, and followed by a final session on November 9), were the product of both accident and intention. *Calypso* was a collaboration with a larger cast of characters, drawn from the now twenty-eight-year-old singer's decade-long career in the performing arts, who all brought key ingredients to a record conceived as an "integrated trip through the West Indies," as Bill Attaway put it in his liner notes, with "songs ranging in mood from brassy gaiety to wistful sadness, from tender love to heroic largeness." The organic-yet-orchestral timbre of the finished tracks—drawn from folk sources and mixed to an impeccable sheen—was created by a group of musicians convened by Harry's bandleader Tony Scott, another close friend from the Sage days.

Scott, born Anthony Sciacca in New Jersey, was an Italian American drawn to Black music who used his chops on clarinet and a network of leading jazzmen, as he later told *DownBeat* magazine, to lend Belafonte's folk records a "jazz feeling." Among those Scott summoned to Webster Hall, alongside Harry's longtime accompanist Millard Thomas on guitar, were the brilliant jazz bassist Milt Hinton and drummer James "Osie" Johnson. Also present were a chorus of Broadway actors led by Brock Peters, who'd sung Belafonte's parts in *Carmen Jones* (and whose singers were also joined, on a few numbers, by the Norman Luboff Choir); Frantz Casseus, the Brooklyn-based "father of classical Haitian guitar" (and contributor of "Merci Bon Dieu" to his repertoire); and Herman Diaz, Jr., the Puerto Rican session leader responsible for moving the drums on "Day O" closer to the room's mics to make them more prominent in the mix. Perhaps most notable of all was Irving Burgie, who wrote—or more accurately, adapted from folk sources—the songs that became Belafonte's most iconic hits.

Burgie was born in Brooklyn to a Barbadian mother and a Black American father: he was a fellow New Yorker with West Indian roots, and a gifted songwriter who shared Belafonte's affinity for turning folk music from the islands into northern pop. After the war, Burgie had used his own GI Bill funds to study classical voice and composition at Juilliard. He'd knocked around the same circuit of folk clubs and union-sponsored hootenannies Belafonte plied in the late forties. And then he built an encyclopedic knowledge of folk songs from across the West Indies—mentos from Jamaica, merengues from Santo Domingo, calypsos from Trinidad— and a healthy store of ballads and love songs, always island-tinged, that he wrote himself.

Burgie was short and unassuming in aspect; he was never destined to break out as a performer. But in 1954 at the Village Vanguard, he convened a group of Caribbean musicians—among them Haitians and Afro-Cubans and a Jamaican piano and penny whistle player, Herb Levy, who would also join Belafonte's *Calypso* sessions—that the club's owner, Max Gordon, dubbed Lord Burgess and the Sun Islanders. Thus did Burgie, now also known as Lord Burgess, gain a sobriquet that recalled the regal monikers of calypso's mighty makers in Trinidad, the British island in the southern Caribbean where the form was born, and where calypsonians battled for supremacy, with witty or ribald lyrics, to be crowned monarch of Trinidad's famed yearly carnival.

This borrowing of the customs and vibe of calypso's home island—a place neither Belafonte nor Burgie had visited in 1956—was in keeping with their project's gestalt.

Notwithstanding its title, only two songs on *Calypso* were in fact calypsos ("Brown Skin Girl" and "Man Smart (Woman Smarter)," both by King Radio but mis-credited here). Of the album's other nine songs, Burgie received a writing credit for eight. Alongside his originals like "I Do Adore Her" and "Dolly Dawn," these were mostly mentos and folk songs from Jamaica whose lyrics or melodies Burgie tweaked for a new frame. He'd learned a few of them, including *Calypso*'s break-out hit, from fellow denizens of the Village Vanguard—which is where, in or around 1953, he and Harry both met the great Jamaican folklorist and singer Louise Bennett.

"Miss Lou," as Bennett was affectionately known, be-came a national hero in Jamaica who did more than anyone, in the years surrounding the island's independence from Britain in 1962, to convince her people that the richness of their own oral culture—from the patois they spoke to the Anansi stories they told and folk songs they sang—held as much value as any book published in Oxford English. Dur-ing a stint in New York in the early fifties, she wrote plays but also worked as a cashier at Macy's—which is where Har-ry's friend Tony Schwartz, whose stomping grounds in mid-town included the department store, met her. After hearing Bennett sing and introducing her to Belafonte and Burgie, Schwartz helped her record an album for Moe Asch on Folk-ways. Called *Jamaican Folk Songs*, it included a recording of

"Day Dah Light" that beat Belafonte's version to the punch by two years (as did another version, by the Trinidad-born singer and actor Edric Connor—who in 1956 made a star turn, as Daggoo the harpooner, in Gregory Peck's 1956 film version of *Moby Dick*).

Irving Burgie, in adapting the folk version recorded by Bennett and Connor for American ears, retained enough of its original Jamaican lines ("Come Mister tally man, tally me banana...") to keep its island feel. He replaced certain of its denser patois lyrics with plainer English, and made one odd change: where the old work song referenced banana "hands"—as bunches of the fruit are logically called—his lyric invoked another appendage ("Six foot, seven foot, eight foot bunch!"). But tweaks to language aside, what most distinguished his version from Miss Lou's was how Harry's was arranged and performed. Miss Lou's "Day Dah Light" hewed near to renditions sung by workmen to keep themselves trudging up Jamaica's docks onto one of those United Fruit Company boats Harry boarded as a boy. Her voice's uptempo lilt, accompanied by little more than hand-drums, is more plea than demand. Summoning the tally man is a lament, in her tuneful staccato, redolent of what Bill Attaway described as "the irrepressible rhythm of a people who have not lost the ability to laugh at themselves." Harry's sloweddown version, on *Calypso*, is different. It's vested with as much pathos and drama as his voice could wrest from a feeling—"Daylight come, and me wan' go HOME"—that here becomes a demand indeed. Harry may have been capable, on occasion, of self-deprecation, but in truth he was never much given to laughing at himself, let alone at his people. And he didn't do so in the number here rechristened "Day O" and also released as "The Banana Boat Song."

His initial cry grabs our attention. Then his lush vocal drifts toward us as if from down the beach, then draws closer. He riffs on the word he's insisting we hear: "Me say day, me say day, me say day, me say day-ay-ay-O. . . ." He descends a note with each line, as if striding downstairs, and then steps down quicker. We've hit the bottom of his range. His voice is still warm and full. He exhales the reason we're here—daylight's come, he wants to go home—with a last extended "O." We're ready, now, for this dynamic preamble to end, and for the song to begin in earnest, that is, with a rhythm set by the next line—"Work all night / and I drink a rum!"—that the chorus and drums, which hit just as the rum does, pick up. Voices gather around Harry's. They keep time with the congas' steady march and reply to his rum line with the refrain they'll repeat ("Daylight come, and me wan' go home") for the rest of song: "Stack banana till the morning come!" ("Daylight come, and me wan' go home"). And so it goes as the tally man arrives and the black tarantula does, too—before this tired singer and his cohort of harmonizing friends and a conga that sounds like rain eases off down the beach.

We feel, as the record ends, the exhaustion of ending a workday at dawn—the weary yet insistent note that greeting the sun's rise entails. But part of the magic of pop, and of records that resonate for as many people as this one did, is their power to do so in ways that vary across context and time. Harry turned a workman's lament into a prideful demand, but when "Day O" echoes as a singalong chant across Yankee Stadium today, it sounds more like a taunt—a clip of familiar Americana that underscores to the opposing team that the home side's winning—the same sentiment as Ray Charles's "Hit the Road Jack." Such novelty uses, to his mind, didn't change what the song was about—and nor did the moment, decades after he first recorded it, when the rapper Lil Wayne scored an infectious hit, "Six Foot Seven Foot," by sampling its chorus. Harry's signature tune didn't belong to him, he said, any more than to Lil Wayne; it belonged to working people in the Caribbean with whom it was born. He was just glad to see a new generation embrace "a song about struggle, about black people in a colonized life doing the most grueling work." This, he told Gwen Ifill in a 2011 interview on *PBS News Hour*, is what made him proud. "I took that song and honed it into an anthem that the world loved."

10

In 1956, "Banana Boat (Day-O)" was *Calypso's* second single and reached as high as #5 on the charts. Its first, "Jamaica Farewell," was a sweet ode to lost love on an island "where sun shines daily on the mountaintops." In his onstage patter in the fifties, Harry liked to say he'd learned that one in his boyhood from sailors on Kingston's docks. He hadn't: "Jamaica Farewell" was penned by Burgie in 1955 (albeit with a melody borrowed from the old Jamaican mento tune "Iron Bar," as Burgie was later forced to admit in court). Burgie deserved his writing credit on that one. The same wasn't as plainly true with the pop-ified version of "Day O," notwithstanding his swapping of the folk version's "hands" for "feet," whose lyrics he copyrighted with Attaway. But it was Burgie who got rich off its publishing, as he confirmed to me at a café in Greenwich Village, decades later, a few blocks from where he became Lord Burgess at the Vanguard in the fifties.

By the time I met him, Burgie was a spry octogenarian in a peaked cap who'd leveraged his outsize success with Belafonte to enjoy later triumphs, as a proud Brooklyn immigrant's son made good, that included being asked to pen Barbados's national anthem when his mother's home island won its own freedom from Britain. Burgie rolled his late model Buick to a stop on MacDougal Street, and, after ordering a cappuccino, was a picture of self-satisfaction as he explained how mechanical royalties work. "Every time they play 'Day O' in Yankee Stadium or the Garden, you know who gets a check? Me!"

If Harry was salty about losing out on those royalties to a collaborator with whom he spoke rarely after they fell out in the sixties, he didn't talk much about it. His greater concern was being dubbed America's "King of Calypso"—a crown, granted him by his marketers and the press, that he roundly rejected. Harry was at pains to explain that most of the songs on *Calypso*, including his biggest hits, bore little relation to the music the album's title invoked. "Two of my biggest records right now are not even calypso," he told *Newsweek* at the time. "'Jamaica Farewell' is a West Indian folk ballad and 'Day O' is a West Indian work song." Calypso on its birth island of Trinidad, by contrast, had deep ties to the country's carnival and local politics, and functioned there, as Harry also explained, as "a kind of living newspaper." He loved calypso and insisted he'd continue to sing calypsos as he liked, but warned against what would happen to the music, in an American context, once "the fast-buck guys hop onto it." In early 1957, he wrote a column for the *New York Mirror* to say more: "The present hysterical type of fervor for any melodies that even remotely resemble calypso will wear out and drive it to premature obscurity," he wrote. "I wish to be accepted strictly on my merits as an artist who sings songs of all the world, rather than be representative of any specific area— and certainly not as a symbol of a contrived craze."

His disavowals—and warnings—weren't heeded. Over the latter half of 1956 and the first part of the next year, many pop music mavens became convinced that calypso was destined to beat out rock 'n' roll as the dominant fad among America's teens. This putative craze emerged just as "teenagers" entered the national lexicon as a distinct group of consumers; it may have been illusory from the start. But such was its currency in Hollywood that by early 1957, four Hollywood studios were readying to release "teen-pics" about calypso's putative hold on American youth—among them *Bop Girl Goes Calypso,* from United Artists, *Calypso Joe* from Allied Artists, and *Calypso Heat Wave* from Columbia. The latter's cast included a young singer and dancer of Trinidadian extraction named Maya Angelou; she went on to win fame as the author of *I Know Why the Caged Bird Sings*, but her first and last album as a singer, released that year, was called *Miss Calypso*.

Broadway producers, too, got in on the act. One launched a revue, at Loew's Metropolitan Theatre in Brooklyn, called *Caribbean Calypso Festival*. Its star was the mighty Trinidadian dancer (and future Bond villain) Geoffrey Holder—a performer who'd made his name in New York in a Caribbean-themed musical, *House of Flowers*, written by Truman Capote and in which Holder played the lord of the cemetery in Haitian vodou, Baron Samedi. For this new revue, music was by Tito Puente's orchestra; Maya Angelou was also on the marquee. But the failure of *Caribbean Calypso Festival* to take flight, or reach the Great White Way, signaled its namesake fad's demise.

When *Calypso* was knocked from atop *Billboard's* Top Pop Albums in April 1957 by—who else—Elvis Presley, there were no other calypso records on the charts. The contrived competition between calypso and rock 'n' roll was over before it began. Americans who'd enjoyed so-called calypsos like "Day O" and "Jamaica Farewell" had little appetite, it turned out, for the real thing from Trinidad—or even for ersatz calypso by performers other than Belafonte. Among his rash of imitators was the actor Robert Mitchum, who in 1957 released an LP called *Calypso—Is Like So* . . . featuring loving covers of Trinidad classics by the likes of Lord Melody and the Mighty Sparrow. But apart from Rosemary Clooney's campy "Mangos" and Terry Gilkyson's "Marianne," no one succeeded in scoring a calypso-flavored U.S. hit. The closest anyone came was the Tarriers: a white folk-pop group, led by the young Alan Arkin, whose own version of "The Banana Boat Song"—which featured the chorus from another Jamaican folk song, "Hill and Gully Rider"—reached #4 on the pop singles chart, besting even Belafonte's version, which peaked at #5.

Harry had disavowed the putative "craze" from the start; he'd even predicted its demise. But no matter. In the United States, where *Calypso*'s hits brought his voice and image into millions of households, he was to remain linked to the Caribbean from then on. In the Caribbean, *Calypso*'s impact was also profound. After "Day O" and "Jamaica Farewell" hit, no hotel band in the British West Indies could get away without knowing both tunes. During carnival in Trinidad in 1956, the calypsonian King Solomon called him out. "Harry Belafonte!" King Solomon sang. "Hear what the critics say! They are positive, you know, that Trinidad is the mother of calypso." But other leading lights of the form there, like the great Mighty Sparrow, credited him with furnishing an invaluable boost to the island's music. *King Sparrow's Calypso Carnival*, the latter's first full-length LP, was released in 1959 in the West Indies and the U.S. by an American audiophile and calypso enthusiast, Emory Cook. It included a tune called "No More Rocking and Rolling," on which Sparrow hailed the truth that, as he put it, "I say calypso sweeping the place, like if she come out of space!" He continued:

> *Calypso sweeping the place, like if she come*
> *out of space*
> *I can remember rock-and-roll had the whole*
> *place under control*
> *But since calypso leave Trinidad, rock-and-roll*
> *really suffering bad*

Many folksingers before Belafonte had gained success via the nostalgia-soaked evocation of a landscape from their youth. Woody Guthrie, for one, had made his name evoking his arid Oklahoma boyhood on *Dust Bowl Ballads*. What separated Belafonte's record from the work of many folk purists (apart from its sheer popularity) was that Belafonte was not at all concerned to present his music as an authentic re-creation of Jamaican or any other island's culture. Rather, *Calypso* evoked a generic pan-Caribbean: a fantasy

island-world easy on the ears and minds of Americans, with
their predilections for sand and sun, but with enough aspects
of island tradition, too, to tap into the nostalgia and realities
of West Indians in New York. The political climate in the
Caribbean and its diasporas during the 1950s shaped Belafonte's music in ways more atmospheric than concrete. But
as evinced by his ties to Louise Bennett, a key cultural figure
in the era of Jamaica's drive toward winning independence
from England in 1962, Belafonte's *Calypso* was the product
of a distinct historical moment in the region defined by the
islands' movement toward ending colonial rule, on the one
hand, and by a continued mass exodus of their people, on
the other, for Northern cities in the 1940s and '50s.

Belafonte may have been at pains to disavow his false
"King of Calypso" crown. But he would soon return to the Caribbean in his music, on records like *Belafonte Sings of the
Caribbean* (1957) and *Jump Up Calypso* (1961). Moreover, in
the next movie he agreed to make for Hollywood, he played
the same role he enacted when performing songs like "Jamaica Farewell": as idealized Caribbean man and acceptable object of white affection. The platform his celebrity
now afforded him in American culture was unprecedented
for a Black entertainer—and coincided with the rise of a new
mass movement for equal rights whose foremost leader
Harry met, for the first time, just as *Calypso* hit stores.

In the spring of 1956, Belafonte became a pop star of pop stars. He was also still a young man of twenty-nine. But that gave him a couple of years on a young preacher from Atlanta who'd begun to make national news as the minister of a Baptist church in Montgomery, Alabama. The Reverend Martin Luther King Jr., then all of twenty-seven, was leading a campaign to desegregate Montgomery's buses in the wake of the Supreme Court's landmark 1954 decision, in *Brown* v. *Board of Education*, to overturn the doctrine of "separate but equal" and declare state-sponsored segregation of public schools illegal. The Reverend King placed a call to Belafonte to let him know he was coming to New York. The occasion was a sermon King was giving for fellow clergy, at the Abyssinian Baptist Church in Harlem. His aim was to attract support for his campaign, which had been launched by the refusal of Rosa Parks, a few months before, to cede her bus seat to a white rider.

King wondered if "Mr. Belafonte," as the polite young preacher addressed Harry, might like to come see him speak. About that, he needn't have worried. Harry had been following developments in Montgomery with keen interest. He'd also heard that King was quite an orator. Harry wasn't a church man himself: in fact, his lack of faith was yet another source of tension, in his tension-filled marriage, with the devoutly Catholic Marguerite. But he was a lover of stagecraft

and speechifying who'd long been fascinated, both as a thespian and an ally to labor organizers, by the question of how
to vest spoken words with magnetic moral force. At Abyssinian Baptist, he was duly bowled over by hearing King speak.

The two repaired to the church basement after King descended from his pulpit. The reverend made his pitch: "I
have no idea where this movement is going," he said. "I need
your help." Harry offered it: he wrote a big check that same
afternoon to the Montgomery Improvement Association.
More importantly, he gained a friendship that would, over
the next twelve years, prove vital to his and King's lives; to
the larger movement they built; and indeed—it's no over-
statement to say—to a society forever changed by their bond
and their work together.

If America was changed by their friendship, so was Harry:
he would credit Dr. King, whom he soon came to call Martin
and then called his best friend, with giving him a school for
living and a model for social action that became, for Harry,
akin to a religion he didn't know he needed. "I wasn't nonviolent by nature," he'd say, "or if I was, growing up on Harlem's streets knocked it out of me." At first, nonviolence
struck him "more as a shrewd organizing tactic than anything else." But it would become, for Harry, something more.

"As I got to know Martin better, and saw nonviolence put to the test, I would come to appreciate its spiritual and emotional value. I'd find I wanted to live by those values myself, both to help the movement and to wash away my personal anger."

In the event, and as he'd admit elsewhere, "washing away" his anger was perhaps less possible, and less desirable, than channeling it. And what he came to owe to King's movement, even as he began to delve more deeply into his anger's roots, was that channel *par excellence*. "Perhaps in the end," he reflected in *My Song*, "where your anger comes from is less important than what you do with it." Thus he came to feed the guiding emotion of his youth—the anger he felt toward his parents and his peers, but also toward his own self and the racist society that shaped him—into his work as a performer and then, in the years after he met Dr. King, also as an activist whose work on behalf of civil rights would come to occupy much of his time and money.

The comment, as a summation of his life's arc written as an old man, ties things up nicely: "where your anger comes from is less important than what you do with it." But at twenty-nine and in 1956 he was still a young one, bedeviled by demons, with a failing marriage, struggling to process how people who'd previously ignored him or met his gaze with suspicion—white women, especially—now followed him adoringly down the street. He went so far, in 1957, as to describe these developments as "traumatic." "Here I was," he told a reporter from the *New York Post*, "a Negro, being accepted by people of all denominations, in all walks of life, by millions as a performer and an artist. Yet in my personal life, I was nowhere, not ready for it. I have a swell group of friends of mixed color and denomination—but a small group. I wasn't prepared for this universal acceptance. All of a sudden there are crowds coming to see you, hundreds of faces looking at you wherever you go, other performers coming to see you work. You're suddenly this special kind of thing. I was too strong to collapse physically, so I collapsed mentally."

Amidst these disorientations, and as he wrestled with how to square his celebrity status with his broken home life and an only-enlarged determination to serve causes he believed in, Harry's search led him to the young Dr. King. It also led him, less fortunately, to a shady pair of characters whom he came to lean on heavily, for a time, in his confusing quest to square his newfound fame with his anger at the society that gave it to him.

Harry's exposure to psychoanalysis, whose mores and insights were essential to Method acting, dated to his time at the Dramatic Workshop and to an era when, he said, "talk of blocks and breakthroughs was as much in the air at Greenwich Village parties as politics and cigarette smoke." His pal Marlon Brando had begun analysis in 1948; now Harry had the will and means to take this leap himself. He'd met Janet Alterman Kennedy, the shrink he began seeing in 1955, after seeing her lecture at a resort, in New Hampshire's White Mountains, where he also had a gig. He got to know her and her charismatic husband better in New York after the pair came backstage, after a performance of *3 for Tonight,* to congratulate him—Jay Richard Kennedy was particularly moved by his rendition of "John Henry." Janet was affiliated with the psychiatry clinic at Columbia Presbyterian Hospital, where she specialized in treating Black and working class patients. Harry was intrigued, and asked if she'd take him on as a patient.

By now he was spending most of his time, when he wasn't on the road, not at the house he'd bought for Marguerite and their girls in Queens, but at sundry friends' places in Manhattan. He often visited Janet Kennedy's couch in the late afternoon, when their sessions could segue easily to cocktails and dinner, at her and her husband's swish apartment on Beekman Place, with this curious couple who encouraged their young charge to call them "mom" and "dad." Harry's psychic debt to Janet Kennedy, the first person to whom he'd fully unburdened the pain of a boyhood defined by his actual parents' withholding of approval and of love, quickly grew deep. He also confessed to his shrink that he was overwhelmed by how to handle his earnings. She suggested she knew someone who could help. He soon decided, after visiting Jay Richard Kennedy in his impressive office on Wall Street, to allow Kennedy—who talked a good game about investing in soy beans and also handled the money of a few other Hollywood stars—to handle his paychecks.

Jay Richard Kennedy, beyond his apparent bona fides as an investor, was also a successful writer; he had a popular mystery series on the radio, a novel, and two screenplays to his credit. Soon enough, he would insinuate himself not merely into looking after Harry's paychecks. Mr. Kennedy—one half of a pair who during this period seemed, as a friend of Harry's put it, to hold him "spellbound"—began acting as his manager, handling his bookings for concerts, and serving as a key consigliere on new projects: "He couldn't make the smallest decision on his own, he wanted Jay Richard Kennedy to make them all." None of this went over well, needless to say, with Harry's old manager. By now Harry had acquired a fancy Hollywood agent to handle his film and TV work, but he'd retained Jack Rollins to look after his nightclub bookings. Rollins sued for breach of contract, as was to be expected in their rough-and-tumble business. It didn't help Harry smell a rat. What eventually did was that Kennedy produced his booming career's one definitive bomb.

Sing, Man, Sing! was a musical revue inspired by *The Family of Man*, a hugely popular exhibition of photographs, curated by Edward Steichen and which hung in the Museum of Modern Art for much of 1955, beneath an entranceway bearing a quote from a Carl Sandburg poem: "There is only one man in the world / and his name is All Men. / There is only one woman in the world / and her name is All Women. . . ."). The show's five hundred images aimed to depict, in dramatic tableaux from around the globe, the full range of human experience "from birth and love and parenthood to poverty, war, and death"—and it featured not a few potent photographs, an impressed Harry noted, by the Black photographer Roy DeCarava in Harlem. He thought it could be good to craft a show that dramatized its sense of human universality, in a grand narrative reaching from prehistoric times to the present. His new manager seized on the idea—and wasn't shy about asserting his involvement in a show named *Jay Richard Kennedy Presents Harry Belafonte in "Sing, Man, Sing!"* This may have been a Belafonte vehicle, but as its press materials emphasized, Kennedy's involvement ran to "producing, writing, directing, and supervising every facet."

Its brand of universalism fell flat. The sanctimonious numbers, in which Harry played the role of He, opposite soprano Margaret Tynes as She (and with their parts also mirrored by a young dancer named Alvin Ailey as He, and one named Mary Hinkson as She), didn't "illustrate the basic likeness of all men by illustrating their very differences," as Harry, that summer, described his own folk repertoire's aims to a journalist. They flattened those differences to nothing. One Kennedy-penned song, "The Blues Is Man," found Harry not extolling that idiom's roots in Afro-America but claiming "the blues don't need a flag or race, just a lonely heart and a haunted face."

Reviewers weren't kind. A critic in Washington, D.C., where Harry and his producer brought *Sing, Man, Sing!* before New York, voiced a consensus view when he bewailed the "stifling banality" of the whole enterprise. To make matters worse, *Sing, Man, Sing!*'s New York premiere, at BAM in Brooklyn, coincided for its star with the onset of an ailment—nodules on the vocal cords—that would torment Harry for decades. Jay and Janet Kennedy didn't voice concern for his well-being; they found a doctor to coat his throat with ether, doing lasting damage to his instrument, so that he could go on with the show. This he did, for several performances—before informing his producer that he had no desire to bring this poor experiment to Broadway. Kennedy responded with rage—and Harry, now determined to extract himself from this harmful relationship, asked a savvy lawyer he knew from the labor movement to dig into his Svengali's background. What he learned was shocking.

Jay Richard Kennedy, who claimed to have been an Irish laborer and Dust Bowl refugee, wasn't who he said he was. In fact, he was a Jew from Bronx named Samuel Richard Solomonick who in the 1930s had been a stalwart member of the American Communist Party. He'd worked for a time as circulation manager of *The Daily Worker* and served as the treasurer of the party's Chicago branch—before then absconding with its funds and becoming involved, from a new home base in Mexico, in a fraudulent investment scheme that caught the attention of the FBI. Its agents quickly learned of Solomonick's past and offered him a choice: to serve hard time or join their cause as a spy. His brief in the latter role, after the Bureau helped him change his appearance and invent a new identity, was to befriend and inform on left-leaning actors with suspected communist ties.

Given Harry's politics and past associations, it was by that point a minor miracle that he hadn't earned a permanent spot on the McCarthy era's blacklists. He suspected he'd only managed to do so by paying a personal visit to Ed Sullivan before appearing on his show in 1954—when he evidently succeeded in impressing on the king of TV, a key arbiter of whether or not his guests' activities were in fact un-American, that while Harry was a passionate foe of racism and backer of progressive causes, he in fact was not a communist. How and whether information absorbed by Jay and Janet Kennedy made its way into his FBI file, which would grow thick in ensuing years, remains unclear. But Janet Kennedy had always been curiously insistent about probing Harry's links to Paul Robeson and others. And now he knew why.

Livid at their betrayal, Harry wanted to go straight to the press—but didn't, thanks to the wise counsel of a lawyer friend who helped extricate him from the Kennedys' clutches, with the help of a severance agreement and an NDA, with his bank accounts, if not his pride, intact. Harry soon found another therapist, whom he'd see for decades; that therapist, Peter Neubauer, became his life's most consistent ally and friend. But he resolved never to entrust his money, or major decisions about his career, to another manager again. Which is how it came to pass, in the fall of 1956 and with *Calypso* ruling the charts, that he became his own manager and launched an outfit called Belafonte Enterprises to create projects—on stage, on film, and in the ascendant medium of TV—of which Harry himself would be "producing, writing, directing, and supervising every facet."

11

In early 1957, Harry was on top of the world—or at least of a certain massive slice of American pop. The owner of the country's #1 and #3 albums (*Belafonte* had re-climbed the charts on the coattails of its follow-up) was also its most popular and highest-earning nightclub act. Plus he had another big movie heading for theaters—and this one, unlike *Carmen Jones*, had an interracial cast.

In fact, *Island in the Sun*, starring Harry Belafonte and Joan Fontaine, made him the first Black actor in an A-list Hollywood production to appear opposite a white star. (Its plot also featured a Caribbean love affair, for parity's sake, between a secretary played by Dorothy Dandridge and her English boss, John Justin). That spring, the film would famously be banned across much of the U.S. South because of the scandalous on-screen relationship it implied between Belafonte's character and the blond Fontaine. *Island in the Sun* was set in the Caribbean, but it wasn't hard to read as being about the United States: a kind of exporting, in a fantasy island milieu not unlike the one in *South Pacific*, of U.S. racial mores and anxieties—with the idealized West Indian, a charismatic labor leader and folk-singing man of the people, standing in for the more troubling U.S. Black. In the film his character's name may have been David Boyeur, but in every particular, down to his sailor's belt of interlocking rings, he looked a lot like Harry Belafonte.

Island in the Sun was a pet project of Darryl Zanuck, who'd snapped up the option to Alec Waugh's bestselling novel and then made turning Waugh's book into a blockbuster movie a priority. Given that Zanuck was Hollywood's most powerful producer, its chances of being made were excellent. But this didn't make coming up with a workable script from Waugh's material—a drama-filled portrait of the postwar British Caribbean, replete with political unrest and forbidden love and anticolonial ferment—any easier. In 1954, the Motion Picture Production Code had lifted its old ban on "miscegenation." But its new standards still urged that interracial romance be handled "within the careful limits of good taste"—a phrasing whose perfect opacity left much room for interpretation. "Good taste" of course varied in different parts of the country. Zanuck's company received a letter from the MPCC even before his screenwriter had set to work, voicing concern that *Island in the Sun* "could reasonably inflame Negro people."

Whether or not such concerns shaped Zanuck's thinking, it was the producer's own instincts that led him to enforce a key change to that story's plot: whereas in Waugh's novel both interracial pairs consummate their love, in the film their affairs' final resolution of marriage—John Justin leaves the island to wed Dorothy Dandridge—is only afforded the white man. Belafonte's character attracts and returns the love of a white woman from their island's colonial class, but he's ultimately forced to choose, as a Negro fighting for justice, between bedding her and uplifting his race. ("We should get a lift from the fact the Negro gives up the white girl he could have had," is how Zanuck put it in a script conference, "in order to devote himself entirely to the welfare of his people.") Harry, before signing a contract to appear in the film, had advocated for his character's love affair to at least come to fruition before coming to grief, and for other changes, too. But he was still figuring out how to wield his leverage with Hollywood, and even he saw that the more important goal was to make history by making the film. He had to content himself with trying, once he and his costars landed with their drunken director, Robert Rossen, in the

West Indies—shooting took place in Grenada and Barbados, in October and November 1956—to tweak their shooting script by ad-libbing new scenes and lines, as much as they could get away with, on set.

Zanuck's controversial film, whatever the particulars of its script, also signaled a new American interest in the Caribbean growing from a confluence of factors that had also fed into Harry's outsize *Calypso* success. For the generation of Americans whose sense of the world beyond America's shores was shaped by World War II, conceptions of the Caribbean were formed by the experience and stories of thousands of American servicemen who alighted in Trinidad during the war to build a naval base there and were charmed by the island's culture—its calypso and carnival and women. They also found they had alighted in a place that, along with other islands in the region, was beginning to move toward agitating for independence from the European powers that had long owned them as plantation colonies. America's military presence during the war was supposed to guard the Caribbean's waters from German U-boats. But it also hastened a sense, with the English and French now fading from the scene and the Spanish already gone, that the region was poised to become "an American lake": an archipelago under the sway of a new imperial power whose culture's influence was felt in the islands, as the British travel writer Patrick Leigh Fermor observed after a postwar swing through the region, in the form of "Coca-Cola advertisements, Frigidaires, wireless sets, and motorcars." Just as ever more emigrants from the Caribbean would settle in American cities, ever more Americans would begin heading in the other direction on vacation.

In Trinidad, one cultural outgrowth of the base the U.S. Navy built outside the island's capital, Port of Spain, during the war, was the advent of a musical instrument that became a prideful hallmark of Trinidadian culture. The inventors of "steel pan" drums, whose mighty bands of players still ply Port of Spain's streets at carnival time, built those drums from fifty-five-gallon oilcans whose fuel powered the Navy's boats. But this cultural exchange, even then, was a two-way street. In 1945 the American pop trio the Andrews Sisters scored a #1 U.S. hit with "Rum and Coca-Cola," a cover of a beloved calypso from Trinidad that presaged Belafonte's similar successes. The Andrews Sisters' producer, Morey Amsterdam, had learned "Rum and Coca Cola" on a U.S.O. trip to Trinidad in 1943: its originator was the calypsonian Lord Invader, who'd penned a typically wry and topical commentary on how well-paid American midshipmen, seeking their pleasure in Port of Spain's brothels and bars, lured the island's

women away from Trinidad's men. Key to the song's pop appeal was its lilting melody. But Lord Invader's risqué lyrics
("Both mother and daughter / are working for the Yankee
dollar") helped their version—notwithstanding their claiming not to know what those lyrics meant—sell seven million
copies. (Morey Amsterdam registered a U.S. copyright for
the song, but Lord Invader and the tune's Trinidadian composer, Lionel Belasco, successfully sued to get their due).

Seventeen years later, when Trinidad and its sister island,
Tobago, won their sovereignty from Britain, the presence of
the U.S. base there—whose control was now ceded to the
new nation—was foretold in the era's most memorable calypso. On "Jean & Dinah," the great Mighty Sparrow proclaimed that "Yankee gone / and Sparrow take over now."
But before Trinidad gained its independence in 1962, its
musical scene and self-image were deeply influenced by a
New York–based singer with Jamaican roots who exposed
the world to Trinidad's music and was anointed, ludicrously
in many Trinidadians' eyes, calypso's king. The touchiness
with which some reacted to that fact, compounded by the
baggage of "Rum and Coca-Cola"– style cultural theft, was
understandable. It wasn't surprising that when he visited
calypso's home island for the first time, during a layover on
his way to begin shooting *Island in the Sun* in nearby Grenada, Harry faced some pointed questions.

At Port of Spain's airport, Zanuck's PR flacks arranged a press conference for the foreign press they'd brought along to cover the production and a coterie of local journalists as well. One of these, on this proud island whose brash culture has never encouraged holding one's tongue, posed the question, "I'd like to ask you, sir—have you any conscience?" He recalled her attacking him for "[taking] the songs of the people of this region, cheapening them, changing them, and singing them in a way no has ever heard of, and then [having] the audacity to steal the title 'King of Calypso' with no regard for the culture of the region."

It was a moment he'd ruminate on for years: he "had to explain who and what I was and what I felt". The first part of his reply, in that hushed room, reiterated a point he'd made before: "First of all, let me say that I have never personally laid claim to be 'King of Calypso.' That was the decision of those I work for." But his embarrassment at how RCA had promoted him aside, Harry, who was never one to pull punches, went further. "But even if I could be the true King of Calypso, I wouldn't want to be. Because although I admire how clever and how interesting calypsonians can be in the songs they write and sing, I also find that most of those lyrics are not in the interests of Black people." This latter talking point, which found him decrying calypso songs that reinforced "the mythology [Europeans] have that we're all lazy, living out of a banana tree, fucking each other to death," was one he'd repeat. For calypso's exponents in Trinidad, whose ribald and humorous songs weren't aimed at Europeans at all, this made no sense. His misperceptions of their art form, which he'd never witnessed in Trinidad, perhaps derived from his sense of how calypso's more ersatz purveyors abroad—with their performative emphasis on straw hats and lewdness—did not project the image of Black dignity that he thought crucial. (Decades later, in a documentary film on the history of a music whose name if not its authentic sound he did more than anyone to make world-famous, Harry was at pains to make nicer with its originators. "Those who possess the calypsonian art are men of remarkable gifts, and there is a specialty to it that I am not privileged to embrace" is how he put it in *Calypso Dreams*. "What I did do was to use the environment of Caribbean lore to put us on the map at another level that I thought was instructive and creative for us, and in that service, if I have offended you, then I beg your forgiveness.")

The island where *Island in the Sun* was set, in any case, wasn't Trinidad. It was a fictional one, called Santa Marta, that bore on two old English colonies where the film was shot and whose people's push toward independence, like

Trinidad's and Jamaica's, was then nearing fruition. Barbados, whose old great houses and palm-fringed bluffs provide the backdrop for Harry's love scenes with Joan Fontaine, would win that independence in 1966—and ask Belafonte's old collaborator, Irving Burgie, to write its new national anthem. It's hard to imagine Burgie getting that gig without the hits he wrote for *Calypso*, and the new song he wrote for *Island in the Sun*—a signature tune for the film's protagonist, David Boyeur, whose ode to his island's denizens and shining sands became a staple of Belafonte's own repertoire. "This is my island in the sun," went Burgie's lyric, "where my people have toiled since time begun."

Burgie's theme song was but one of the bravura numbers with which Harry's David Boyeur, the singing folk hero of Santa Marta, paid homage to his home. In another, by the island's docks, he rallied its workers with "Lead Man Holler." Boyeur seeks the support of his island's black majority in an election against a son of its old elite and falls in love with the admiring daughter of its richest white family. But in the final cut of the film, and despite Belafonte and Fontaine's insistence on filming a few earnest love scenes, they don't even kiss: their most intimate moment involves drinking from the same coconut.

Boyeur's ultimate rejection of his love interest ("My own people wouldn't understand") seemed to reinforce the day's anti-miscegenation norms in the U.S. —norms that had long been looser, as Harry's own mixed heritage showed, in the Caribbean. But this didn't prevent *Island in the Sun*, even as it triumphed at the box office, from bestirring controversy and attracting death threats for its stars. (Zanuck, as a canny producer, wasn't above using controversy for publicity—he offered to cover fines for any theaters that dared to show it down South). And that controversy was augmented by events that had nothing to do with the film. Such was Harry's celebrity by then that his own life was a kind of spectacle for public consumption. And that spectacle's dramatic turns, in the event, didn't hew to those of a film that landed in theaters just as news hit the papers that he'd divorced Marguerite—and not only that. As Harlem's *Amsterdam News* put it: "BELAFONTE WEDS WHITE DANCER."

12

The white dancer in question was Julie Robinson. Julie had come of age in the same arty Manhattan milieu as her new husband, whose path she first crossed in his Dramatic Workshop days. The pair met properly when Marlon Brando, who'd been Julie's dance student and then her on-off boyfriend, asked his pal Harry to squire her to lunch out in LA. She'd grown up not far from where Harry did in New York, as the red-diaper daughter of Marx-reading Russian Jews in Washington Heights who sent her to the Little Red School House in Greenwich Village. A sharer of Harry's political passions, she was also no stranger to racial integration carried out in public, thanks to her work with the pioneering Black choreographer—"I never thought she'd integrate her company," she said of Katherine Dunham, "but I knew I was a good dancer"—who became Julie's mentor. Her first photo shoot with Harry seemed timed to underscore his cross-cultural appeal; it appeared in the same issue of *Look* magazine, in June 1957, that declared him America's "first Negro matinée idol."

The underlying causes of the divorce Harry and Marguerite had finalized in Las Vegas, earlier that spring, were clear enough. But his change of spouse nonetheless dealt his popularity a blow. "Many Negroes are wondering," blared *the Amsterdam News*, "why a man who has waved the flag of justice should turn from a Negro wife to a white wife." Harry was moved to pen a cover story for *Ebony* called "Why I Married Julie" (his simple answer: "I was in love with her"). That particular baleful column, in Black America's flagship glossy, appeared alongside a feature in which the magazine asked a cohort of prominent Negroes—Eartha Kitt, Duke Ellington, Mahalia Jackson—if they thought "interracial marriage hinders integration." Their unanimous reply: no.

To that point, the Black press had covered Harry's rise with pride, wondering at his success in negotiating the white establishment and winning white fans—rather than with the enthused interest reserved for Black performers like Fats Domino, Sarah Vaughan, or Nat King Cole, who were beloved by Black publics. When news broke of his "Holiday in Trinidad" special in 1955, the Black press emphasized that

Harry would have "complete say about the style and presentation of the half-hour segment . . . on an important show to be aired nationwide." Appreciation for his import and advocacy grew as he became increasingly outspoken about how TV, as he told one interviewer in 1955, was a medium on which "Negro life does not have an adequate representation and could be drastically increased." In August 1956, the *Chicago Defender* had published a series of interviews in which he connected his work as an entertainer with his determination to change American society. His refusal to perform in segregated venues and to play "Uncle Tom roles" in films or on TV, he emphasized, was of a piece with how he would always "maintain artistic integrity and public responsibility as a Negro"—which meant being "truly deeply proud of the traditions, achievements and stamina of his race" while also, as a member of the human family, remaining "truly deeply militant against bigotry in all its forms." Now with *Island in the Sun* in postproduction, he enthused about the movie he'd just shot. "This is the most important sociological film ever made," he told a journalist in London. "In the film Joan Fontaine is in love with me—and I reject her."

When Harry saw Zanuck and company's final cut with its neutered love affair, though, he was appalled. "It stinks," he said of a film he now declined to promote and that he described to the *New York Post*, in July 1957, as "a terrible picture based on a terrible bestselling book." He was now more determined than ever to decide for himself what stories—and which images of Blackness—he wanted to enact on-screen. That summer, he angrily turned down an offer to play the male lead in Samuel Goldwyn's big-budget adaptation of Gershwin's *Porgy and Bess* (Sidney Poitier took on Porgy in his place). Instead, he set up a company to manage his affairs, Belafonte Enterprises, and launched HarBel Productions, within it, to make films. It was the first Black-owned production company to make pictures with Hollywood's studios, and it made Harry the first Black person to gain such sway over the images Hollywood projected onto America's silver screens (at least until Poitier leveraged his own distinct success in the sixties).

———

Belafonte had wanted to take this step well before he had the resources to do so. In the late forties, he became involved with the Committee for the Negro in the Arts, or CNA. Founded in 1947, its mission was to "expose racial discrimination in the radio and television fields." Now he was in a position to pursue that vision; he asked old friends from the CNA and other fellow travelers to help. Among these was the Harlem-based writer John O. Killens, whose bestselling 1954 novel *Youngblood* gave us the phrase "kicking ass and taking names." With Killens and other collaborators, Harry developed pitches for a Western about freed slaves peopling Kansas after the Civil War, starring himself and Marlon Brando; for a biopic on that great man of Russian letters, Alexander Pushkin; for an adaptation of Eugene O'Neill's *Emperor Jones* that would reveal the play's hidden roots in Haiti and recount the revolution of Toussaint L'Ouverture.

None of these got made. But the project Harry did see green-lit as his first with HarBel was brought to him by a producer named Sol Siegel, who won MGM's backing to make a film he was calling *The End of the World*: a postapocalyptic yarn in which Harry would play a Pennsylvania mine inspector who, trapped underground when a nuclear bomb decimates the eastern seaboard, emerges to find a world devoid of life and makes his way to a deserted Manhattan whose silent streets, lined by empty buildings, echo like canyons as he cries out for fellow survivors.

The film, which by the time it entered production was mysteriously called *The World, The Flesh and the Devil* (a phrase from the *Book of Common Prayer*), was pitched to a moment of peak Cold War paranoia about the prospect of nuclear apocalypse. What drew Harry to the project, beyond the fact that he wouldn't have to leave New York to make it, was that his part in the story hadn't been written for a Black man: his and Siegel's feint toward color-blind casting, he felt, could furnish "a new way forward for Holly-wood." His character restores power to a Manhattan apart-ment house and revives an abandoned radio station over whose airwaves he tries to reach other survivors. The script called for his character to meet and fall in love with one sur-vivor, played by the Swedish-born actress Inger Stevens, be-fore they're joined by a third, an injured white man played by Mel Ferrer. There was real potential here, Harry felt, both to surmount old societal norms and to evoke, in these characters' relations, a new anti-racist dawn.

Unfortunately for him, HarBel's first contract with MGM meant that the latter's executives, rather than the star they'd hired, still had final say over the film's shooting script. And partway through production, those higher-ups blanched at rushes depicting the blooming romance between him and Stevens and changed the film's ending. It was one thing to have a Black man play a paragon of civic and courtly virtue at the end of the world. But far be it, in 1950s America, for him to actually get the girl: its now-nonsensical third act, contra-dicting the thrust of its rising drama to this point, found Ste-vens' character coupling not with the man who's saved her life, but the privileged white one whose Black rival stands down for the sake of peace—and the reification, even in a film that imagined a society freed from old dogmas, of per-sisting norms. It was *Island in the Sun* all over again.

Having come within an inch of quitting this picture in the midst of filming when he realized where it was heading, he also learned a lesson: in the next film his company produced, he made extra certain that final script approval rested not with the production's backers in Hollywood, in this case United Artists, but with him. *Odds Against Tomorrow* was a crime movie that hewed to the by-then hoary conventions, and black-and-white color palette, of film noir—but with the twist that its most sympathetic character, played by Harry, is a successful jazz musician who can only meet his debts to the mob and his responsibilities to his ex-wife and child by turning to crime. He falls in with a pair of would-be bank robbers, played by Ed Begley and Robert Ryan, who hatch a plan on the gray streets of Hudson, New York, where the film was shot, that will only come off if they can learn to heed their Black companion's wisdom.

With a script by the blacklisted writer Abraham Polonsky but credited to Harry's friend John O. Killens, *Odds Against Tomorrow* was directed by Robert Wise of *West Side Story* fame and featured a score by John Lewis of the Modern Jazz Quartet. Its credit roll and other qualities reflected HarBel's mission, with Black talent both in front of and behind the camera, of using Hollywood's largesse and reach to tell different kinds of stories. But as a moody crime flick that doubled as a racial melodrama, it bombed at the box office. In a year when moviegoers could choose to see that or Sidney Poitier in MGM's *Porgy and Bess,* they opted in droves for the latter.

Harry resolved, after *Odds Against Tomorrow,* to stay away from making films for a while: the 1960s were full of other callings. He wouldn't make one for the next eleven years. But television was another story. In the wake of his success with *Calypso*—success that began with a TV special—this was a happier hunting ground. "With his bestselling recordings he got America to sing his songs," as the wag who compiled his archive years later put it. "Through television they came to know who he was." He didn't merely become a master at crafting extended prime-time segments seen by tens of millions; he wielded his leverage with the networks in ways that would afford him—at least for a time—an astonishing amount of creative freedom in exchange for lending his image to advertisers. When, in June 1956, Harry did his old ally Ed Sullivan the favor of appearing on a special toasting the eighth anniversary of TV's most popular show, he used the occasion to tell the *New York Herald Tribune* how TV had to change. "An industry as vast and powerful as television needs the Negro and the Negro needs it," he said. "It is not enough for a singer like 'King' Cole to just appear occasionally and sing some pretty tunes." He set out, in the ensuing months and years, to show why.

In August 1957, Harry accepted an invitation from Nat Cole to appear on Cole's own variety show—a short-lived attempt on NBC to grant a top Black entertainer his own slice of prime time. Harry supported Cole by joining him for a jolly rendition of "Mama Look a Booboo," a tune he'd learned earlier that year while filming *Island in the Sun,* and whose composer, the calypsonian Lord Melody, he would later hire to help him write songs in New York. This ditty about an ugly boy, by a singer beloved in Trinidad for his cheery wit and homely looks, had a different resonance in Harry's hands. Thanks to a kinescope that's now on YouTube—with Harry at his most beautiful, hamming with Cole for the camera—you can see how his performance on TV of the song, which became a minor hit that year, ironized Melody's lyric in ways his recorded version never could.

Harry resolved only to appear on TV if allowed to perform "songs taken from the ethnic sources of all nations" and to lend his repertoire, from his stage show, its "proper setting." In 1958, Steve Allen handed over a twenty-minute segment of his popular program to Harry, who devoted this airtime, in ways that *The New York Times* said gave Allen's show "a tremendous lift," to a familiar medley of ballads and spirituals and work songs from Ireland and Israel and the

West Indies and beyond. A similar extended segment of Belafonte-ia, on the first *Bell Telephone Hour*, went over similarly well. Having embarked on a triumphal tour of Europe in the summer of 1958, he also taped a suite of songs in London for the BBC: they did well and helped his recording of "Mary's Boy Child" become, in England, a pop Christmas anthem to rival "White Christmas." Later that year, he signed a contract with Britain's flagship network to produce a series of shows there, over the next five years, for which the BBC, according to *Variety*, "[shelled] out the highest individual fee paid to one performer in its history." Finally, in the summer of 1959 and back home in America, he won an offer to produce the kind of extended special he'd long envisioned: he was able to convince CBS and Revlon, the cosmetics company that sponsored what became *Tonight with Belafonte*, to back his vision for sixty minutes of uninterrupted TV, buttressed between two three-minute ads for mascara and compacts, devoted to "a portrait of Negro life in America, told in song."

Ambition, in those days, was Harry's middle name. But the "portrait" he ended up producing for the makeup magnates who enabled it was, by all measures, a triumph. If the films he produced in this period earned mixed reviews and scant attendance, the idiom of the TV special was ideally pitched to his talent both for interacting with the camera and for lending songs a kind of stagecraft and dramatic arc borrowed from theater and the idiom of the Broadway revue. When the show aired on December 10, 1959, an audience of millions tuned in to absorb what seemed, from the soothing tones of "Shenandoah," sung by a harmonizing chorus over the opening credits, to be a dulcet piece of Americana—only then to be confronted, as the show began, by an unsmiling Belafonte, dramatically lit on a darkened soundstage, singing the chain gang holler "Bald Headed Woman." Behind him, a group of dancers were silhouetted in spotlight, enacting the hammering motions of shackled Negros at work. This history and its music—there was no mistaking the assertion being made—was America's story, too.

To direct his special, Harry had enlisted a young Norman Jewison, years before the young Canadian director made *In the Heat of the Night* and *Fiddler on the Roof.* Its music was conducted and arranged by Robert De Cormier, who by then had spent over a year leading the Belafonte Singers, a choral group who'd become a key feature of his concerts and recording dates. Its corps of dancers featured Arthur Mitchell, then the sole Black dancer in the New York City Ballet. Between segments, the camera scanned over large panels drawn by the artist Charles White, an old friend of Harry's from the Committee for the Negro in the Arts, depicting archetypal moments in Black life—children at play; couples in love; workers at work—to underscore their themes. The beloved bluesmen Sonny Terry and Brownie McGhee lent an authentic timbre and harmonica to "Jump Down, Spin Around." Most memorable, though, was the singer who amounted to Harry's costar on the program.

By the late fifties, Odetta already had made a name for herself as a folk singer. Born in Alabama and raised in Los Angeles, she'd cut her teeth at venues like the hungry i in San Francisco and New York's Blue Angel. Her first solo LP, *Odetta Sings Ballads and Blues*, had appeared in 1956 and became a touchstone for aspiring folkies; Bob Dylan would later credit it as the record that moved him to become one. For her third album, *My Eyes Have Seen*, Harry wrote an introductory note in July 1959. "There are many singers with fine voices, great range, and superb technique," he wrote. "Few, however, possess that fine understanding of a song's inner meaning, which transforms it from a melody to a dramatic experience." But she wasn't much known to the culture's mainstream when, after Harry followed his opening number with Lead Belly's "Sylvie," backed by his chorus, a spotlight turned toward a poised Black woman, her kinky hair cropped short, holding a guitar. She loosed a cry ("Waterrr boy!") that she answered herself, with a strum on her guitar, to announce a uniquely powerful voice and presence—that of a Black woman whose body wasn't thin and whose hair wasn't straightened—whose like hadn't been seen before, except in mammy-guise, on national TV. Soon enough, Odetta would become known as the Voice of the Civil Rights Movement. Here, she joined Harry for a kids' tune and a charming rendition of "Hole in the Bucket." She also loaned her deep and mighty instrument to "Jericho", during the spirituals segment of the program, and to a rousing closing number in which she joined Harry and his multiracial chorus in bidding the show's viewers, "Fare thee well."

The show received both rave reviews and strong ratings. At a time when TV was coming in for growing critique as a mindless medium, here was a special, wrote the entertainment reporter at the *Los Angeles Times*, "as good an excuse to own a television set as I can imagine." *Variety* hailed a "truly delightful and refreshing experience." Many reviewers, like one at *The Philadelphia Inquirer*, praised both the show's content and its sponsor's tact: here was "a fascinating hour of vocal and visual artistry," blessedly free of "mood-shattering interruptions." But perhaps no review was so quotable as a rave from A. S. (Doc) Young, a venerable figure in Black media whose column, The Big Beat, was then appearing in the *Los Angeles Sentinel*. "In about 55 minutes," Young wrote, "Belafonte climbed history's highest peak of achievement by a Negro showman." And this wasn't, in his eyes, by accident. "The Belafonte show was zenith, acme, and all that because, for the first time, a Negro was the production company head, as well as the star performer, in a televised spectacular seen in millions and millions of American homes. For the first time . . . a Negro production company head had the major say-so about what televiewers would and would not see in this prime time spectacular."

Tonight with Belafonte didn't just make Belafonte the first Black producer of a prime-time special on American TV; it won him an Emmy for the year's Outstanding Performance in a Variety or Musical Program. Revlon's marketers, for their part, may not have been wholly pleased that department stores across the South removed Revlon products from their shelves. But the company and CBS were so happy with the show's larger success that they gratefully signed Harry up, again with unheard-of terms allowing him to fill their airtime however he wished, in five more such hourlong specials. All these rewards, to Harry, no doubt meant a lot. But what its larger success meant to him was evinced most strongly in a bound leather scrapbook I found in his archive at the Schomburg decades later, embossed on its cover with the phrase *TONIGHT WITH BELAFONTE*.

In the scrapbook's overstuffed pages there were production notes and sketches for the show's striking sets; song lyrics and contact sheets full of photos; several dozen pages of press clippings and awards; and then, in the volume's most personal section, page after page of telegrams, addressed to his new home on Manhattan's West End Avenue, bearing congratulations and praise from associates and friends. His daughters Adrienne and Shari sent kudos from their mother's house in Queens:

> DEAR DADDY WE STAYED UP TO SEE
> YOU TONIGHT WE ENJOYED EVERY
> MINUTE OF THE SHOW WE THINK
> YOU'RE WONDERFUL AND WE LOVE
> YOU VERY VERY MUCH.

One Richard Ashby, public affairs producer at CBS's Hollywood affiliate, spoke for many in the industry (if not down South):

> THANKS FOR THE GREATEST HOUR
> I'VE EVER [HAD] ON TV AND PRAISE
> TO REVLON FOR THEIR TACT.

Said Harry's collaborator Charles White:

> THE WHOLE SHOW WAS A TRIUMPH
> PROUD TO BE ASSOCIATED WITH IT
> HIGHLIGHT OF MY LIFE.

Joan Blondell, the veteran actress:

THANK YOU FOR THE ADULT
MAGNIFICENCE THAT YOU
BROUGHT TO TELEVISION.

Mr. and Mrs. Billy Eckstine were more jocular:

ABSOLUTELY ONE OF THE MOST
ENTERTAINING SHOWS I'VE SEEN IN
MANY A MOON KEEP GOING OLD BUDDY.

Sidney Poitier sent two.

WE HAVE COME A LONG WAY, AND THIS
NIGHT WE HAVE ARRIVED AT ONE OF
THE STATIONS ON THAT LONG ROAD
TO FULFILLMENT

went the first.

The second was more succinct. It referred to discus-
sions they'd evidently had about Sidney joining the show.
Said Harry's old friend:

YOU NEEDED ME LIKE A HOLE IN THE
HEAD. LOVE, SIDNEY.

13

The address to which those telegrams were sent—300 West End Avenue—was a stately red-brick apartment building near the Hudson River at 74th Street. Harry and Julie had recently moved there from the cozy bachelor pad where they'd lived as newlyweds after they resolved, in the fall of 1958 and with their son David nearing his first birthday, to find a more spacious place in Manhattan. They set out first to do so on the Upper East Side, but when Harry made inquiries, brokers and building owners in that bastion of tony Waspdom made it clear that he and his family might feel more welcome elsewhere. By now he was a prized performer and welcome guest at the Waldorf Astoria. But New York's housing market was as racist as ever. He lodged a complaint with the city that became public when Eleanor Roosevelt, in her

JOSHUA JELLY-SCHAPIRO

nationally syndicated column, decried the fact that this great New Yorker couldn't find a home for his lovely family.

Turning down Roosevelt's kind offer to take them in herself, Harry and Julie expanded their search to the more liberal (and more Jewish) West Side—only to be confronted, when they found an apartment that they liked on West End Avenue, with a racist landlord there, too. This time Harry had his white publicist apply for the apartment in his stead and acquire a lease, which Harry then signed himself. He and Julie moved into their new flat not long before his *Tonight with Belafonte* triumph—and then went one better. They hatched a plan, before that lease expired and with the help of a few of their fellow tenants, to buy the entire building from its racist owner—as it happened, a son of the Dominican dictator Rafael Trujillo. Then Harry converted all its apartments' renters into owners of shares in a larger enterprise he financed to create one of the Upper West Side's first co-ops—and combined adjoining apartments into a palatial home for him and Julie that occupied the building's entire eighth floor.

Soon enough, "Harry's building" would also become home to Lena Horne and other friends, like the great jazz bassist Ron Carter. But the larger significance of the home Harry and Julie made there for decades, apart from 300 West End Avenue being where they raised their kids, David and Gina, was the role it came to play for Martin Luther King—who for the next decade stayed there whenever he was in New York—and for the "kitchen cabinet" of a movement whose leaders often convened, if not in Harry and Julie's kitchen, then at least by the oak bar in their red-walled living room nearby. The energy and savvy with which he'd sought to use and expand his fame from that home base was massive. So was the feedback loop of adrenaline and praise, not always healthful, that his nonstop schedule won him. Now he'd segued from the role of performer to that of producer. But it was as an activist that he would soon most identify, as he came to feel that "for all the passion I still showed onstage, as a man, I felt far more immersed in a movement that could not—must not—fail."

In May 1957, Harry traveled to Washington, D.C. to hear Martin Luther King, from the steps of the Lincoln Memorial, address some 30,000 people gathered for a "Prayer Pilgrimage" organized by A. Philip Randolph and the just-born Southern Christian Leadership Conference. It was a key harbinger of the "I Have a Dream" speech he'd give from these same steps six years later—and the first time many Americans, tuning in to news reports of what occurred, heard his voice. Seventeen months later, in October 1958, Martin was recovering from being stabbed in New York and couldn't lead the 10,000 students, both white and Black, who marched to the White House to demand that the federal government enforce the desegregation of America's schools. Harry, just returned from a European tour on which he'd repeatedly been asked by journalists about when and how the government would uphold the Supreme Court's decision in *Brown*, made the trip to D.C. again to help. When the marchers reached the White House's gates, Harry made a show, for the watching TV cameras, of asking a guard who refused his group entry—President Eisenhower was out playing golf—to give his assurance that a petition signed by thousands calling for the immediate integration of schools and colleges across the South reach the president's desk.

If Harry's political and producing work were now occupying much of his time, his career as a recording artist was by no means through. The LP he released in 1958 didn't hit. Belafonte wasn't a bluesman, and on *Belafonte Sings the Blues*, it showed: lacking both that idiom's rootsy grit and the plush range of his Caribbean hits, it was a fine-sounding record but also an album on which, as one critic put it, "one number erases the next." The same couldn't be said for the eclectic stage show he now brought to the world's top concert halls, backed with dynamic precision by a well-drilled band and his own chorus, the Belafonte Singers. And in 1959, he recorded a concert at Carnegie Hall, given to benefit a school founded by his friend Eleanor Roosevelt for unprivileged boys, that became a landmark. Captured in glorious "Living Stereo," the recording of *Belafonte at Carnegie Hall* was directed by a pro-

ducer, Bob Bollard, who'd also overseen Emory Cook's seminal recordings of carnival in Trinidad—and was now working
with RCA to bring the wonders of stereophonic sound to the
masses. The resulting album awakened many to that technology's power to evoke, with magical fidelity when the right
mics were used for recording and the right speakers for playback, the three-dimensional experience of hearing music
performed in one of the world's great concert halls. Prized by
audiophiles for the aura of "presence" the record lent Harry's
voice and accompanists, and the crowd they charmed, it also
heralded the rise of a new kind of LP—the "live" album—that
became a staple of the record business.

Belafonte at Carnegie Hall also gave sonic form, in the
rousing rendition of "Matilda" that closed out the concert, to
the breadth of his appeal. "Women over forty!" he entreated
during its call-and-response chorus. "Now the intellectuals!"
This merry calypso about a woman robbing her man's money
was no kind of protest song. But given the growing role of his
politics in his public reputation, and the movement then
building across the country, the communal form he gave to
such songs resonated both for his live audience and for the
millions who heard them singing along with him on this
album and its equally popular 1960 sequel, *Belafonte Returns
to Carnegie Hall*. Here was a singer, wrote the critic Nat
Hentoff, whose uniqueness lay less in singing material "with

protest in it" than in cueing white audiences "to understand this is a protest they are invited to be a part of." And Harry, for his part, had similar thoughts about the ideas and ideals his fans projected onto him, and which he cultivated in turn. "Folk songs were anthems of the dispossessed, rallying cries for justice," he reflected of his songs from the 1950s. "And when white audiences listened to this black singer bring them to life, they were doing more than enjoying the tunes, or the way I sang them, or even the sex appeal I brought to the mix. If you liked Harry Belafonte, you were making a political statement, and that felt good . . . If you were a white Belafonte fan, you felt even better. You were connecting with your better angels, reaching across the racial divide. Consciously or not, you were casting your vote for equality."

Equality, as a cause and ideal, is not the same as integration. And integration, when it comes to battling racism and as recent generations of activists remind us, is not the same as racial justice: the acceptance into white spaces of certain Negroes—the tickled laughter of those "women over forty" in Carnegie Hall, crushing on Harry—should never be mistaken, on a systemic level, for redressing inequities affecting millions. But in those early days of the civil rights movement, when its leaders were galvanized by insisting that the country enforce its own Supreme Court's will, "integration" was a buzzword that Harry, too, espoused as a goal whose halting realization also fed his affection for the multicultural melting pot that was New York City.

In his first triumphal TV special for Revlon, he had presented "a portrait of Negro life in America, told in song." He prepared to produce his second, in the fall of 1960, after returning from a hugely successful world tour that brought him from Japan to Australia to Moscow. He decided to present a portrait of life in New York that celebrated the great array of cultures and songs one could encounter on a single stretch of the city's blocks. His inspiration came from his old friend Tony Schwartz, the agoraphobic genius of audio who in 1954 had released an album with Folkways called *New York 19*—a record of all the varied lifeways and sounds to be found in the Manhattan postal code from which Schwartz rarely strayed on the west side of midtown. Including a chunk of the theater district and blocks of Hell's Kitchen long peopled by Irish immigrants and now home to many Puerto Ricans, New York 19 also included wharves where ships and people from around the globe landed near the Palladium Ballroom, where mambo was the rage. Here was the city as world—and as setting for a TV special that, in Harry's riff on Schwartz's record, featured "Guantanamera," "Hava Nageela," and selections from a show, *My Fair Lady*, that was then tearing up Broadway.

The ratings and reviews for Harry's TV version of *New York 19,* which aired on CBS on November 20, 1960, weren't as rhapsodic as they had been for *Tonight with Belafonte.* But they also weren't bad. What put paid to the contract he'd signed with Revlon to produce four more such specials—he had visions for specials celebrating the music of Africa, and folk traditions from around the world—was how *New York 19* enacted its premise: by making a blatant show of depicting both grown-ups and children all playing and singing and dancing together (where in the first special, Arthur Mitchell had twirled and bounced with a fellow Black dancer called Mary Hinkson, now he did so opposite Julie Robinson Belafonte). Such displays of integrated life weren't wholly new to TV. On *Tonight with Belafonte,* a year before, the corps of backing vocalists that supported Harry and Odetta's renditions of Negro folk songs and spirituals included white singers as well as Black ones. Its great victory, observed A.S. Young, lay in not bragging about this fact but instead presenting its integrated cast as being "natural as a morning sunrise." But including a few white members in one's chorus, evidently, was one thing; displaying white and Negro and brown children playing together and mixed-race pairs of dancers engaged in kinetic flirtation was another.

Some weeks after *New York 19*'s airing, Harry was called in for a meeting with Revlon's CEO. Charles Revson was a Jew and a great fan of Harry's; he made a throat-clearing show of sharing how he'd been subject to his fair share of prejudice himself. But then he came to his point: The angry noise he was hearing from CBS's affiliate stations in the South meant he had a request. He and those stations would have no problem, going forward, with shows featuring an all-Black cast; what they couldn't abide was another program that made such a spectacle of integration. This, to Harry, was anathema. "If you asked me to put on a flowery shirt and sing more calypso tunes because that's what white people like," he'd recall telling Revson, "I would consider it. But when you tell me no whites, you've crossed a line: morally, socially, and politically. There's no way to square it. I cannot become re-segregated."

With that, he gave up the remarkable platform furnished by television—for the time being. But with the big check Revson cut him to cancel his contract, which saw Belafonte paid in full for his unmade specials, he had other endeavors to fund. As the 1960s got under way in earnest, he turned to combating segregation not on TV but on the ground. Having devoted a great deal of energy and money to trying to integrate the images that colored Americans' lives, he would credit his fallout with Revlon with helping him realize that culture could change only so much before the society its media reflected also evolved. "To change the culture you have to change the country," is how he put that epiphany's lesson.

14

————

The dichotomy proffered by that line—between changing the culture and changing the country—implies needing to choose between them: Harry concluded that his energy might be better spent, for a time anyway, confronting America's racial politics head-on. He would prove to be as deft a political operator as he was a cultural one. But Harry's own career, in which he never halted his cultural work entirely, proved what political theorists like Antonio Gramsci and Stuart Hall have long argued: that the dichotomy between culture and politics, when the goal is large-scale social change, is a false one. Stuart Hall was a Jamaican contemporary of Harry's whose parents left the island not for New York but England. He made his name as an intellectual and broadcaster there by insisting—from his pathbreaking perch at the BBC—that a "long march through the institutions," and through England's culture industries specifically, was as important to advancing the lot of Black Britons as formal politics was. And the huge strides Harry made in that long march, in the U.S. in the fifties and after, were vital to the flourishing of the political movement that became central to his and so many others peoples' lives in the 1960s.

Around that decade's start, Harry shifted from devoting most of his time and energy to his career in entertainment to serving, in whatever ways he could, the cause and goals of Dr. King. He never tired of insisting that this leap, for him, really wasn't one: he'd been an activist before he became an actor, he said, so turning the dial back was no big deal. But what defined his involvement in, and importance to, the roiling politics of those years weren't activities common to celebrities who embrace the "activist" tag. To be sure, he was a prodigious fundraiser and funder of the movement. He was also a hardcore lefty who was a folksinger and a union man: he loved a good march (preferably undertaken while singing). But what made him most vital to the movement's successes weren't activities that in some instances can seem to have more to do with moral vanity than making change. They were activities born of his vocation as an overtly *political* actor—as bridge and go-between, and mediator and manipulator of forces, both for personalities within the movement and in vital exchanges between its leaders and the federal government.

In both these realms, 1960 furnished a crash course. His correspondence from the first months of that year evince a man working furiously to leverage his connections and fame, in New York and across the country, to bolster the cause and ideals of Dr. King and his organization, the Southern Christian Leadership Conference. One way he did so was to help found a New York–based organization, chaired by A. Philip Randolph and Bayard Rustin and with Nat King Cole in the role of treasurer, called the Committee to Defend Martin Luther King, Jr., and the Struggle for Freedom in the South. Harry volunteered to lead the committee's Culture Division, and enlisted Sidney Poitier to help. The minutes of their meetings and the flurry of appeals they sent to prospective backers that spring suggest not just days but weeks devoted to the cause. Most of the stars to whom they reached out signed on with gusto. A few didn't. Harry and Sidney weren't shy in those cases about voicing disappointment. They sent Sammy Davis Jr. an upbraiding letter for flaking on a meeting. "It is unfortunate that in the current struggle for civil rights and liberties, [to which] you could contribute so much, that you can't be more disciplined." They closed with a succinct note of sarcasm: "Thanks a lot."

Dr. King. sent a letter to Harry, dated March 9, 1960, to thank him for all was doing to aid their struggle. It became one of Harry's prized possessions. "You and Julie have certainly given me renewed courage and vigor to carry on,"

Martin said. "I can assure you that your personal concern and support will remain meaningful to me so long as the cords of memory shall lengthen."

———

By the time Harry received that letter from King, he was also readying to aid the cause down south, whose youthful members' tactics and determination Harry first learned of that February in his kitchen on West End Avenue. He opened the paper, as he recounted to me decades later, to see that a brave group of students down in Greensboro, North Carolina had sat down at a lunch counter in a Woolworth's there and refused to leave until they were served.

Those students' bravery, and photos of their being jeered by white counterparts who dumped ketchup on their heads, didn't just galvanize Harry. Their successful sit-in model spread across the South—and made clear that young people had a key role to play in a movement whose essential internal dynamic, to that point, had pitted the deliberative nonviolence of King's SCLC against the even more cautious tactics of old-guard organizations like the NAACP. The organization that those students from the sit-ins founded a short time later, the Student Nonviolent Coordinating Committee, or SNCC, was launched by young veterans of King's movement—notably, Ella Baker, who'd been with King since the Montgomery

Improvement Association. But the "SNCCers" embrace of Ghandian tactics meant avowing more aggressive forms of what Baker and her comrades called "direct action"—demonstrations meant to provoke mass arrests—and they voiced frustration at certain of their elders' ways, including the preacherly piety and top-down nature of Dr. King's leadership. Harry's involvement with SNCC—and with mediating between these young upstarts and Dr. King—began at its birth; he wrote his first check to the group in April 1960, at SNCC's founding conference. Weeks later, in a seemingly unrelated development, a young senator from Massachusetts reached out to seek Harry's support in his campaign for president.

Where Harry's role within the movement was to serve as a bridge between its radical youths and pious elders, he was now asked, by John F. Kennedy, to connect his campaign to Black America. In the run-up to that summer's Democratic convention, Harry was squarely in the camp of Kennedy's no-hope progressive rival, Adlai Stevenson. He also had little reason to think that Kennedy was interested in the cause that mattered to him most: as a senator, JFK had in fact voted against the Civil Rights Act of 1957. For that reason, another Black celebrity whom both parties viewed as essential to cultivating the Black vote—Jackie Robinson—had already come out in favor of the presumptive Republican nominee, Richard Nixon. At first, Harry resisted meeting Kennedy. But eventually he acquiesced to a meeting—and informed him clearly, when the senator arrived with the Secret Service to ask for Harry's support in the general election, that the real key to the Negro vote wasn't Harry Belafonte or Jackie Robinson. It was Dr. King.

Kennedy had paid this visit to assure Harry that he was now a friend of civil rights. He also belonged to a party whose Southern wing was staunchly segregationist: an overt alliance with Jim Crow's foremost foe in Dixie, at least before he took the White House, wasn't one Kennedy could readily make. He hadn't considered, as Harry urged him to, that there were in fact millions of other votes on offer in Southern states—Black ones—that could be his if he supported the right of disenfranchised Negroes to cast them. But both left that initial meeting, a summit as replete with mutual suspicion as mutual respect, convinced that they had reasons to keep talking. And so began a fateful dance, between the Kennedy and King camps, that Harry first served by urging Martin to meet with Kennedy—they did so a few weeks later, in June 1960—and then by brokering what would prove, for both camps, a vital political partnership.

Advising Dr. King to withhold his formal backing for JFK, Harry offered his own after the convention. He taped an advertisement with the soon-to-be-president in Harlem. Nodding along as the patrician senator voiced his suddenly ardent support for civil rights, Harry then turned to the camera and let its target audience—his fans, and Black voters—know: "I'll be voting for Kennedy. Will you?" And then, two weeks before the general election, King was arrested in Atlanta. He'd taken part in a sit-in at a Rich's Department Store—and then saw a judge in another Georgia county, where he'd committed the putative misdemeanor of driving in Georgia with an Alabama license, order him imprisoned for breaking the terms of his suspended sentence for the earlier infraction. Helping secure King's release, before he came to harm in prison, became a test that the Kennedy camp—after Harry got his pals Frank Sinatra and Sammy Davis to impress its urgency on them—ultimately passed.

At this point, Bobby Kennedy, John's soon-to-be attorney general, was not a known or trusted entity to Harry or other of Martin's close advisers: in fact he'd been an active participant in Joe McCarthy's Senate Subcommittee on Investigations, and was a figure of suspicion. But Martin's mantra with regards to Bobby Kennedy was one Harry liked to repeat: "Somewhere in this young man sits good," Martin had told him. "Our task is to find his moral center and win him to our cause." Actually pulling him to their cause would take years. But his action in this instance went some way to convincing Harry and Martin that it was possible. Bobby Kennedy placed a call to the judge who'd locked King up, and quietly reminded him that denying bail to a citizen arrested for a misdemeanor was unconstitutional.

Martin's release on the election's eve, for Harry and others, was a signal moment. Martin's father, "Daddy King," immediately transferred his own backing in the election from Nixon to Kennedy—and thought his son should do the same thing. But Harry urged strongly that he *not*: "If you anoint him and become his Black mouthpiece," he recalled telling Martin, "you'll pay a huge price if he lets us down." Martin released a letter thanking the senator for his help but held back his full endorsement, per Harry's wise counsel, the better both to remain officially above the fray and to grow his political capital by doing so. It was a decision that infuriated the Kennedys—but also earned their respect. "We circled each other for a long time" is how Harry described his approach to Bobby Kennedy to me, years later. "But we saw there were ways we could be useful to each other." Locating Bobby's moral center, as King urged, would take time. But the ways that he and Harry could be useful to each other were reinforced, from the start, by the results of an election that Bobby's big brother won by a whisker. The weekend before he did so, preachers in Black churches across the country received an urgent communique from the SCLC concerning Dr. King's gratitude for the Democrat's role in securing his release. A great many urged their congregants to vote accordingly.

15

At Kennedy's inaugural ball, Belafonte serenaded the dashing young president and his wife Jackie alongside Frank Sinatra and Gene Kelly and Laurence Olivier. Over the years, his dance with JFK and his brother, now installed atop the Department of Justice, would take many turns—and the Kennedys would seek to keep Harry close even as they frustrated him by seeming as concerned with limiting conflagrations on their watch as actually advancing the cause of civil rights. If those dynamics shaped his ties to the administration at home, he also became an emissary of its agenda abroad. On March 1, 1961—Harry's thirty-fourth birthday—Kennedy signed the Peace Corps into being, and Belafonte agreed to serve as the organization's "cultural adviser," focusing on Africa. By that time, he'd grown close with the South African singer Miriam Makeba, whom he'd met in London but who'd moved to New

York and now often joined him onstage during his concerts. Her presence in his orbit became a way not merely to call attention to the fight against apartheid in her homeland, but to propound his own agenda with the Peace Corps: connecting the fight to decolonize Africa to the struggle of African Americans, in the United States, for civil rights.

In his capacity as the White House's unofficial ambassador to the continent, Harry helped organize a series of airlifts that brought young people from Kenya and elsewhere to study at U.S. universities —including the young man who became Barack Obama's father. He also visited and bonded with Sékou Touré, president of the newly independent nation of Guinea. Touré, later known as a despot, was at the time a charismatic Pan-Africanist whose nation-building project, before Guinea was pushed to the Soviets by the Cold War's illogic, Harry urged Kennedy to support. Those entreaties fell on deaf ears—as would Harry's call to the president's younger brother in the spring of 1961 to ask that the federal government furnish protection to young activists from SNCC and other groups who were boarding interstate buses, at Greyhound and Trailways stations across the south, to test the Supreme Court's recent ruling that segregating public transit violated the Fourteenth Amendment.

Bobby Kennedy's reply to this request, to protect what became known as the Freedom Rides, was disappointing: he had no authority to send in National Guardsmen, he told Harry, if Southern governors didn't request them. More than that, the attorney general wondered: was it really the time for confrontation? To this, Harry replied in kind: he had no authority, he said, to tell John Lewis and Bob Moses and Ella Baker what to do. And more than that, whatever his semiofficial role for the Kennedy Administration in Africa, he was also a private citizen with money. That May, he wrote SNCC a check for $40,000—and presided over a crucial meeting between SNCC's leaders and Dr. King. King had supported and praised SNCC's launch. But he'd also declined to join the Freedom Rides. His deliberative ways and love for quoting scripture inspired these impatient upstarts to nickname him "De Lawd." Harry was an avowed MLK man who was also now SNCC's foremost backer: he was in a unique position to mediate. And one day the next winter, at his place in New York, he hosted a dozen SNCCers to hear their grievances, after which he insisted that they respect and work with King's SCLC. He then welcomed to their gathering a humbled Dr. King, fresh from a stinging defeat in the SCLC's campaign to desegregate Albany, Georgia. The détente was brokered between the two organizations in Harry and Julie's red-walled living room, and they agreed to choose their next target and campaign together.

In these ways and others, he played a pivotal role as a behind-the-scenes nexus and arbiter in the roiling politics of those years when Bobby Kennedy also finally came around. During the Freedom Rides, the attorney general called out the National Guard to disperse a mob menacing movement members in Montgomery, Alabama, and guaranteed their safety on their onward journey to Mississippi—and eventually insisted, to the Interstate Commerce Commission and in defiance of Dixie's governors, that "WHITES ONLY" signs be removed from their bus stations. Harry also helped broker Dr. King and SNCC's vital shared decision, in the spring of 1963, to train their next campaign on "the true nerve center of the Jim Crow South": Birmingham, Alabama. Their ensuing sit-ins were at once menaced and helped by the intemperate violence of Birmingham's commissioner of public safety, Eugene "Bull" Connor; his aggression prompted waves of local young people join the demonstrations. Those young people's bravery, in facing down Connor's hoses and dogs in pictures that circled the globe, marked the movement's turning point. Birmingham was also where its aims and ideals, articulated with grace by Martin in a famous letter from his jail cell, won sympathy from many Americans, and people across the world, who theretofore had cared little.

In Harry's archive at the Schomburg, years later, I found the typewritten draft of a telegram he sent to President Kennedy that April after King and Abernathy were jailed in Birmingham. With edits made in Harry's own hand, the letter was addressed to the president but meant for public consumption. "Americans and men of all lands look aghast," it read, "as public officials in Birmingham use the power of their office to do violence to the poor, blind, ministers of God and to all who seek freedom under the constitution." It continued:

> Those who have committed their lives and their honor to the cause of freedom throughout this land will not falter or be deterred until their cause is won.
>
> The unleashing of dogs against people seeking to secure their freedom as citizens and their dignity as men degrades not only those directly responsible but those who countenance or fail to oppose such violence.
>
> In these times there is great need of moral leadership to strengthen those like Dr. King who are leading the fight for all men and to make clear the knowledge that this land will not permit the continuing denial of freedom to any of its citizens or the abuse of those who are lawfully seeking such freedom.
>
> We call on you as president of all the people to exercise your leadership to end the reign of terror in Birmingham and the south that is darkening our land.
>
> We call on you as president to use the power of your office to help strike off the shackles that have too long done violence to the freedom of our brothers in the South.

On the letter's last page, the list of few dozen concerned citizens who'd signed on included Harry's celebrity pals, judges, rabbis, and other worthies ranging from Ralph Bunche and Joanne Woodward to Anthony Quinn. They shared this missive with the president's brother, too, as a direct appeal to the attorney general. They called on Bobby Kennedy to "take immediate measures to ensure the personal safety" of Dr. King and others who'd been arrested in Birmingham, and "to protect the exercise of their rights guaranteed to them under the Constitution of the United States for which we the undersigned hold you responsible."

That wasn't Harry's only contact during those frantic April days with the attorney general. Crucial to the resolution of the crisis-cum-victory that Birmingham became was their steady stream of calls. And now it was Bobby Kennedy, his moral center found, who picked up the phone to make a request: could Harry, to forestall a growing crisis and in discreet fashion, furnish $5,000 to bail out Dr. King and his aide Ralph Abernathy? Harry could (though in the end, he didn't need to—a Birmingham businessman did). The attorney general's next request, even more sensitive, was one he'd make only of someone he trusted: he asked Harry to serve as the point person for gathering a far greater sum—$160,000—that was needed to bail out the hundreds of children also in Birmingham's jails whose continued detention, the attorney general feared, might spark a riot. With the AG leaning on a slew of powerful labor bosses to supply what was needed, Harry received calls from the likes of the New York Transit Workers' chief, Mike Quill, and gathered funds to send to Alabama that the AG, calming an urgent situation by back-channel means, couldn't handle himself.

If those were the highlights of his background dealing, his most prominent public turn in its spotlight arrived six months later. Today the date of the March on Washington, August 28, 1963, is most often recalled for the famous speech that Dr. King, egged on by the great gospel singer Mahalia Jackson ("Tell them about the dream, Martin! Tell them about the dream!"), gave from the steps of the Lincoln Memorial. But at the time, just as remarked upon—and as symbolically important—was the crew of celebrities whom Harry inveigled to come at King's request. "The effectiveness of the march can be tremendously aided," said Martin in a telegram Harry received from him on the road in Vancouver, in late July, "by the presence and participation of a large number of theatrical and artistical personalities of our nation." Harry delivered on the personalities, and the large number—and then made sure to arrange them on the Mall so that their faces were the first the TV cameras caught. Paul Newman and Lena Horne, Sidney

Poitier and Sammy Davis, Shelley Winters and Tony Curtis, James Baldwin and Leonard Bernstein—all were present. And so too, in a symbolic coup, was Charlton Heston: a prominent member of Hollywood's right wing and future head of the NRA whom Harry had leaned on Marlon Brando to invite by asking Heston if he'd like to serve, with Marlon, as the honorary cochair of the march's Hollywood delegation. Here was a cause, avowed by the star of *The Ten Commandments,* that not just all of Hollywood but all Americans should support.

If the March on Washington was Harry's most visible moment as a leader of the movement, the most dramatic occurred the next summer in Mississippi. After JFK was assassinated in 1963, volunteers from SNCC and allied organizations sought, in the run-up to the elections in 1964, to register rural Blacks across the Cotton Belt to vote. What was billed as Mississippi's Freedom Summer had, by that August, turned bloody: local police were working in concert with the Ku Klux Klan to intimidate young volunteers, and three such young people had disappeared in June—and turned up dead. On August 4, those volunteers' mutilated bodies were found in a shallow grave. Harry received a call from Jim Forman, the de facto head of SNCC's volunteers in Greenwood, Mississippi: his brave crew, though frightened, had no intention of leaving Mississippi. Doing so, at the summer's end, would feel like they were giving in to the Klan's intimidation. Those young people, mourning their brethren in this cauldron of hate, wanted to stay—and they were running out of money.

Harry had helped get Freedom Summer underway by raising funds and organizing benefit concerts the spring before. But now SNCC's volunteers, to keep gas in their cars, needed more money fast—at least $50,000, Forman told Harry, ideally delivered within the next seventy-two hours. Harry told him he'd get it. He flew to Chicago and, with the help of an influential newspaper columnist there, raised $35,000 from liberal donors horrified by news of the murders in Mississippi. He got $20,000 more from friends to the cause in Montreal. Julie organized a snap fundraiser, at 300 West End Avenue, that pulled in another $15,000. And then Harry, with no way to convey $70,000 to Dixie by the deadline other than to carry it there himself in cash, called on an old friend to act as his sidekick. Sidney Poitier's reply, when he picked up the phone, was Harry's favorite beat in a story he never tired of telling. "I'll do it," Sidney told him. "But after this: never, ever call me again."

Harry had called Bobby Kennedy, he assured Sidney, to inform him of their mission. What he didn't say was that federal protection wasn't guaranteed—Kennedy's deputy AG for civil rights had simply told him, in a non-committal way, that they'd send federal marshals to keep an eye on things. Had Sidney known, he likely wouldn't have met Harry at Newark Airport for the evening flight they boarded to Mississippi.

When they landed in Jackson and boarded a single-engine plane to fly into a darkened airport in Greenwood, there was no protection to be found. The ensuing ride into town, in a car their SNCC hosts had buffed to a dull shine so as not to reflect pursuers' headlights, was harrowing. As soon as they pulled onto the road, lights flickered in the car's rearview mirrors. A group of menacing pickup trucks, driven by Klansmen or their cronies, vroomed up behind them. One had a two-by-four strapped to its bumper; it rammed them from behind. Sidney and Harry's heroic driver from SNCC zigzagged in the road, not allowing their gun-toting pursuers to pull up alongside the celebrities in his back seat, even as he watched warily for local cops, along the roadway's edge, with whom the Klan was in cahoots. Their lives were only saved, or so it felt to Sidney, by a convoy of SNCC cars that rode out to meet them. The pickup trucks' frustrated drivers, aiming their rifles at Harry and Sidney or into the sky—it wasn't clear—fired into the night.

In the tale of that narrow escape, another of Harry's favorite beats was the fact that he and Sidney, in an SNCC safe house that night, slept head-to-toe in a single bed (he let Sidney have the inside). But it was all made worth it by the joyous reception they received from young volunteers who were terrified but determined to remain: they thrilled to the arrival of these two heroic figures who'd appeared in their midst with a black duffel bag that Harry overturned on a table, to riotous cheers, dumping bundles of cash at the volunteers' feet. They sang several songs to celebrate as they tucked into a late dinner of chicken and ribs. But there was one that felt inevitable, there in that barn outside Greenwood, Mississippi—and it wasn't "We Shall Overcome." The volunteers cried out for it, and Sidney egged him on. "Go on then," Sidney said. Harry, rising to his feet, let them have it.

"Daaaayyyyy O!"

Those delirious civil rights workers weren't waiting for the tally man to count bananas; they were there to register the downtrodden people of Mississippi to vote. But the chorus of Harry's signature rang out with the sense of weariness but also of resolve and of hope, he'd recall, that they all felt that night.

"Daylight come!"

they sang along with their hero,

"And me want to go home."

They sung another version, too:

"Freedom, freedom come, and it won't be long . . ."

16

The 1960s were nearing their midpoint. Harry, not yet forty, had already enjoyed a decade-long run as one of America's most popular entertainers. By some alchemical feat, he'd turned a work song from the West Indies into an American pop hit—and an unofficial anthem of the civil rights movement for which the royalties from his hit records furnished a vital and ongoing resource. By now, Harry and Dr. King—whose speeches Harry still listened to each morning for inspiration, years after he passed —were calling each other best friends. Such was Harry's closeness to Martin, and concern for his family, that he bought them a $50,000 insurance policy on his life. Whenever Martin was arrested, Harry's first call was to Coretta: he wanted to ensure that Martin's proud if long-suffering wife, raising their family on her husband's modest pastor's salary, had what she needed. During one such call in 1963, after Martin was locked up in Birmingham, Coretta confided to Harry that she had no one to help her with her kids and shopping. He duly arranged for a housekeeper and driver who would, on his dime, look after the family for years.

It says a lot about both Harry's priorities and business acumen, after he became his career's own manager in 1956, that when the IRS raided his office looking for off-the-books assistance to King and other radical allies, they found nothing untoward: his payments to the Kings' domestics, per the exacting habits of Harry's accountant, Abe Briloff, had been done completely on the books, with the government's share withheld from every check remitted to the Kings from Harry's coffers. When in July 1964 Lyndon Johnson signed the Civil Rights Act into law, the movement to which Harry had devoted much of his energy and funds for a decade reached both a great victory and an inflection point. He was all of thirty-seven years old. What he'd achieved and how he'd helped change his country's culture and its society alike was already enough, or should have been, for the entire life of any one entertainer or activist or citizen. But what defined his own memories of those years—the dramas leading up to the movement's ensuing victories and the tensions surrounding their aftermaths—were the questions he asked himself about where to channel his anger, and his ambition, next.

The word "anger" and its variants appears no fewer than ninety-two times in Harry's memoir. Some of these invoke the emotion's presence in people near him—his mother's anger at his father's philandering and failings; his brother's anger at her abandonment; the anger of his movement's members at history's ills, at Bull Connor's dogs, at a racist world. But his oft-repeated enunciations of ire most often refer to himself: they index a feeling that functioned, in Harry's story and life, with operative force. Anger fed his hurt at Millie for leaving him to care for his brother; his determination, as a young actor more often overlooked for roles than chosen for them, to succeed; his rage at the belittling equivocations voiced by too many politicians he knew when it came to questions of racial justice. But if anger was an engine for his defining involvement in the civil rights movement, he also credited that involvement with giving him the joy depicted in a photo he kept in the front hallway of his last apartment on the Upper West Side over the Apple Bank on 72nd Street.

Taken in the early sixties, the photo shows him with MLK at Madison Square Garden. Their mouths are open; their waists are bent in mirth. Someone has just said something hilarious. Here are two pals, cracking each other up. Also, two men whose public personae were serious indeed but whose bond, in intimate spaces like Harry's living room, with a bar he kept stocked with Martin's favorite sherry, Harveys Bristol Cream, relied on sharing each other's private selves. The reason Harry kept this photo on his wall, he liked to say, was as a reminder of humor's crucial role, even in the midst of grave political struggle, as a source of sustenance. That was surely so: after Martin's release from Birmingham's jail it was only apt to share a laugh about, say, the droning snores of Martin's heavyset aide-de-camp, Ralph Abernathy, in their shared cell. But the photo, more simply put, suggests this pair's human goofiness when they were together—and the ways they confided in, and relied on each other, behind closed doors.

In this vein, Martin didn't speak much, Harry would recall, about the sexual compulsions that made extra-marital trysts a habit that menaced his reputation and saw his security compromised by the FBI. This aspect of Martin's private life, known to all his intimates, caused him shame. But he did share with Harry, his divorced friend, how he'd fallen in love at seminary with a young woman—a white one— whom it was unthinkable for him to marry. If that white girl was the one who got away, the Black church girl whom Martin had wed—Coretta—was the one he stuck with. Coretta was loyal to her man and his movement and the conservative mores of the Baptist Church. She was Martin's Marguerite, but party to a marriage with a very different fate. Harry was a denizen of the secular north, and of show business: once his life's proclivities no longer matched his first love's, flying to Las Vegas to get a divorce became both thinkable and wise. This wasn't the case for Martin, an upstanding pastor whose wife's faith grew only more important, as his public profile rose, to the projecting of his own. His marriage to Coretta, no matter its sometime unhappiness, was for keeps. And as glad as he was to bond with Harry in New York and Dixie, he never followed him to seats of sin like Las Vegas—a town that became, for Harry, a second home.

As the pull of politics began to outstrip that of performing, Harry had mostly phased out club dates. These were replaced with triumphal tours of concert halls in Europe and the Far East—and one gig he never forswore: his annual month or more in residence in Vegas. Throughout the civil rights years and after, he and Julie spent a chunk of each summer in the best suite at the Riviera (and later, after Caesars Palace opened, in similarly plush digs there). The money—upward of $100,000 a week—was too good to eschew. But his affinity for the adult mischief to be found in this town, where he also brought his kids for family vacations, ran deeper. Weekends may have been spent waterskiing with young Gina and David on Lake Mead, but Harry spent his nights, after leaving the Riviera's stage in his mohair jacket, risking his earnings at blackjack and craps. Being comfortable with gambling and gangsterdom, he liked to say, was in his blood. His people ran numbers; no one's swagger had so impressed, on Harlem's streets, like his uncle Lenny's. One night at the Riviera in 1957, he'd caught the thrill of getting hot at blackjack and watching a white pit boss squirm as his stack of chips grew. After this, he couldn't get enough of the adrenaline high he caught, win or lose, from matching dollars and wits with scowling high rollers in ten-gallon hats.

Of course, he lost more than he won: there's a reason that the Riviera's manager, a senior member of the Chicago syndicate named Gus Greenbaum—a jovial Jew who called Harry "Hesh" and loved talking politics and Israel with Julie—urged him to stop giving his Vegas earnings right back to the mob. Greenbaum told him to instead get himself a stake in the action, and in where the Strip was heading, by buying a tract of desert outside town. Before Harry could act on this sage advice, Greenbaum was found with his throat slit. But this was also the town where he'd honed his act and earned great sums; cemented a warm if wary friendship with Frank Sinatra, who also became a backer of civil rights and useful fellow-friend to the Kennedys (at least until they broke links with Old Blue Eyes, in 1962, thanks to his mafia ties); and played the best man at the sham wedding of Sammy Davis Jr. to a Black showgirl enlisted to serve as a kind of racial beard for Davis, who was embroiled at the time in a torrid affair with Kim Novak. Harry didn't much care for Davis's self-loathing shtick—he called Sammy "the clown in Frank's court." But their own complex friendship, like many of Harry's essential bonds in show business, ran through Las Vegas.

Among the others he brought there for vacation, or at least a few days of R & R, were members of King's inner circle and SNCCers he flew out to give tickets to his show and cash to blow in the casino. Martin himself, though, was never among them. His public friendship with Harry, as enacted with dignity in Manhattan and at marches down South, was one thing. But they were both keenly aware of not wanting their friendship to be seen—whether by the public, the FBI, or Martin's own family—as involving a debauched showman leading his Christian friend to temptation. Harry was keenly aware of his own status as a role model. But safeguarding his own reputation, in the more libertine world he inhabited, was more about discretion than behavior: his lasting fondness for late nights in Vegas and flirtations with women not his wife were between him and Julie. For the leader of civil rights, as they both knew, the stakes were different. "Martin's pedestal," as Harry put it, "was a lot higher and more fragile than mine. He wasn't just a role model. He was a moral leader."

That may have been so; but Harry was conscious of the pedestal on which he too was placed, comparatively modest in moral height though it was—and of its psychological effects. When he looked back on that era, he described a sense not of discrete memories but rather the whirl of them—the gala gigs and dramatic marches; the high-stakes meetings with Panthers and presidents; the high-rolling stints in Vegas; the trips to Africa and Washington and to recording studios in LA or Greece to nurture new talent. "I wanted to do everything, and I did," he'd recall. "But why? Why race around trying to please every constituency, like that guy I remember from *The Ed Sullivan Show*, spinning plates on sticks, trying to keep them all spinning so none would fall?" It was a question he spent much time exploring on Peter Neubauer's couch—and whose answers he came to attribute less to qualities innate to his personality (though his energy was prodigious) than to the cumulative effects of the fawning admiration that filled the days of a beloved star who also came to be seen by many as a paragon not merely of sex appeal but of justice. No human's body, the writer Hilton Als has observed, is equipped to absorb that much love. But the particular blend of praise and approval that Belafonte received differed from that bestowed upon most celebrities, as did the way he metabolized it. This, as he later put it, was "bigger. More complex. It wasn't just adoration I was getting. People were investing faith and hope and trust in me. I was being anointed." For anyone, this would be a lot; for a man who'd grown up poor and black with dyslexia and a stutter and self-esteem issues to match how he was treated by the world, it was even more so.

"Of all the black kids in Jamaica and Harlem," he'd ask, "why had I been the one chosen to sit with leaders of state, who solicited my opinion?" The answer he reached, with a big hand from his therapist, was hard-won. "I felt driven to justify people's respect, and with Peter's help, I saw how that had become a cycle. The more I did, the more they respected me; the more they respected me, the more I felt compelled to do." The almost manic drive that resulted, as he pondered on Neubauer's couch, also owed more than a little to his mother—a woman who was no less headstrong in her old age than she'd been in her youth. By the early sixties, she'd given up the nice house out in LA Harry had bought her and his custodian stepfather, and returned to a one-room apartment in Harlem, where she lived until her death, refusing further help from her famous son and deeply attached to the hardworking habitus of a poor and driven immigrant. Her son now wasn't poor in the least, but his own compulsive drive—and the exalted standards to which he held himself and those around him—had repercussions. Some of those repercussions, for the many constituencies he served, were fruitful and long-lasting. But for his musicians and associates, beratements were frequent. His children also suffered, in ways that left marks, from the inconstant ways of a father who, as David Belafonte put it, "was serving two families: us and the family of Man."

If Harry's frequent absences and harsh ideals hindered his capacities to parent, his self-image as a loving dad was also based in a determination not to repeat the behavior of the first person—his own father—he saw turn anger into violence. That particularly masculine process was one in which Harry, during his rambunctious youth, grew quite versed. But his embrace of nonviolence, thanks to Martin Luther King, had gone beyond political tactics to become a philosophy for life. He'd seen nonviolence put to the test and win. He'd made King's philosophy central to his own values as an activist and as a complicated man driven to "wash away my personal anger." The tension between violent and nonviolent ways of channeling rage had been present in Harry's own breast and mind from boyhood. It was also a tension that defined the 1960s, demarcating the decade's first half, when peaceful marchers brought King's dream to America's mainstream, from its latter years, after 1965, when radicalism and riots burned its cities.

In historiography of the era, the decade's midpoint is often recalled as an inflection point: the summer month in 1965 when Lyndon Johnson signed the Voting Rights Act was also the month Watts erupted in riots and Stokely Carmichael of SNCC, sick of being arrested in Dixie, began thinking in terms not of equality but of "Black power." Those tensions in the movement were present well before then, both among Black advocates for change and between them and certain powers-that-be who engaged their cause. And those dynamics had a telling airing in an apartment on Central Park South whose doorbell Harry rang, on May 24, 1963, after walking over from the West Side to attend a gathering convened by the unlikely pair of Bobby Kennedy and James Baldwin.

17

The apartment was owned by Kennedy's father, Joe, and had served as the family's New York base during JFK's campaign for president and since. Now it was to host an "off-the-record chat" between RFK and an assemblage of leading Black activists and public figures who, the younger Kennedy hoped, might help him better understand Black rage, Baldwin told Harry when he called to ask him to attend. "There's so much anger out there in the black community," Baldwin said to Harry. "Even Martin can't get his arms around it. Bobby wants to understand that anger better, to know how to respond." Baldwin and Belafonte were good friends: both Harlem-bred, they'd met in the early fifties through their shared involvement in the Committee for the Negro in the Arts. Harry was a deep admirer of the great writer's essays and elan. But he confessed to being a bit puzzled by Baldwin's call from RFK's Virginia estate. The attorney general had invited the author of *The Fire Next Time* to his estate, Hickory Hill, to address the larger outlook of Black America after Birmingham. Over their lunch, Bobby had suggested that Baldwin invite others to voice their views in Manhattan the following night. Baldwin's role in organizing this confab seemed, to Harry, born of "froth combined with naivete." Baldwin gathered a group that included, Harry saw as he arrived, Lena Horne and Lorraine Hansberry, the playwright; young activists from CORE and SNCC; and the psychologist Kenneth B. Clark, a leading authority on the effects of segregation on children.

Harry had been speaking with Bobby regularly for two years; he wondered about his real motives. What exactly did he hope to learn about racism's ill effects on Black Americans that he didn't already know? The impetus for this listening session had to be more baldly political. And so it proved. JFK and his brother, notwithstanding their helping secure bail money for Birmingham's marchers, remained as concerned with protecting the president's political capital as with civil rights. They didn't think it feasible or wise, given dynamics in Congress, to push for a federal civil rights bill yet. Their hope, in Birmingham's wake, was that the movement's leaders might appreciate what the administration had done and would continue to do, behind the scenes, for their cause. And this is what Bobby, hopeful of support, conveyed to Baldwin's Black brain trust. "We have a party in revolt," he told the assembled, "and we have to be somewhat considerate about how to keep them onboard if the Democratic party is going to prevail in the next elections."

That may have been true. But this was a room less concerned with "political reality," as it looked from the White House, than with the lived realities of Black Americans who were turning, in growing numbers, to leaders more radical than Dr. King—Malcolm X was then rising to prominence—for a reason. The conversation, Harry recalled, began civilly enough. But then Bobby made a remark about the United States's prospective involvement in a simmering conflict in Vietnam; young Black and white Americans, he said, might again be serving their country together. The conversation took a turn. Jerome Smith, a young CORE activist who'd joined the first Freedom Rides and weathered police batons and southern mobs' fists as a result, confronted the attorney general. "What you're asking us young Black people to do," he said, "is to pick up guns against people in Asia while you have continued to deny us our rights here." This was not a manner of being spoken to, or a viewpoint, that Kennedy was accustomed to tolerating in his father's parlor. And Jerome Smith wasn't done. If he was going to pick up a gun anytime soon, it would be to defend himself against racist

190

cops—perhaps at a demonstration soon. "When I pull the trigger," he said, "kiss it goodbye."

Bobby was stunned—as much by what this young man said as by how his elders, like Lorraine Hansberry, concurred. "You've got a great many very accomplished people in this room, Mr. Attorney General," the playwright said, before gesturing in Jerome Smith's direction. "But the only man who should be listened to is that man right there." Others nodded—and then piled on. Here was a chance, rare indeed, to explain to one of the country's most powerful figures why its Black citizens might not be keen to defend its flag. A sputtering RFK, minutes later, declared the evening over. Clarence Jones, the SCLC attorney who'd worked closely with Bobby to bail Dr. King's people from jail in Birmingham, lingered to calm ruffled feathers. So did Harry. But Harry cut Bobby short when a flummoxed Kennedy began to chastise him. "You know us better than that," Bobby snapped. "Why don't you tell these people who we are?"

Harry's reply was angry. "Why do you assume I don't? Maybe if we weren't telling them who you are, things wouldn't be as calm as they are." And the last words of the evening, before Bobby stormed from the room, as Harry recalled in his memoir decades later, were also his. "You may think you're doing enough," Harry told the attorney general, who he'd at first circled warily but who was now his most trusted contact in government and a politician who would become a friend and a candidate for high office whom Harry backed to the hilt. "But you don't live with us, you don't even visit our pain. Obviously, progress in America is in the eye of the beholder. What you observe, Bobby, and what you want to see of us, is based upon the needs of a political machine. What we need is well beyond that. The problem is the failure of the power players to see us for who we are, and what we are really experiencing. Those children in Birmingham are our children, not yours."

Back home on West End Avenue that night, he received a call from Jimmy Baldwin—news of their evening with RFK, Baldwin told him, was going to be in the next morning's *New York Times*. Though he didn't admit it that evening, Baldwin seemed to have leaked the story himself and was quoted in the article. Whatever Baldwin's motivations for stirring the pot in this way, Harry had a sinking feeling when he read the piece on the front page, the next morning, under the headline "ROBERT KENNEDY CONSULTS NEGROES HERE ABOUT NORTH." In the story, which described this summit that had occurred at an undisclosed location, Baldwin was quoted accusing JFK of "not using the great prestige of his office as the moral forum it can be." Airing differences within the privacy of this ill-advised gathering, to Harry's mind, was one thing. But Bobby remained a figure with whom the movement needed to be on good working terms. He worried that reproving Bobby and his brother in print was a big tactical mistake. When Dr. King called him that morning to hear about what had occurred, Martin was more sanguine. "Maybe it's just what Bobby needed to hear," he mused. "He's going to hear a lot more of it if the President keeps dawdling on that civil rights bill."

The civil rights bill in question, reported another article in that same day's *Times*, was one that Democrats in Congress were now convinced could pass if the president "worked at it," said Senator Hubert Humphrey of Minnesota. As the paper of record put it, "The violence in Birmingham, coming so closely on the riots at the University of Mississippi last year, [has] convinced many legislators that stronger civil rights laws are necessary." Two weeks later, that growing sense was bolstered by the show that George Wallace, Alabama's Jim Crow–loving governor, made of barring two Black students from entering his state's university. It's hard to say which development mattered more to President Kennedy's thinking—Wallace's display of white supremacist id or the haranguing that Bobby Kennedy received from fed-up Black activists on Central Park South. But both informed the surprise announcement he made on June 11. JFK proclaimed from the White House that he was putting a bill to Congress that would give his Justice Department far-reaching powers to sue states and municipalities seen to be violating the civil rights of citizens with regard to voting, schools, or access to public accommodations and services.

It was a propitious moment for the movement—and one that was quickly shadowed, as many such moments were, by reactionary violence: the same night Kennedy came out in legislative favor of civil rights, the NAACP activist Medgar Evers, arriving to his home in Jackson, Mississippi, with an armful of T-shirts reading "Jim Crow Must Go," was shot and killed by a Klansman in his driveway. His murder underscored what JFK had said in his speech from the Oval Office: the country was facing a moral crisis that necessitated an epochal change. "Our task [and] our obligation," he told the American people, "is to make that revolution, that change, peaceful and constructive for all."

Noble words, devilishly hard to enact: what revolution has ever been experienced by both those who stand to gain and those asked to share their history's spoils as "peaceful and constructive for all"? JFK was fortunate to have, in the august leader of the SCLC, a counterpart who shared his vision (and who was brought to tears, his intimates recalled, by JFK's historic speech). But it was in the aftermath of that speech on June 11, in the fast-moving and operatic drama of those climactic years, that Dr. King decided, with his old friend and mentor A. Philip Randolph, to bring the movement to Washington.

18

The civil rights movement gave the world no shortage of totemic images—of brave children in Birmingham being fire-hosed; of brave men in Memphis declaiming, on signs hung from their chests, "I Am a Man"; of Dr. King at his pulpit. But among the era's icons and innovations, none so shaped our idea of advocating for change as the movement's *marches*. There's an oft-reproduced photograph of Harry and Martin walking together—Harry is tall in black; Martin is jaunty in a sailor's cap—in Alabama. Their arms are touching. Their faces are proud. Behind them is a stream of allies. The image conveys a sense of striding together, as the writer Rebecca Solnit has put it, "toward transformation and into history." The civil rights movement's leaders, *pace* how they're sometimes recalled in schools, didn't invent nonviolence as a mode of engaging in civic discourse: Thoreau published "Civil Disobedience" in 1849. But in mainstream Americans' minds, theirs was the movement that turned walking down the street into a political act.

Before the civil rights era, trade unionists and suffragettes had made picket lines and parades a familiar trope of American dissidence. But it took this movement led by a Baptist minister whose hero was Mahatma Ghandi to lend the symbolism of religious pilgrimage—of a physical journey undertaken for metaphysical uplift—to secular politics and earthly demands. Gandhi had famously done this by trekking from India's inland to the sea, in 1930, to make salt with his countrymen in contravention of British taxes and laws, and to demand an end to British rule. And now Dr. King and the SCLC, whose first prominent visit to Washington had been for the organization's founding "Prayer Pilgrimage" in 1957, resolved to turn another collective walk on the Mall, that August, into their movement's next big step.

President Kennedy and his brother, when they caught wind of these plans, saw them as a perturbation: What more, the Kennedys asked again, did the movement want? Hadn't JFK's civil rights bill, and Bobby's behind-the-scenes maneuvering in Birmingham, proved the administration's bona fides? Martin himself, concerned the march might fall flat, was hesitant. But Harry and others urged him to see it through. Harry would help ensure, by recruiting a troupe of Hollywood stars, that the march had the visibility it needed. Martin, with his almighty oratory, would ensure their message resounded. Still, they had to convince themselves that the risk of a meager turnout, which could stall their momentum in its tracks, was worth the opportunity to take their "last chance to stage a massive exercise in nonviolence," as Harry later put it, "before the streets of American cities north and south filled with rage and resentment, guns and blood."

It's debatable whether the choice really was that dire. But soon enough, Harry would make the same case to RFK. Harry had wondered, after their confrontation in New York, when they'd speak again. But the attorney general called him first. He asked, in imploring tones, whether it was really necessary, with a civil rights bill finally being drafted, to bring the movement's case to Congress's steps. Washington, D.C.'s police force was in no way equipped to handle a march of 100,000 people. The costs the federal government would incur to protect marchers from potential racist foes also drawn to D.C. by their presence were large. Harry's retort was succinct: "Are you telling us," he said to Bobby, "that we should abandon our right to freedom of assembly as a cost-saving measure?" The larger message he underscored to the president's brother: whether the Kennedys liked it or not, the march was happening—and would show Congress that the bill they were considering was supported by a broad cross section of the country.

JFK asked Dr. King to the White House to discuss his proposed march—and to impart warnings, as the historian Taylor Branch recounted in the first volume of his monumental three-part history of those years, *Parting the Waters*. In the Oval Office, Kennedy invited Martin to step into the Rose Garden for a chat—the implication being that he himself was subject to the FBI surveillance that had yielded the intelligence he now shared: J. Edgar Hoover knew, Kennedy murmured to King, that two members of King's inner circle—the SCLC's head fundraiser, Hunter "Jack" O'Dell, and its chief political strategist, Stanley Levison—were active members of the Communist Party. Whether Kennedy believed this information wasn't clear. Nor was where Hoover—the closeted cross-dresser whose snooping into the gay private life of another of MLK's key advisers, Bayard Rustin, had already resulted in Rustin's expulsion from King's circle—had attained it. But information was leverage, and the president's meaning was plain. Two of King's most trusted advisers had to go. And the FBI had their ears and eyes on Martin, too, and on the philandering that could be his downfall.

Jack O'Dell's exit from the SCLC—his past as a trade unionist and member of the CPUSA was well known—had been written on the wall. Days before his ouster, he had conveyed as much to King. "Not the least formidable of the obstacles blocking the path to Freedom," he said, "is the anti-Communist hysteria in our country which is deliberately kept alive by the defenders of the status-quo as a barrier to rational thinking on important social questions." About those "important social questions," King and O'Dell were in fact in accord: as Martin became a more forceful advocate, in his last years, for all victims of capitalism's ills, O'Dell returned to his side. But for now, O'Dell had to go. And so too, the Kennedys made clear, did Stan Levison (even if, as he sincerely insisted, he was not and in fact never had been a card-carrying Communist). When Bobby conveyed as much to Martin's attorney Clarence Jones, Jones breezily replied that they'd simply remove Levison from the SCLC's official payroll: Martin would be just as happy consulting him covertly. A furious Bobby made plain that this wasn't what he had in mind.

Harry's own ties to this scandal and its fallout had a surprising backstory. Levison was a Jew with a law degree who'd succeeded at business (he owned several Ford dealerships

in New Jersey) and donated generously to the SCLC's coffers before beginning to offer tactical acumen and becoming, by the early sixties, the de facto head of King's kitchen
cabinet. As Harry put it, Levison repeatedly gave King "wise
advice that steered Martin away from some pitfall, and toward some opportunity." And it was thanks, indirectly, to
the FBI's snooping that he would learn as much. For although Levison's flirtation with communism in the forties
hadn't led to joining the party, he had briefly married a fellow traveler Harry knew.

Levison had known her as Janet Alterman. Harry knew
her as Janet Alterman Kennedy: his ex-therapist and the
wife of the shady financier and ex-Communist-turned-FBI-
informant Jay Richard Kennedy, who had briefly become
Harry's manager—and with whom Levison, back in the forties, had also briefly been in business. This information
might have been enough to convince Harry that Stan Levison was indeed some sort of double agent. But Harry had
spent too much time in Levison's company, and seen him
mold too many decisions that proved vital to their cause, to
think he had ulterior aims. When Levison told him he was
as shocked as Harry was by his ex-wife's ties to the FBI and
her marriage to Jay Richard Kennedy, as well as the fact
that they'd both crossed paths with this mysterious pair,

Harry took him at his word. "I don't know what it means," Stan told him. "But it happened."

And now Harry found himself responsible for ferrying messages between Levison and King. Martin had absorbed the Kennedys' message: he would have no direct contact, for a time anyway, with Levison himself. But he had no intention of depriving himself of his consigliere's advice—even if Levison's phones, as now also seemed clear, were tapped by the Feds. Now, when Martin had a dilemma he wanted Stan's views on, he often asked Harry to go to a trusted friend's house and place a call to Levison's office, then wait for Levison to walk down the block and ring Harry back from a payphone safe from the FBI's ears to convey whatever Martin needed. Such tactics didn't protect King completely from Hoover's snooping: Bobby Kennedy was so angered by Clarence Jones's flippant reply to his request for Levison's head that Bobby approved Hoover's request to tap Jones's phones. However, Bobby declined Hoover's request to eavesdrop on King's own lines. But the wiretap on his lawyer granted the FBI ears into King's private deliberations and conduct, as Freedom of Information Act requests later lodged by the historian David Garrow confirmed. The Justice Department could have used what they knew, at any time, to torpedo King's reputation and movement. But fortunately for him, and for the country, that August's march on the capital was allowed to proceed.

In recent decades, tromping en masse down public byways—whether to oppose a war or for the Women's March or the March of Dimes—has become a familiar form of political theater. Such gatherings are often predicated less on concrete demands or policy proposals than with registering discontent. But they're all inspired by what happened in Washington that summer: a collective walk whose aims were negotiated with the powerful in advance—and whose success set a lasting model for what voicing political views beyond the ballot box looks like. Walking is interrupted falling, as the essayist Garnette Cadogan reminds us, and thus an act of faith that's long been conceived as such by seekers of higher truth. As a form of collective action, the march was ideally matched to a movement whose leaders spoke the biblical language of redemption and rivers and promised lands. They meant to trek the proverbial deserts of Dixie until Pharoah let God's people go, as the spiritual sung by Paul Robeson demanded. And their aims accorded with their means of welcoming to their March on Washington, and to what Dr. King called their "beloved community," people of all faiths and backgrounds who heard their call.

19

The organizers of the march had hoped, with the help of allies in the labor movement, for 100,000 people to turn up. More than 250,000 people of all shades assembled, as Harry said, "not out of demagoguery, or anger, but hope." Attendees were buoyed by the sight of Harry's troupe of celebrities walking through the crowd, pressing flesh and flashing smiles as they made their way to the Lincoln Memorial. (The exception was Marlon Brando, who toted an electric cattle prod of the sort, he told anyone who'd listen, that Birmingham's cops had used on children). Harry would think a lot, in ensuing years, about the "power of celebrity harnessed to social causes," as he put it, "[and] whether it does any more than give the crowd a thrill and stroke a few stars' egos." Sometimes not, he thought—but it did on that day. Also vital to the march's success was Bayard Rustin's sage insistence on including, in their budget and plans, a system of loudspeakers capable of amplifying the day's speeches across the entire Mall. When his prized system was sabotaged just before the march, the attorney general, now fully invested in the day's success, sent the Army Signal Corps to help set up a new one. Without a single incident of violence, the march's press glowed: it was a day whose mood and mass signaled to the country, with the help of Martin's ringing words, that segregation had to go—and that furnished a massive assist to the civil rights bill which, with JFK's approval, was about to start winding its way through Congress.

That afternoon, the president invited Dr. King to the White House after his speech. Harry, in a hotel suite nearby, clinked glasses with buoyant friends—Brando and Poitier, Paul Newman and Joanne Woodward, Ossie Davis and Ruby Dee. They were all grateful and proud to be present; they also all heartily declined Harry's suggestion that perhaps they should stay on for a few days and lobby Congress to move faster on civil rights ("There I was again," he'd recall, "pushing my friends too hard"). Amidst the astonishment and hope, a TV set in his suite was tuned to a panel on one of the networks devoted to parsing the day's meaning. Harry glimpsed the face of the panel's moderator. He couldn't believe what he saw: chairing this conversation of leading figures and friends of their movement, including James Farmer of CORE, was none other than Jay Richard Kennedy. He had now won Farmer's ear, Harry later learned from Dr. King, and become a close adviser to CORE's chief.

Harry now felt a duty to share what he knew, NDA or not, about Jay Richard Kennedy's mysterious past with Martin and other close associates in the movement—which is how he learned about Stan Levison's past with Janet. Jay Richard Kennedy, as was revealed by FBI transcripts later on, was trying to prop up Farmer as the peaceable and patriotic civil rights leader that he thought the FBI ought to help make the movement's figurehead, at King's expense. This didn't work. But Jay Richard Kennedy would continue to cut his strange swath through the culture: he became Frank Sinatra's financial adviser before ending the 1960s as a lover and political mentor to Elaine Brown, the future chairwoman of the Black Panther Party. When Harry finally won access to his own thick FBI file, years later, the bits related to Jay Richard Kennedy suggested that Harry wasn't a much-valued informant (though there was a communiqué to his supervising agent, dating from after his split with Harry in 1956, in which Kennedy apprised that while Belafonte may have become hugely famous, he was "generally disliked by the Negro people.") In 1964, Kennedy told the Bureau that Harry was, like Martin, "an agent of the Peking government"—but was again met with skepticism: the informant, noted the agent who interviewed him, "would not give any facts to substantiate this information."

Whatever the true effects of this odd character's involvement with the FBI, his backstory and proximity to key figures in the movement underscored its growing climate of paranoia. For its leaders, concern over infiltration and hostile machinations by their foes in government was increasing. Weighing even more heavily on their thoughts about the movement's larger prospects for victory, though, was what Harry described as the almost automatic-feeling way that every one of its triumphs was followed, within hours or days, by "some grievous crime of hate." It was as if, he wrote, "Jim Crow were a living, breathing, snarling being, and the hatred of every last racist in the South were concentrated in him as he pulled another trigger or lit another fuse." After JFK's speech for equality, that June, it had been Medgar Evers's murder. Now, after the exultant aftermath of August's March on Washington, it was a bombing in Birmingham: four little girls, having just finished Sunday school, were horrifically killed by an explosive set to go off during services in their church's basement. Scarcely two months after that, the young American president, who had become a beloved one, and whose backing for civil rights helped make history, would be shot by an assassin in Dallas.

On the night JFK died, Harry was in Paris visiting the set of a new film being directed there by his blacklisted friend Jules Dassin. He first heard the confusing news from a car radio, in French, en route from the Boulogne-Billancourt studio to the apartment, on the Île Saint-Louis, of the American novelist James Jones. Having gathered there for dinner, Harry and Jones's other guests ended up surrounding a blinking TV to watch grainy footage on repeat. His despairing grief was tempered by his instinctual worry, soon assuaged, that Kennedy's assassin might be a Black radical, which would set the movement back years. JFK's replacement in the White House, in the months after his death, sought to push his civil rights bill through Congress. It was initially held up by a filibuster in the Senate, but the bill finally passed and was signed into law by Lyndon Johnson in the midst of that Freedom Summer.

On July 2, 1964, discriminating against any American because of their race, origin, religion, or gender became a federal crime. Segregation of schools and "all public accommodations" was outlawed, and it became official U.S. policy, across every state and county in the land, "to enforce the constitutional right to vote". But on the ground down South, the law's enactment had done little to furnish justice or the franchise to impoverished Blacks in places where Jim Crow's powers-that-were had no interest in following Washington's dictates, and even less to the busloads of young volunteers who alighted in Dixie that summer to confront those powers directly.

By that fall, many of the SNCCers whose efforts he'd bankrolled were exhausted. Harry helped with that, too: in September 1964, he brought a dozen of them—including Bob Moses, John Lewis, Julian Bond, and Fannie Lou Hamer—to West Africa, for what he conceived as a kind of inspirational vacation. In Conakry, Guinea, their delegation was personally greeted by Sékou Touré ("Welcome home," he said). Guinea's president would soon become better known for his regime's corruption and cruelty than for the regal charisma with which he met Mother Africa's prodigal kin. But in 1964, the very idea of encountering a Black head of state was enough to bring Fannie Lou Hamer—a sharecropper's daughter who'd spent her whole life in the state where she'd just helped found the Mississippi Freedom Party—to tears. Harry's love for connecting diasporic dots, and a weakness for charismatic leaders whose left-wing verbiage belied darker sides, would remain with him for life.

Back home, the movement's next major battle was in Alabama. In the city of Selma, a group of students had entered a whites-only movie theater and refused to leave.

Their dispersal by tear gas launched a campaign to desegregate the city, coordinated by SNCC. A local judge issued an injunction that banned any gathering in Selma involving more than two people where conversing about civil rights or granting new voters the franchise occurred. That fall, Martin Luther King won the Nobel Peace Prize. On his way home from Norway, he stopped at the White House. President Johnson intimated to him, as had JFK in similar moments before, that the country could use a break from racial upset. But Martin was already struggling to retain his leadership of young activists less enamored of nonviolence; he couldn't sit back from Selma.

King put his moral weight and that of the SCLC behind what was happening there. In the first days of the new year, his speech to an "illegal" rally of townspeople and activists in Selma sparked a renewed push against the status quo. What ensued was a series of marches, mass arrests, and pitched battles, including one that February in which a twenty-six-year-old church deacon named Jimmie Lee Jackson was killed, and another weeks later in which SNCC's John Lewis had his skull cracked by a policeman's baton after Lewis tried to lead a procession of six hundred demonstrators across the Edmund Pettus Bridge.

Four days after "Bloody Sunday" on the Pettus Bridge, Dr. King arrived to lead a march from Selma to Alabama's capital in Montgomery, fifty-four miles away, to honor Jimmie Lee Jackson and insist that the civil rights of all Alabamans, including the right to register to vote, be upheld. By the bridge, King and 2,000 followers were confronted with the same brutal cops who'd beaten Lewis and many others. He knelt in prayer rather than push on with a larger coterie of fellow clergy he'd recruited for the cause. And then he turned their march back to Selma rather than face more bloodshed. For this gesture of pacifist compromise, King caught much flak from younger comrades. But days later, after a judge granted a permit for their march, King crossed the Pettus Bridge protected from thuggish local police by members of the Alabama National Guard who President Johnson had just placed under federal control. Then King set out, arm-in-arm with his fellows and with the 3,000 marchers allowed by their permit, toward Montgomery.

Their march now had federal protection. But the five-day walk remained long, and scary. Harry would join the last leg of the walk to Montgomery, where those famous photos of him and Martin were taken. But he spent the intervening days working to furnish a morale boost for the marchers that only his largesse and Rolodex could have afforded. The venue was the campus of a Catholic school and hospital, outside Alabama's capital, where they were to camp the night before reaching their goal. Harry placed calls and made travel arrangements for not a few of the nation's leading singers and entertainers. Then he oversaw the construction, in a makeshift muddy campground, of a stage built by volunteers from stacked coffins and plywood. The next day, 3,000 tired marchers and their supporters, having spent four days trudging along Alabama's sweltering blacktop, watched Harry mount that stage of coffins to introduce a remarkable concert. One after the other, friends to the cause sang songs—Johnny Mathis and Nina Simone; Odetta and Tony Bennett; Joan Baez and Peter, Paul & Mary. Other worthies, including James Baldwin, Leonard Bernstein, and Shelley Winters, offered words. Harry sang "Jamaica Farewell"—and then took part in cheerful hijinks that night in the motel where he'd put up his celebrity friends in shared rooms. Harry and his old friends Bill Attaway and Billy Eckstine donned sheets and moaned like ghosts in the halls.

Not everyone was amused by this stunt. But that night and then again the next morning, as the stars joined the marchers for their last miles into Montgomery, the feeling, Harry said, was unmistakable: the movement couldn't be stopped. How could it, when the great and the good of American culture were all pushing it along? Along the three-mile route into town, their foes showered the marchers with epithets from behind the state troopers lining the roadway. When the march and its celebrity escorts reached Alabama's statehouse, Joan Baez climbed onto a flatbed truck to sing "The Star-Spangled Banner" and then "Blowin' in the Wind." Harry took the mic from Baez to proclaim a great day for their movement and for America, too, as Governor George Wallace stewed from behind thick drapes in his nearby office. A great day it may have been. But this time, victory's backlash arrived with the murder of a white activist named Viola Liuzzo.

A mother of five in Detroit, Liuzzo had been moved by the images of bloodshed at Pettus Bridge to drive her Oldsmobile down to Montgomery and help the cause, by shuttling participants in the march to the airport outside town after it was through. Tony Bennett, Harry recalled, would have been the next celebrity she ferried to his flight home if he hadn't demurred on account of having too much fun. Returning from her airport run with a Black volunteer, Viola Liuzzo was set upon in her Oldsmobile by a carload of Klansmen. They wanted to teach this "Nigger lover," and anyone who thought like her, a lesson. They put two bullets in her head.

On August 6, 1965, President Johnson's signing into law of the Voting Rights Act furnished a vital victory for the movement. But for Harry personally, that win's arrival was shaded by costs that would stick. In Detroit a short time later, he performed a benefit concert and invited Viola Liuzzo's bereaved husband and children to his dressing room to share sympathies—only for one of Liuzzo's sons to stride right over and punch him in his crotch. Liuzzo's widower was mortified. Harry was doubled up. But he would dwell often, in therapy as in his memoir, on why this boy's grief and pain were directed his way. ("I came to appreciate that the boy blamed me for his mother's death. He wasn't right, but he wasn't wrong, either.")

That fall, an increasingly militant SNCC made a final push to enfranchise and empower the illiterate underclass Blacks in rural Alabama. Stokely Carmichael, the charismatic activist who the next spring would declare, "What we want is Black power," had by then become SNCC's de facto leader—and officially nixed its credo of nonviolence by changing the organization's name, if not the acronym by which it was known, to the Student *National* Coordinating Committee. "National" ambitions aside, one of the soon-to-implode organization's efforts to put the Voting Rights Act to use was to have Carmichael set up the Lowndes County Freedom Organization in one of Alabama's poorest corners. The outfit's aim wasn't merely to register Black voters but to give them a new party to vote for. Its symbol, per a policy meant to enable illiterate voters to cast ballots—and in a state whose segregationist Democratic Party's icon was a white rooster—was a black panther.

Harry found the "antiwhite" aspects of Carmichael's rhetoric deeply harmful, and his advocacy for bearing arms, soon to be echoed by the Black Panther Party he inspired, "both dumb and dangerous. Mostly dumb." In certain ways, he had much in common with this tall and outspoken young man with whom he shared West Indian roots—Stokely was born in Trinidad—and a Pan-African sensibility that influenced how both men, as proud members of a larger diaspora, approached America's racial travails. Stokely would also become the paramour of Harry's South African protege, Miriam Makeba. But if Harry understood the anger driving Stokely toward violence, his own conversion to Ghandian ideals and tactics as the right outlet for one's rage, was absolute. He blamed Stokely for tearing apart an organization whose foremost builders—Bob Moses, John Lewis, Ella Baker—he dearly loved. But also germane was the fact that Stokely hailed from an island with which Harry, as a Jamaican who'd adopted Trinidad's music to his own ends, nurtured vexed ties. Of the rivalrous disregard that typified their relationship from the get-go, Harry said: "You could take us out of the islands, but you couldn't take the islands out of us."

20

You could take us out of the islands, but you couldn't take the islands out of us."

The admission is striking. It's also a familiar truism, at least to immigrants from the West Indies. It was never going to be easy for Harry's outsize Jamaica-bred ego to share space with Stokeley's Trinidadian one. But the sentiment applied equally to the public perception of Belafonte the entertainer. He tried hard, for years after *Calypso* hit, to avoid the feeling of being pigeonholed as a singing symbol of the Caribbean. By the time he brought the leading lights of American pop culture to Montgomery in 1965, he had been a major figure in that culture for a decade. As a prominent player in other realms of American life, too, and a profound friend to the cause and culture of Black Americans in the

Jim Crow South, he was also arguably the country's fore-most exponent of Black folk culture in a pop context. But on that wooden stage outside Montgomery in 1965, he didn't sing "John Henry" or "Cotton Fields." He sang what every-one wanted him to. He sang "Jamaica Farewell."

People want the hits. Harry may have remained deter-mined to evoke and perform the musical heritage of the "human family": at Carnegie Hall in 1960, and in the stage show he brought to concert halls around the world in those years, his repertoire included "La Bamba" and "Henè Ma Tov" and another Israeli folk song, "Vaichazkem," that he liked singing with the Chad Mitchell Trio. But he was never going to outrun the records that made his name and that had made him famous. One reason, perhaps, is a truth that would become a mantra for the marketers of so-called world music, a couple decades hence: authenticity. His charmful *Calypso* favorites evoked a culture and region of which he was recognizably a part. The year he returned to Carnegie Hall, he released a pair of collections of Afro-Americana—*My Lord What a Mornin'* and *Swing Dat Hammer*, respectively—that didn't hit. What did, in 1961, was a return to the islands. *Jump Up Calypso* featured a new rendition of a classic from Trinidad, Lord Kitchener's "Jump in the Line," that also be-came a favorite of Harry's. It was his last album to be certi-fied gold.

After it was, Harry stepped away again from calypso. His next album, *The Midnight Special*, like his previous forays into blues-based material, was middling as art, but did hit #8 on the charts—and succeeded in granting another young talent his first recording date in New York. In 1962, Bob Dylan had just turned up in Greenwich Village from Minnesota. It was the thrill of his young life to play harmonica on a session led by a singer who, as Dylan would recall years later, he'd grown up revering not only for the range of characters his songs evoked ("lovers and slaves, chain-gang workers, saints and sinners and children . . ."), but for the fact that he "appealed to everybody, whether they were steelworkers or symphony patrons or bobby-soxers—even children." This was praise that, to Harry, meant a lot. And Dylan also felt a strong kinship, as he wrote in *Chronicles*, with Harry's way of dealing with a vexsome cohort of folk purists who were born of the folk revival that produced them both. It was Harry, Dylan said, who taught him to insist that "all folk-singers were interpreters." In accounts of his inspirations, names like Woody Guthrie and Robert Johnson and Ramblin' Jack Elliott commonly feature. But there was another artist, as Dylan revealed in *Chronicles*, who shaped how he sought to evolve folk's ethos and sound for a new decade and a new generation.

In February 1964, Dylan released *The Times They Are*

A-Changin'. The next month, Harry enjoyed what he'd later describe as his last hurrah at pop culture's peak: Ed Sullivan handed over his stage and his audience of millions for a full twenty-two minutes, during which Harry ran through a medley of tunes met with warm applause. That same winter, the Beatles had appeared on the same program to show Sullivan and America, in their six-minute bow before a crowd that lost their minds, where the culture was heading. Harry had released an album the summer before, *Belafonte at the Greek Theatre,* that was nominated for a Grammy. But it was his last LP to crack the top 40.

If this was the season of Harry's life during which activism outweighed entertainment, he also grew as devoted to turning other recording artists into stars as he was to polishing his own. His political work had taught him that as much could be accomplished from behind the scenes as by taking center stage. Skills and habits he learned effecting change from the shadows now fed his desire, in show business, to place others in the limelight. The decade had begun with him visiting Africa for the first time, under the aegis of Kennedy's State Department. He would return repeatedly, under no aegis but his own and the larger cause of Black people everywhere, to nurture ties to African leaders who were battling the legacies of colonial rule in their own nations.

From boyhood, Harry had sensed that something profound joined the Black residents of the two nodes of diaspora—Jamaica and Harlem—he knew best. Now he grew occupied, as he would remain for decades, with uncovering and enacting what linked them to Africa both historically and in a present wherein many on the continent were also moving to transcend white supremacy. No such struggle, from the early sixties on, so energized him as that of Nelson Mandela and his African National Congress to end apartheid at the continent's southern tip. It was perhaps only fitting, then, that the African artist with whose career and life he became most engaged was from Johannesburg.

His first encounter with Miriam Makeba, and with the larger cause and cultural heritage he helped her come to symbolize to many, occurred in London. There in the fall of 1959, Harry was cornered at his hotel by the Reverend Trevor Huddleston, an Anglican priest who'd returned from a stint in South Africa determined to launch a movement in Britain against apartheid—and was now helping promote a film about the situation that had just premiered at the Venice Film Festival. The film's New York–based director, Lionel Rogosin, made *Come Back, Africa* by telling South

Africa's racist government he wanted to shoot a film promoting the country to tourists. While there, he'd collaborated with apartheid's foes to do anything but.

Harry watched Rogosin's film. He was knocked out—and by one scene in particular: it featured an entrancing singer in a humble shebeen, performing what sounded like a beguiling mix of jazzy American soul and tribal African music. He wasn't the first or last foreigner to feel enamored with these sounds that emerged in South Africa's urban townships from the intermingling of global pop with Zulu harmonies and Xhosa melodies. And his impression of how its musical styles like mbube and mbaqanga might hit American ears, in tandem with Miriam Makeba's striking presence and beauty, were only confirmed when he met the twenty-seven-year old singer in person. Makeba was sheltering in London with a few of the student-activists featured in *Come Back, Africa*, who'd come to Europe to help promote it. For the South Africans, returning home would mean sure imprisonment by the apartheid regime. Harry promised Makeba that he'd do all he could to help her and her friends get visas to come to the United States, and to help make her way once she got there.

In the event, he didn't need to help his new protégé with that first part: Lionel Rogosin, the director of *Come Back, Africa*, had already helped her get a visa to come perform in

New York at the Village Vanguard. Her first gig there was a disappointment: ill-advisedly, she tried to win over its crowd of hepcats as a straight jazz singer with a South African accent. It was after Harry saw her fall flat there—and leaned on his music critic friends not to write her off just yet—that he was able to make good on his latter promise.

Makeba was a denizen of Johannesburg's famed nightlife district, Sophiatown: she was versed in the jazz songbook. But she hadn't become her homeland's best-loved singer by mimicking Ella Fitzgerald. She'd done so by showcasing her "click-singing" and unique sense for vocalizing her Xhosa forebears' rhythms in a contemporary context. Makeba had been raised in deep poverty by a single mother with whom she spent the first six months of her life in jail. Makeba's mother had landed there for making home-brewed alcohol, and her daughter's upbringing was full of privation and abuse—but also an education in African rhythms and phrasing that she lent the vocal groups in Sophiatown, the Manhattan Brothers and the Skylarks, with whom she first made her name. In New York, Harry took Makeba on a long walk and convinced her to let him help her develop an act that would appeal to this new crowd not by obscuring her roots but enacting them in fresh ways. He also bought her out of the extortionate contracts she'd signed with her label in South Africa, and with the managers who'd brought her to New York. Determined to break her out in America, Harry set her up with a new record contract, with George Marek and RCA, and opened a bank account for her whose ledger he filled with what he described, to this wowed young woman who began calling him "Big Brother," as an advance against their future earnings together.

She brought her new act to the Vanguard's small stage in a resplendent faux-African gown. Harry had had it designed for her by a costume-maker friend of his and Julie's—Katherine Dunham's husband, John Pratt. Makeba's new set succeeded, at least with the music mavens and actor friends Harry packed the place with. It also went over well when he got her a slot, seen by millions, on *The Steve Allen Show* on NBC. By the next spring, Makeba was sharing a stage with Harry at Carnegie Hall. Her performance there of "The Click Song" was one she'd reprise, with him, in concert halls around the world. In 1965, they recorded an album together, *An Evening with Belafonte/Makeba,* that won a Grammy. The record, despite its title, didn't document a live concert. It was a studio session featuring folk songs—or riffs thereupon—that the pair sang in Zulu, Sotho, and Swahili, along with a newer tune by a martyred ANC activist named Vuyisile Mini. Mini's composition "Ndodemnyama we Verwoerd" comprised a warning to apartheid's figurehead ("Beware, Verwoerd!") and became an anthem of the movement against his regime.

The Grammy that album won was in a category—for Best Folk Album—whose advent Harry's own rise had enabled (and in which he'd been won a statue for *Swing Dat Hammer* in 1961). But like Harry's similar effort with his Greek protégé Nana Mouskouri—*An Evening with Belafonte/Mouskouri* landed in 1965—it was also a landmark in the prehistory of another curious genre which, nearly three decades later, would gain its own category at the Grammys. In the 1980s and '90s, "world music" became the tag under which Makeba's music was marketed in the West. She bristled at being grouped with musicians from far-flung cultures with whom she shared nothing but non-Western roots. In the sixties, Harry's attempts to help turn her into an American pop star didn't hit big; her solo albums for RCA never sold like her mentor's. His vision of hipping Americans' ears to the foreign-yet-familiar-sounding glories of South African pop wouldn't happen in earnest until Paul Simon went to Johannesburg to record *Graceland* in 1985 (and got into hot water for going against Harry's advice that he get permission in advance, from the ANC, to break the cultural boycott that remained in place until apartheid's end). But the success Makeba did win under his tutelage—including a 1967 hit that became her signature, "Pata Pata"—helped turn her into "Mama Africa": a global symbol of her continent and a key figure, in those years' dashiki-wearing gestalt, in articulating ties between Black Americans and Africa.

Harry's own impulse to draw those connections also animated an ambitious endeavor that had begun when he convinced George Marek and RCA to back a box set that he'd conceived, at the height of his popularity and power with his label in the fifties, as a kind of Afro-diasporic reply to Harry Smith's *Anthology of American Folk Music*. He envisioned an anthology of Black music that would recount, in sound, the saga of Black people in America from the arrival of its first slaves to the twentieth century. After years of preparation and of hunting for songs and artists to feature, he began work on what he called "the anthology" in 1961, before spending a decade of sporadic toil, with his choral director Leonard De Paur and friends like Bessie Jones and Brownie McGhee, on sessions that saw them record scores of songs from across the Americas and Africa—only for the project to be shelved when executives at *Reader's Digest*, whom George Marek had convinced to help release a planned-for box set of five LPs, pulled out of their agreement to do so.

America at the sixties' end was a different country than

it had been a decade prior; so was Harry's role and reputation in its culture. His early albums for RCA may have, as he said, "proved that Americans were more ready than had been assumed to hear the voices of others or the culture of other people." But by now those same Americans, at least as appraised by *Reader's Digest*'s gauge of the mainstream, were perhaps less ready to embrace Black American history as their own than they had been, once, to sway along to sunny folk songs from long ago or far away. The staid but hopeful aspects of the civil rights years had given way to riots and radicalism, to Black Power and protests against the war in Vietnam. Harry had become as well known for his politics as for his pop star's smile. Able to move fluidly between these worlds, Harry was a star who knew how to sit back and help others shine and who was as adept at working an adoring crowd, at a political rally, as he was working a green room of his peers.

21

The Tonight Show. A Thursday night in February 1968. Sitting behind Johnny Carson's rosewood desk isn't the show's usual host but a stand-in: a beautiful, brown-skinned man whom Carson has invited to hold down his chair at 30 Rock for an entire week. It's Harry Belafonte. America's "King of Calypso" is suave and smiling in a natty suit. He's been among the country's biggest celebrities for a decade—ever since 1956, when he rowed his banana boat song ("Day-O!") up the charts to become a pop star beloved not just on America's metropolitan coasts, but in living rooms from Iowa to Maine, where his LPs are fixtures. He's visited this set before, to cross his legs on Carson's couch and engage in repartee. But his role this week is different. Now Belafonte is holding Carson's microphone himself, exuding gravitas and glamour. He's the easeful arbiter and éminence grise, for a week at least, of American culture: the honcho and host of a television program that a huge portion of Americans who haven't gone to bed early and who own TVs are tuning into.

Belafonte flashes his famous smile under his famous widow's peak. He looks like a million bucks. Carson's gambit has already paid off. The ratings on Monday night were among *The Tonight Show*'s highest ever. And they've climbed each night since. Carson has brought him here to welcome a range of conversations and guests that the show's usual host, that paragon of midwestern affability and easeful wit, couldn't welcome himself. Johnny Carson was, by his own account, an "Eisenhower Republican." But he was more forward-thinking, with regards to race, than many people of that description. And he had, by the winter of 1968, grown plainly and publicly opposed to the disastrous war in Vietnam. Belafonte, for Middle America, may have been a cherished entertainer. But he was also an outspoken lefty and a known confidante of Martin Luther King: Carson knew that Belafonte would address issues then roiling the country that would, that summer, explode into riots. And he'd convinced his bosses at NBC to let Belafonte, as a condition of his accepting the gig, invite on whomever he liked.

Harry had asked his friend Robert F. Kennedy, at the

week's outset, to be among them: his hope was that Bobby would use the date to announce a much-anticipated run for president ("You've said that those who dare to fail greatly can achieve greatly," the singer teased the demure senator. "Do you believe that in 1968 . . . we will have a choice to back a candidate who will dare greatly?"). He didn't get RFK to bite. But he did get him to wax regretful that an administration in which he'd served—his late brother's—had launched a war that Bobby now strongly opposed. Ensuing nights weren't just dotted with show-business friends who shared Belafonte's politics (Marlon Brando), or complexion (Cosby) or both (Sidney Poitier); Belafonte also brought to Americans' living rooms a who's who of the Black public sphere. He had Diahann Carroll and Dionne Warwick; Wilt Chamberlain and Aretha Franklin; Lena Horne and Freda Payne. He had Black comics whom many white Americans knew (Cosby, thanks to *I Spy*) and Black comics whom many didn't (Nipsey Russell). He had them all the share the couch, as was *The Tonight Show*'s wont, with other decidedly non-Carson-like guests like the blacklisted Jewish actor Zero Mostel and the Cree folksinger Buffy Sainte-Marie (she sang "Now That the Buffalo's Gone"). And he's saved his foremost lineup, on Thursday, for last.

Paul Newman has never appeared on a talk show before; he hates the glib side of showbiz. But Belafonte has asked his blue-eyed friend, well known for his commitment to liberal causes, to come and discuss more substantial matters than promoting films: why, Belafonte wants to know, should a top movie star stick his neck out for civil rights? "What do you do," Newman replies, "give up your citizenship when you become an actor?" His presence here is its own coup. But the simple sight of Newman wedged on the couch between Belafonte and two lesser-known Black entertainers—the folksinger Leon Bibb (who's just offered a lovely rendition of "Suzanne") and the ventriloquist Aaron Williams (with his sidekick Freddy)—is something to see. The white man is the minority, at least on this night, in America's living room. And now Belafonte rises to furnish his coup de grâce: "Ladies and gentlemen." He dips his head. "The Reverend Martin Luther King Jr."

Dr. King is stocky and shorter than his lithe friend. He smiles in his dark suit. "I'm delighted to be here, Harry," King says in precise preacher's tones. "And I'll tell you one of the reasons. I flew out of Washington this afternoon, and as soon as we started out they notified us that the plane had mechanical difficulties. And I don't want to give you the impression that as a Baptist preacher I don't have faith in God in the air." Beat. "But it's simply that I have more experience with him on the ground." The crowd's laughter at King's joke, and the smoothness of his delivery, seems to surprise them. Harry asks his close friend a question whose answer he knows: "How old are you, Dr. King?" King can scarcely push out his reply (he's just turned thirty-nine) before Newman exclaims, "You're a young fella!" From the couch: cross talk and good-natured ribbing. Then the conversation turns serious.

"I guess I could use some of this time to get into pleasantries," Belafonte begins, "to talk about the many experiences I've had with you not only here but in Europe and other places." This, it's clear as he pauses to raise his head, isn't what he wants to do. "What do you have in store for us this summer?" Now King joins in the crowd's nervy laughter: the summer of 1968, everyone seems to sense, is going to be a doozy. And America's foremost activist for justice is glad to explain, by way of a capsule history of the past few years in American life, what he's focusing on now.

King says that the passage of the Civil Rights and Voting Rights Acts were great victories. But they've done little, in the three years since the latter's passage, to redress inequalities built over centuries. And his approach to battling such ills doesn't just involve confronting unjust laws. "I feel," he intones, "that we are in the midst of a most critical period in our nation. And the economic problem is probably the most serious problem confronting the Negro community, and poor people generally." King insists that America's inability to confront poverty at home can't be disconnected from its waging immoral wars abroad. He has a sound bite ready: "The fact is we spend approximately five hundred thousand dollars to kill each Vietcong soldier while we spend only about fifty-three dollars a year for every person characterized as poverty stricken." And now his plan is to use the same methods he used to advocate for civil rights for Black Americans to confront more far-reaching ills: "I think the time has come to bring to bear the nonviolent direct action movement on the economic conditions that we face all over the country."

Now the studio audience is silent; these aren't joking matters. But one can sense, in the crowd's silence, something more. Liberal Americans are accustomed to looking at King with the admiring respect evinced by Paul Newman as he signals concentration, from the couch, on King's words. But backing his eloquent calls for equality and fairness, a few years earlier, was one thing. Questioning capitalism is another. In the crowd's silence, and King's tired look as he tries to explain why it's necessary to do so, one can sense how beleaguered he feels, in his life's final year, from trying to use the moral platform he's built to train his admirers' eyes on a broader movement for justice that his friend Harry

Belafonte has long served not merely as a core member of King's kitchen cabinet but as a benefactor. And Harry's next question, one can tell from his friend's face, is unexpected.

"Do you fear for your life?"

Martin pauses, shoots Harry a look. Then collects himself. "We have lived with this a number of years now. Since we started out in Montgomery, Alabama, in 1956, I had to deal with this problem because if I moved around worrying about it, it would completely immobilize me." He's speaking softly, but his words echo sentiments to which he'll soon give rousing voice in a famous speech. "And so I've come to the point where I take this whole matter very philosophically. I'm more concerned about doing something for humanity, and what I consider the will of God, than about longevity. Ultimately, it isn't so important how long you live, the important thing is how well you live."

Two months later, King was felled by an assassin's bullet. Two months after that, Bobby Kennedy (by then a candidate for president) was, too. King's interview with Belafonte is the last one he gives on TV. But what's remarkable about it, and about Belafonte's weeklong "sit-in" on *The Tonight Show*, was what it signaled both about where American society was heading, and how a changing culture helped it get there. For not only was Harry Belafonte the only figure in that culture who one can imagine conjoining the worlds and figures he did, with heft and charm, on Carson's couch. This was also a fact inseparable from the particular nature of his success as an entertainer and as a public figure in this era when TV—a medium to which his charms, both superficial and profound, are preternaturally given—had become the center of American life.

That he also seems to be a nice person, per Johnny Carson and as perceived by people at home, is of course key. But it's the outsize stature he projects—the moral authority and self-regard that comprise his charisma—that attracts admirers by the busload. It's also a big part of why Harry, for those closest to him, isn't always the easiest to be around. But when his contemporaries and friends give themselves over to what can happen in his presence, in public acts of alchemy, the results make history.

22

———

The Sixties," as a period, is more often invoked to recall the heady hopes of the decade's middle years—a span stretching from "I Have a Dream" in 1963 to 1967's Summer of Love—than those vibes' grim denouement amidst assassinations and riots, confusion and fear. If the March on Washington represented the country's last best hope to avoid its cities' streets being "filled with rage and resentment, guns and blood," as Harry put it, it's telling that the movement's greatest legislative win was met, two years later, not with rejoicing in the streets but with violence. Days after Voting Rights became law in August 1965, Los Angeles was aflame. The unrest that came to be known as the Watts Rebellion was sparked by the undue arrest of a young motorist in that Black enclave; it resulted in thirty-four deaths, 3,000 arrests, $40 million in damage, and took 14,000 members of California's Army National Guard to quell. Those events in Watts, like a similar uprising that gripped Harlem a summer before, also set a template for rebellions in ensuing years and in cities across the country, from Newark to Detroit, Chicago to Kansas City, Philadelphia to Washington, D.C.

If the sixties for many white Americans were marked by the rise of flower power and free love, of flashing peace signs and protesting war, the era to many Black ones—and not only those living in communities strafed by violence—signaled other shifts. Not the least of these, in an era when Black pop stars engaged racism head-on and the Black Panthers became paragons of "radical chic," was a new entwinement of politics and culture. Harry's reply to these developments was to dip a toe back into the world of prime-time specials— the last ones he would ever produce—on network TV. *The Strollin' 20's* was a paean to Harlem's cultural riches in its namesake era that aired on CBS in 1966. It was written by Langston Hughes and narrated by Sidney Poitier. It was a direct response, Harry said, to other images of the neighborhood then filling people's screens and misperceptions of its residents and history. He himself was a product of Harlem, he told reporters, and it was vitally important to him to show that the neighborhood where he'd grown up, like other so-called Black ghettos now known for being "on the path of head-on collision with the white world," also contained "humor, love, and personality that remains unseen." Whether white audiences internalized that message may be hard to say. But *Strollin's* fond account of the world that Blacks who migrated from the South to Harlem made there in the 1920s—a world of dancing at rent parties and of convivial streets and literary riches; of Ellingtonian swing and sophistication—did earn strong enough ratings to convince ABC to green-light a more refractive attempt to reframe America's understanding of Black culture, and Black joy, at a time when phrases like Black rage, and Black power, felt much more common.

For *A Time for Laughter*, Harry gathered Black humorists both storied and new—Moms Mabley and Diana Sands; Redd Foxx and Nipsey Russell; Dick Gregory and Richard Pryor—whose acts were at once forms of coping with and of resisting American racism. Abiding by his belief that "the American white can only become acquainted with the American Negro through his art," Harry presented Black comics who'd honed their acts before Black crowds. Radically, the show played most directly to Black viewers who could appreciate the fine line between self-mockery and mocking a white society's absurd views of Black life. Redd Foxx reminded Moms Mabley, dressed as a princess and looking in a mirror, that she'd never be as fair as Snow White; Diahann

Carroll sat in a faux witches' pot circled by white cannibals eager to eat her up; Harry himself, dressed in a doctor's gear, performed surgery on a watermelon. One senses from watching the show's sketches and reading its quizzical reviews that this was the moment when Harry realized, as would the corporate backers who soon stopped handing him the keys to their networks, that he'd pushed the mainstream's envelope as far as it could go.

The same April week in 1967 that *A Time for Laughter* appeared, Martin Luther King visited Manhattan's Riverside Church to give a historic speech proclaiming his opposition to the war in Vietnam. That speech, which King composed on yellow legal pads in the guest room at Harry and Julie's apartment on West End Avenue, effectively ended his relationship with a livid Lyndon B. Johnson. It also marked the pivot that would define his life's last year, as he moved from decrying American racism to linking its causes, and effects, to larger iniquities wrought by the American empire and American capitalism. This shift in King's outlook, and in his message, cost him many allies. These decidedly did not include Harry. His vision for how fighting racism fit within the larger cause of building a just society for everyone was in accord with King's new stance—even as he grew increasingly wary, as the zeitgeist moved away from hopeful idealism and toward a more militant politics, of the confusions and contradictions that shift augured for people across the diaspora whose dots Harry had worked so hard to connect.

Soon after Miriam Makeba's arrival to New York, she married another South African émigré who became an eminence of world music: the trumpeter Hugh Masekela. By the late sixties, though, that marriage had unraveled, and her relationship with Harry would also be tested by her fondness for harder living and harder politics than his. Where Harry remained a firm ally of the African National Congress of Nelson Mandela, Makeba's New York apartment became a haven for partisans of the more radical Pan-Africanist Congress. She dated Huey Newton, head of the Black Panther Party. Then she took up with Harry's old nemesis from SNCC, Stokely Carmichael. Carmichael left SNCC in 1967 on account of his rogue acts and refusal to work with white allies, and would later change his name to Kwame Ture. He served briefly as the Panthers' honorary prime minister and then exchanged his old work shirts for a tailored Nehru suit, mahogany cane, and massive bejeweled ring that he wore backstage during one of Makeba's concerts on the night Harry realized they were an item. In 1969, Carmichael and Makeba, who'd married the year before, would declare themselves done with America's racist society, and decamp for West Africa. They settled in Conakry, Guinea, where their host was none other than Harry's old friend Sékou Touré—

who by now was known less as an apostle of African social-
ism than as a vain and vengeful dictator with a penchant for
imprisoning his foes when he wasn't sentencing them to
death. Touré made Makeba his ambassador to the UN.

It was Stokely Carmichael, in a 1967 book he coauthored
with Charles V. Hamilton called *Black Power*, who coined
the phrase "institutional racism." For the revolutionary who
had coined the phrase "Black Power," institutional racism
was a tool for indictment: a way to describe racism not as an
attitude or idea, but a systemic ideology embedded in, and
enforced by, America's institutions. Harry's stance, vis-à-vis
the institutions he spent his career engaging—America's
media and its government; its TV networks and its Hollywood studios and blue-chip corporations—was different.
Those institutions' racism was a fact he railed against—but
also that he worked from within, with guile and brilliance,
to change. His success changed the culture. It also pointed
up a compelling alternate definition of Carmichael's catch-
phrase. When Harry took his seat behind Johnny Carson's
desk, for that historic week hosting *The Tonight Show* in
1968, and used that platform exactly as he pleased, Alfred
Duckett, one of Harry's oldest admirers in the Black press,
wrote in the *Chicago Defender*: "Harry Belafonte is Black
power."

23

The novelty and impact of watching a Black man engage America's most pressing social questions from Johnny Carson's chair was huge for white viewers. It was even bigger for Black ones. "Television was the only thing that connected any of us with the larger world," recalled Henry Louis Gates Jr., of the partly segregated hamlet where he grew up West Virginia. "Night after night, my father and I stayed up to watch a black man host the highest-rated show in his time slot—history in the making." They weren't alone. *The Chicago Defender*'s Alfred Duckett praised "the best damn shows I have ever seen on TV." The power Harry embodied, Duckett wrote, was the power "of being so respected that you can say anything that comes to your mind. The Power of being proud black and letting non-black know you're not putting him down if he too has soul. The power to joke about the Problem without being bitter but getting the message through." The British critic W. J. Weatherby, writing in *The Guardian*, opined that during his stint in Carson's chair, Harry "became the tightest link between the streets and show business for a whole week."

Many felt exhilarated witnessing what Harry's presence, and encouragement, elicited from "eloquent fearless guests," as Weatherby described them, who "discussed everything from soul food to Vietnam with no pulled punches." Harry had made clear that his role as host would not extend to reciting ads or thanking the show's sponsors (a duty handled for the week by Carson's sidekick, Ed McMahon). Robert F. Kennedy ignored the show's sponsorship by Philip Morris Inc. to accuse the tobacco industry of killing Americans, while Harry used his interview with Buffy Sainte-Marie to decry the suicide rate among despondent Native Americans. And between them all, Harry shared home videos of his interracial family waterskiing on vacation in Las Vegas—which may not seem radical until you consider what happened when Harry returned to NBC weeks later to guest-star on a prime-time special with the English singer Petula Clark: her special's sponsor, the Chrysler Corporation, threatened to pull out when its executives learned that their white star had touched Harry's elbow as they sang "On the Path of Glory."

In the visual archive of King's luminous journey across American consciousness in the 1960s, there are two surviving bits of footage that showcase the prophetic nature of the great man's will to ponder his own death. One occurred in a conversation with one of his closest friends that happened to be filmed for broadcast on national TV—and was thankfully recorded as a kinescope in that era before VCRs and TiVo, which later appeared in *The Sit-In*, a 2020 documentary about Harry's week on *Tonight*. It was during his appearance on *The Tonight Show* that King first tried out his line on how the length of a life, or its premature curtailment, should not be its measure ("it isn't so important how long you live, the important thing is how well you live"). The other such moment was the famous "Mountaintop" speech he gave at the Memphis headquarters of the nation's largest denomination of Black Pentecostals, the night before his assassination. That's the sermon, delivered at the city's Mason Temple with a shining brow and in a preacher's voice aquiver and booming at once, wherein he proclaimed that he'd seen the promised land. "I don't know what will happen now," he said of his outlook in the face of what he now seemed to sense was coming, "but it really doesn't matter with me now, because I've been to the mountaintop." He continued:

Like anybody, I would like to live a long life; longevity has its place. But I'm not concerned about that now. I just want to do God's will. And He's allowed me to go up to the mountain. And I've looked over. And I've seen the Promised Land. I may not get there with you. But I want you to know tonight, that we, as a people, will get to the Promised Land. So I'm happy, tonight. I'm not worried about anything. I'm not fearing any man. Mine eyes have seen the glory of the coming of the Lord.

The day after King evoked the mountaintop from Memphis, Harry was at home on West End Avenue when his and Julie's Jamaican housekeeper told him to come look at the TV. Martin may not have feared any man. But a meek and twisted one checked into a boardinghouse across the street from the Lorraine Motel and shot him. In a chair in his living room where, a few nights before, he and Julie had sat talking with Martin as the latter sipped his Harveys Bristol Cream, Harry sank into a chair, rocked into stillness. But not for long. His first call was to Coretta. By the next morning, he was in Atlanta with Martin's widow and her four shocked children.

Caring for Coretta, offering solace to her kids, pulling a dark suit from Martin's small closet full of them to give to the funeral home for his casket—these were born of his loyalty to, and love for, her husband. It was loyalty to Martin's movement and ideals that also spurred him to convince Coretta to fly with him to Memphis, on a plane the CEO of Fabergé loaned Harry for the week, to take part in the march that Martin was meant to lead. Harry's calculated hope was that Coretta's arrival there—to march with striking sanitation workers and then deliver a dignified speech that she gave with Harry at her side—would be vital not merely for showing that the causes and means of engagement Martin backed hadn't expired with his death. "The country's going up in smoke," he recalled saying to her, "and your presence, and what you say, will have enormous impact on what this nation will do." Whether or not Coretta's brave trip to Memphis, and footage of her speech on the news nationwide that night, in fact helped tamp down emotions—one hundred American cities and towns, in ensuing days, would be singed by unrest— is hard to say. From what did occur, it's clear that a contrasting sentiment was rising: Stokely Carmichael, in Washington, gave a press conference in which he assured America, in tones that would have been anathema to his old mentor, that King's killing would prompt violence. And so it did—though perhaps not in as sustained and widespread a fashion as it would have if not for the efforts of his widow and the singer and activist who'd become his most trusted friend.

Of all the signal images of mourning from King's funeral in Atlanta—the mule-drawn wagon that carried him
three miles from Ebenezer Baptist Church to Morehouse
College; the thousands who lined the roadway to watch
it pass—perhaps none so distilled the nation's grief like a
photo of a wet-cheeked Harry sitting next to Coretta, her
own face stony behind a black veil, with his fist in his mouth
to keep from sobbing. Harry and Julie's involvement in what
happened in Atlanta that week, and in supporting the King
family through what came next, was even bigger away from
the cameras. When Coretta's close friend Xernona Clay-
ton returned from a trip to a downtown department store to
buy some dresses for the week, and rang the doorbell at the
King family home, it was Harry who answered and gave her
money to pay for them. When he and Julie accompanied her
to inspect Martin's open casket at Spelman College before
viewing was opened to the public, it was Julie who lent her a
powder puff to touch up the mortician's sloppy job of putty-
ing the wound on King's face. When Harry was appointed
one of his estate's three executors, along with his attorneys
Stan Levison and Harry Wachtel, it fell to him to settle the
affairs of a man who'd won a Nobel Prize and written bestselling books but whose bank accounts—since all that he
earned went straight to the SCLC—held some $5,000. Thus
did it also fall to Harry, after he and Stan Levison divvied

mementos from Martin's last effects, including his tie clip
and an envelope on which he'd scrawled notes for a speech
he never gave, to lend his own bank accounts to ensure that
Martin's family had what they needed, at least until they
could set up a foundation in his memory to pay Coretta's
bills.

In Atlanta that week he served, alongside King's close
associates Ralph Abernathy and Andrew Young, as de facto
host of a funeral that brought to Georgia a panoply of prominent citizens resembling the one at the 1963 March on
Washington. All the Brandos and Poitiers and Kennedys
you'd expect were there; the movie stars and pop stars were
also now joined, in the pews, by U.S. Senators, foreign dignitaries, and "candidates, former candidates, and hopeful
candidates," as the writer Elizabeth Hardwick put it, "exposed to the public on prime viewing time, free of charge,
free, certainly, of the cost of a past contribution or a future
pledge." (President Johnson, concerned that his presence
would inflame protests against the war, sent Vice President
Hubert Humphrey and his attorney general, Ramsey Clark.)
For Harry, this solemn gathering was also marked by a char-
acteristic urge that seemed to grip him whenever the great
and the good gathered in one place—to see them do more.
He proposed an all-night vigil, in an Atlanta stadium and
featuring a slate of famous speakers, to hail King's legacy of

nonviolence and turn the nation's attention to a new cause—the Poor People's Campaign for economic justice—that King had been readying to launch that spring. This idea was met with enthusiasm by all his celebrity friends—except one. Sidney Poitier felt that pulling off a dignified funeral was enough. Harry was so livid at his old twin's hesitancy, which ensured that the vigil wouldn't happen, that they didn't speak for two years.

That sad spring after Martin's death, which would be made sadder still by Bobby Kennedy's murder in June, was a season of deep pain and confusing transitions. The last time Harry and King had been together, a few days before Martin left for Memphis, they'd held a final planning session at Harry and Julie's place in New York for the Poor People's Campaign. Despairing of the will toward violence he saw rising in the Black community, King was determined to turn his movement toward combating the iniquities of capitalism by joining with impoverished Americans of all creeds and colors—poor whites from Appalachia, Chicano farmworkers from California, American Indians from everyplace—to erect a shantytown on the National Mall to urge Congress to pass an Economic Bill of Rights. This wasn't a bit of legislation that President Johnson, with whom he was already on the outs over Vietnam, would give the time of day. Nor was it a campaign that his more conservative advisers, like

Andrew Young, who said as much that night on West End Avenue to Martin's deep frustration, thought wise. But both Harry and Julie—often the only woman in these conversations—backed Martin's plan to launch his new campaign against poverty.

In the event, the Poor People's Campaign was launched with King's heir-apparent in charge of the SCLC, Ralph Abernathy, presiding. But Abernathy's failings as a leader didn't just derive from the truth that, like most mortals, he lacked King's charisma and vision; his conservatism led him to court ties with politicians who Harry loathed, including Richard Nixon (and, later on, to endorse Ronald Reagan's campaign for president). His ascent was the beginning of the end, at least by Harry's lights, of the SCLC. The Poor People's Campaign did erect a shantytown in Washington called Resurrection City, but it was soon bulldozed from the Mall, along with King's envisaged movement for economic justice, with little fanfare or fight. A similar declension of his vision awaited the King Center in Atlanta that Harry had helped set up, for Coretta and the family, after King's death. Where Harry and others hoped that foundation might advance King's causes and vision, the family was more interested in embalming, and perhaps monetizing, his greatness. Harry ended his involvement with the center the next year when he learned that among its first annual gala's sponsors was the CEO of Ford Motor Company, an outspoken apologist for, and business partner of, the apartheid regime in South Africa. It was a nudge for Harry, amidst the foundering of American organizations he'd done so much to support, toward focusing on the affairs and causes in Africa that would occupy him for ensuing decades. It was also the start of a slow unraveling of his relationship with the King family that would culminate, four decades later, in squabbles over those personal effects that he and Stan Levinson were gifted in 1968 and in Harry's being disinvited, in 2006, from a memorial service for Coretta on account of the family's not wishing to offend a sitting President—George W. Bush—whom Harry had recently called "the greatest terrorist in the world."

Such were the dramas of 2006. But in the summer of 1968, the aftermath of Martin's death was made sadder still by the murder of the onetime attorney general who'd become a close friend and who that spring had indeed launched a presidential campaign of which Harry was an ardent backer. Harry's downcast state of mind, in an interview he gave the *Los Angeles Times* that July, was palpable: "I'd like to take my family, go and live in Africa," he said, "and be able to stop answering questions as though I were a spokesman for my people. I hate marching and getting called at three a.m. to bail some cats out of jail, or sitting on panels to talk

---

about America's racial problems." All he wanted to do now, he said, was "watch grass grow, and leaves change color, and see my children grow up."

In the event, and in that year that Hugh Masekela scored an unlikely pop hit with "Grazing in the Grass," Harry didn't move his family to the continent. He did begin spending more time at the Hudson Valley retreat he'd bought several years earlier in a bucolic town not far from where his elder daughters, Adrienne and Shari, went to boarding school. Chatham, New York, may have been an excellent place to watch the leaves change color. But Julie, a city girl to her core, didn't love it there. And much as David and Gina, now eleven and seven, enjoyed weekends in the country, their childhood memories of their workaholic dad, notwithstanding the sentiments of that despondent summer, would remain as typified by absence as presence. And his bitterness, as he looked to dust himself off and prepare for whatever was next, was deeply felt. "For me, the miracle in America was Martin Luther King," he said. "In the years that King and SNCC were coming to the people with love, the people didn't believe. They finally believed when it was too damn late."

24

•

The first time Americans saw Harry cry was also the first and last time his daughter Gina did, she told me decades later. Gina was six when she watched Harry weep for his friend at home in New York, before he flew to Atlanta to sit by Martin's widow at his funeral with a fist to his mouth and wetted cheeks. "Your best friend gets assassinated," Gina said, "at a time when you're working so hard to free not only yourselves but your community—it was devastating. But I don't think he ever gave himself the opportunity to mourn Dr. King. My father didn't often give himself the opportunity to feel sadness. Showing sadness, in his misogynistic West Indian body, was a sign of weakness, as opposed to a shared emotion of empathy."

What he did do, in that moment and then for the rest of his

life, was turn his grief into action. Harry's relationship with Bobby Kennedy, with its backstory of wariness and calculation, was different from his relationship with King. But it had grown in concert with Bobby's evolution, after he left the Justice Department, into an eloquent crusader against poverty and injustice and imperial wars—an evolution crucially aided by his having communed with the poor of Appalachia and in America's cities, at Harry's urging. Harry's involvement in JFK's run for the presidency in 1960 was born of mutual usefulness. By contrast, his relationship to RFK's campaign—which he'd joined as a vigorous ally and adviser from the start—represented a chance for his worldview, in the person of a politician with whom he enjoyed a close and hard-won friendship, to gain the White House. But then, not two months after King's demise, Bobby was also gone. "Assassinations seem to be a big part of the American horror story," Harry told the makers of the film about his week hosting *Tonight*. "The loss of Dr. King, coupled with what happened with Bobby Kennedy . . . changed the American climate severely."

The loss of both men left him at least briefly adrift—a movement man without a movement or party to bankroll or shape. Perhaps, if King's organization and the progressive wing of the Democratic party had finer heirs apparent waiting in the wings, another outcome would have been possible. But in both cases the replacements paled alongside the originals. Where Vice President Hubert Humphrey was a craven opportunist, in Harry's eyes, and a hawk on Vietnam who relieved Harry of his Peace Corps role on account of his opposition to the war, Eugene McCarthy "said the right things, [but] in person was cold and detached." At the SCLC, Ralph Abernathy voiced Dr. King's piety but none of his vision. Harry had little use for any of them.

Years later, Henry Louis Gates Jr. observed, in a profile for *The New Yorker*, that "Harry Belafonte was radical before it was chic and remained so long after it wasn't." He was right. But, paradoxically enough, Harry also struggled to find his feet in a cultural moment that was defined by radicalism. The issue, for Harry, wasn't hesitancy about the idea of Black Power or the creed of Afrocentrism: his investment in the Continent, as homeland and as cause, had begun with his first trip to Guinea in 1961, and was now only growing. But he was a King man to his core. The operative word in his moral mentor's devotion to nonviolence was "love": love for justice; love for humanity; love, too, for their white allies who had their own stake in equality—and whose own love, and donations to the cause, Harry had become so expert at winning. All of this, observed Elizabeth Hardwick, made no sense to "new black militants who were determined to break the dependency of the black people even on the cooperation, energy, and checkbooks of the guilty, longing, loving whiteys." She continued:

Everything separated the old Civil Rights people from the new militants, even the use of language. The harsh, obscene style, the unforgiving stares, the insulting accusations and refusal to make distinctions between bad whites and good—this was humbling and perplexing. Many of the white people had created their very self-identity out of issues and distinctions. They felt cast off, ill at ease with the new street rhetoric of "self-defense" and "self-determination."

Harry may not have felt cast off by young militants he'd shunned. Over the preceding decade and a half, he'd formed a crucial bridge between "the old civil rights people" and the North's restive streets. But his success as both an entertainer and an activist was staked on nothing so much as the cooperation, energy, and checkbooks of white people. Now north of forty himself, he was one of those "old civil rights people," whose thirty-nine-year-old figurehead was gone. The world without King was feared—not least by the West Indian son of Harlem who'd made the preacher his compass and his comrade. It was hard not to view their bond as a kind of miracle: how had it happened, really? How had this secular paragon of showbiz and of Manhattan, this streetwise West Indian, fallen in love with the righteous godhead of Southern Christendom, a figure as plodding and peaceful in

affect as Harry was sharp-tongued and spry. Their differences seem to have been as enlivening, as in all successful
partnerships, as their mutual recognition. "Perhaps what
was celebrated in Atlanta," Hardwick wrote, "was an end,
not a beginning—the waning of the slow, sweet dream of
Salvation, through Christ, for the Negro masses." The end of
that "slow, sweet dream" left Harry wondering, in more
realms than one, what role to play.

One answer he reached, in returning to film work for the
first time in eleven years, was to play an angel. *The Angel
Levine*, based on a short story by Bernard Malamud, was set
between Manhattan's Black and Jewish precincts, which
Harry had traversed his whole life, and at whose cultures'
nexus he still dwelled. It was as close to home as a project
could be for this sometime movie star who still had the juice,
thanks to his lingering production deal with United Artists,
to mount a production that didn't merely reflect his personal obsessions but let him continue to push, in the talent
he hired and the interns of color he insisted on having on
set, to diversify Hollywood. Its script was by Bill Gunn, a
black writer who'd just penned *The Landlord*, a subtly hilarious and layered look at the interracial dramas that played
out on New York's streets. Together with the picture's

Slovakian director, Ján Kadár, they endeavored to tell the story of a Jewish tailor with a bad back and a dying wife who, one afternoon while trudging home from the welfare office, witnesses a fateful robbery.

On the sidewalk, a woman is relieved of her furs. Mishkin, looking on, cries out. The robber, a lithe man in a black leather coat, runs into the street—and is clobbered by a car. His death is upsetting. But not as upsetting, for the schlubby tailor, as what happens when he returns home. In his kitchen, he's visited by a black man in a black leather coat who looks suspiciously like the Harlem hustler he's just watched die (and a lot, too, like Harry Belafonte). This visitor is a Jewish angel-in-training named Levine, he explains, who's been sent the incredulous tailor's way on a mission from God: to perform a miracle that the tailor, whose faith has been severely tested by his life's trials, will recognize as such and thereby grant Levine his wings.

Malamud's slight story centered on the perspective of a Jewish protagonist whose redemption depends on his capacity for avowing the humanity—rather, superhumanity—of the *schvartze*-angel he initially disdains. The film Harry wanted to make, and that he'd asked Bill Gunn to write, vested that *schvartze* with a human backstory and arc and love interest to counterbalance his neurotic costar in a yarmulke who was also, in real life, Harry's neighbor on the

Upper West Side. Zero Mostel walked with a limp won from a bus that crushed his leg on West 86th Street, and was best known by the late 1960s for star turns in *Fiddler on the Roof* and Mel Brooks's film version of *The Producers*. But he'd won the admiration of peers like Harry, a decade before, for how he'd handled being blacklisted: not only had Mostel refused to name names or renounce his political views when hauled before the House Un-American Activities Committee, he'd had the gumption, in ridiculing its members' putative worry that he'd give acting secrets to the Russians, to tell HUAC to piss off. On Capitol Hill as on Broadway, he was a great comedic actor and a huge personality—and an odd fit for a film which, as an effusive pan in *The New York Times* put it, felt "so nervously at odds with itself, so timid in its impulses, and so mistaken in its choices."

In the film, the health of Mishkin's wife, Fanny, improves. But the tailor refuses to credit Levine with her resurrection. Levine disappears, and Fanny's health declines once more. Mishkin rushes after him to beg amends, venturing into Harlem to find his guardian angel. There he encounters a curious crew of fellow Jews—Black members of the Commandment Keepers Ethiopian Hebrew Congregation—whose existence and eschatology remains little known, even now, beyond their synagogue on 123rd Street. In Malamud's short story, the tailor finally credits his black guardian angel with being a miracle worker, Levine gains his wings, and the tailor returns home to find his wife cured. "Believe me," he tells her, "there are Jews everywhere." But in the film, Mishkin fails to find Levine, and ends his search in a vacant lot near the Commandment Keepers shul, where a black feather drifts down from the heavens, leaving the audience as confused as Mishkin is.

Watching *The Angel Levine* today, it's not hard to understand why the film—which veers unsettlingly in tone from sentimental to sanctimonious to strange—struck many critics as an odd multiculti takeoff on *It's a Wonderful Life*. It's amazing that this oblique postcard from Jewish New York, decades before *Seinfeld* conquered the heartland, opened on screens nationwide. White critics hated it. The black press ignored it completely. Audiences of all hues stayed away. Harry spoke in press interviews, before leaving for a Brazilian vacation that coincided with its opening, about how badly he'd felt the need, after Dr. King's passing, to make a film exploring his dream of using shared faith to engender brotherhood. He was likely well aware, even before the film came out, that it was "an advertising man's despair," as one journalist put it, that would struggle to find an audience. But Harry would recall that the film had been worth it: on set, one of the interns of color he'd insisted on employing on the picture had handed him a script that prompted him—for the first time in two years and after their falling out at Martin's funeral—to call his estranged best friend in showbiz.

Sidney Poitier liked the script that Harry sent him, which was called *Buck and the Preacher*, as much as Harry did. He was also looking for projects to fill out his own production deal with Columbia Pictures. He agreed right away to help Harry turn *Buck and the Preacher* into a kind of black reply to *Butch Cassidy and the Sundance Kid*.

Before *Buck and the Preacher*, other Hollywood movies born of that most hallowed and hackneyed of American genres—the western—had featured Black leads. Poitier himself had starred in one in 1966: *Duel at Diablo* may have been the only film released by a major studio that year, of the eighty Hollywood produced, to feature a black lead. But it showed Poitier's costar James Garner, of *Maverick* fame, seeking to avenge the scalping of his Comanche wife, and belonged to a surge of "revisionist Westerns" in which even John Ford, the foremost creator of Hollywood westerns as cinema and as ideology, began to unsettle the genre's white supremacist tropes. In 1960, Ford made *Sergeant Rutledge* with Woody Strode, an ex-NFL player who played a stoic member of the U.S. Army's detachment of Black cavalrymen, known as Buffalo Soldiers, whose complex role in taming the West, later eulogized by Bob Marley in reggae form, was little known. *Buck and the Preacher*, though, was the first bona fide western from a major studio to feature a pair of A-list Black stars as protagonists rather than servile sidekicks or loners. And it was a film that underscored the will of Black pioneers and cowpokes in the old West to claim a share of the continent's vast acreage for themselves. It explored the relations between those Blacks and the Indians that the westward expansion of the United States was pushing from the land. And in doing both those things, it aimed to reframe the history of those frenzied and violent decades, between the Civil War's end and the 1920s, that birthed not a few of the guiding myths and images of American culture, and turned the continent's western half into a part of the barbarous nation headquartered in Washington, D.C.

For both of its principals, too, *Buck and the Preacher* was a watershed. For Harry, who had to that point played only handsome love interests and charming hustlers on screen, it was a chance to darken his teeth and play a grubby "preacher"-cum-con-artist with matted hair and no resemblance, in his shady morals or huckster's mien, to Harry's public personae as glamorous singer and paragon of progressive thought. For Sidney, *Buck and the Preacher* became his chance, after the production's hard-drinking first director flamed out after a few days in Mexico, to helm a movie himself—and to hop up from his director's chair to play a righteous wagon master whose raison d'être, in late 1860s Kansas, is to protect newly freed slaves from the shady white soldiers who want to prevent them from establishing homesteads on Kansas's plains and instead scare them back into bondage. His character's name recalls the Reconstruction-era figure of the "black buck"—a virile and violent black man with no respect for white authority or laws who'd also become an archetype, in D. W. Griffith's *Birth of a Nation*, of American cinema. Poitier's Buck is more upstanding than virile, and among the challenges he must surmount with his faithful wife, played by Ruby Dee, beyond contending with his frenemy the preacher's rivalrous tricks, is negotiating safe passage for his charges from local Native Americans with whom he is alternately allied and at odds.

Harry and Sidney were determined to depict their film's Indians, like its Blacks, as agents in their own history. They enlisted Julie—whose skin was olive and who often wore her hair in braids—to play a savvy squaw. They might have done better to find an Indigenous actor for the role. But Julie had grown deeply involved with the burgeoning American Indian Movement, and took the part seriously indeed. She learned her Apache lines with the help of audiotapes, recorded by a native speaker, that her daughter Gina watched her practice with before they flew down to Durango for a shoot that doubled as a family vacation. When the film's stars went on *Dick Cavett* to flog its release, Sidney was at pains to underscore that as much as their film sought to inject Black humanity into the West, he'd also been deeply concerned to "present to the American public an image of an Indian man and Indian woman as whole human beings, as people."

Upon its release in April 1972, *Buck and the Preacher* didn't do too much better at the box office than *The Angel Levine*. But unlike that downbeat dramedy, Poitier's directorial debut was dynamic entertainment that went on to enjoy a cherished life in the golden era of grindhouse cult classics and late-night TV that was even more pronounced beyond America's shores, perhaps nowhere more so, strikingly enough, than on the island where Harry, as a boy, had absorbed Hollywood's offerings. In Kingston throughout the 1970s and 1980s, as friends of mine who grew up attending triple features at the Carib and Odeon cinemas recall, *Buck and the Preacher* became a firm crowd favorite. On an island where the spaghetti westerns of Sergio Leone were also wildly popular, Harry and Sidney's black cowboy show shared bills with *Car Wash* and kung fu flicks and won a resonance in the culture attested to by no less an authority than the reggae deejay I-Roy, whose eponymous 1973 ditty "Buck and the Preacher" ("Come down Jamaica way...," he toasts, "and see this kind of black movie!"), wasn't the only reggae jam to hail its charms.

Another film featuring the pair would inspire more. *Uptown Saturday Night* (1974), also directed by Sidney, was a vital box office redemption for Poitier—its release grossed some $10 million, big money in those days. His second directorial effort fit squarely within the burgeoning genre of blaxploitation: *Uptown Saturday Night* proved that both white and Black moviegoers had far more appetite for a movie with an all-Black cast, playing pimps and gangsters and P.I.s and whores, than attempts to diversify typically white genres (let alone highbrow dramas). Harry, for his part, hesitated when Sidney asked him to draw on boyhood memories of his uncle Lenny, and his underworld doings, to play a Harlem don called Geechie Dan Beauford. He only agreed after convincing Sidney to take a note from the playbook for his *Time for Laughter* TV special by asking a bevy of leading black comics—among them Bill Cosby and Richard Pryor—to play bit parts where, in brief madcap appearances meant to keep the audience engaged, they'd riff on the scenes they entered however they wished.

The tack worked. Harry stuffed orange slices in his cheeks, channeling his old pal Marlon Brando's look in *The Godfather*, to play Geechie Dan as a gravel-voiced riot with gravitas. At the church social that concludes the film, he informs a rival hood that "I haven't had this much fun since reform school." Decades later, at the end of our first lunch together, Harry laughed as he gave me the email address he was using at the time: geechiedan@aol.com. There was good fun to be won from playing a crime boss, and he would memorably return to a similar role twenty years later in his pal Robert Altman's *Kansas City*. Harry's misgivings about blaxploitation as genre led him to decline to take part in Poitier's two successful follow-ups, *Let's Do It Again* (1975) and *A Piece of the Action* (1977)—both of which featured Bill Cosby. The striking Bahamian-born actor Calvin Lockhart, who played Harry's rival don in *Uptown Saturday Night,* starred in *Let's Do It Again* as the gangster Biggie Smalls, inspiring the nickname of another New Yorker of Jamaican descent—the Notorious B.I.G., né Christopher Wallace—whose mother brought him to Jamaica for extended visits in the late seventies and eighties, when Lockhart's blaxploitation films were a staple in island cinemas.

When it came to Harry's stop-start career in the movies, he remained as allergic to being typecast as he was to sitting still. His always-challenging relationship with Hollywood was shaped by his oft-frustrated will to "evolve as an artist" in a degraded industry in which his shelf life as a leading man was nearing its end. The same worries seem to have bothered him less in his career as a singer: his bread-and-butter gig, from the late sixties on, was an annual residency at Caesars Palace. Such remunerative tenures in the music business are based not in sharing pathbreaking sounds but cashing in on a performing persona that liquored-up gamblers on vacation already know and love—for Harry it was the worldly folkie and sex symbol from the islands, which he'd first perfected in Vegas and would return with for decades.

As a new generation's tastes ran away from his brand of folk and toward rock 'n' roll and Woodstock and Sly and the Family Stone, Harry's run as a bankable and prolific recording artist for RCA Victor neared its end with a series of albums—from *Belafonte on Campus* to *Belafonte Sings of Love* to *Belafonte—By Request*—that collected old folk tunes with newer folkish hits like "The Circle Game" and "Scarborough Fair," and felt like retreads. On his penultimate album for RCA Victor, 1971's *Calypso Carnival*, he returned for a final time to the region and idiom that made his name. By then, his old musical brain trust of West Indian New Yorkers was no more: Harry had fallen out with Irving Burgie in a dispute over royalties and lost his most trusted accompanist and bandmate, Millard Thomas, to cancer. But among a new crop of acolytes and craftsmen he pulled to his cause was a young Harlemite, of Trinidadian stock, who wrote and arranged most of the songs on *Calypso Carnival*. Ralph MacDonald would go on to pen hits for the likes of Roberta Flack and Rod Stewart, but he had both songcraft and carnival in his blood. His father was the vaunted calypsonian

Macbeth the Great, who composed "Don't Stop the Carnival"—which MacDonald arranged for Harry and made the central tune in the "carnival medley" with which he would close his stage show for the next twenty-five years.

And if Las Vegas is where Belafonte's songs of the Caribbean completed their transformation into bona fide Americana, it was beyond America's shores that he would cement his status as a symbol not merely of his natal islands, but of America and civil rights and the vitality and sadness and beauty of Africa's diaspora in the New World. Harry's first experiences performing in Europe dated from his initial rise to fame in the 1950s. In Germany in 1958, he'd gotten over his wartime biases to perform a show in Berlin where an adoring crowd stomped along to "Hava Nageela" and chanted the name of one of the first major American entertainers to puncture their isolation after the war. The goodwill imparted then, when a one-night gig at the city's Titania-Palast became three because so many young East Berliners traversed Checkpoint Charlie to see him, had lasted. But none of that prepared him for what he encountered in Hamburg, in 1976, when he launched a new tour of the continent. That European tour was arranged by an enterprising young Danish promoter, Arne Worsøe, who became a key figure in Harry's life and career, during a decade when, having had his heart broken by America, he spent increasing amounts of time and energy abroad. This was an entertainer who knew adoring crowds. But he'd never experienced anything like the love they showed him, in Hamburg and then in Brussels and Bonn and across the continent, by starting their standing ovation even before he began to sing. For a onetime pop idol whose star had begun to fade in the U.S., those Hamburgers' love was a harbinger of joyous gigs he would play across Europe in the 1970s and '80s, returning nowhere more frequently than Germany—mostly its Western half, but then also to the East, where young people behind the Iron Curtain revered him as a totem of free thinking and justice.

Across the 1970s and into the 1980s and '90s, decades when he came to function as a kind of global eminence grise, his foremost engagements as an activist involved the movement to end apartheid in South Africa and nuclear weapons everywhere; famine relief in Ethiopia; and supporting the flawed revolution of a Communist *barbudo*—Fidel Castro— with whom he nurtured a thirty-year friendship after alighting in Cuba for the first time, in contravention of the U.S. embargo and to attend Havana's famous film festival, in 1974. Through it all, and even as his concert bookers in the U.S. grew more likely to send him to universities and provincial arts centers than to Carnegie Hall, he would return to Europe for triumphal tour after triumphal tour of a continent whose people couldn't get enough of him.

25

When Harry accepted an invitation in 1983 to headline a World Peace Concert in East Berlin, in the huge concert hall that doubled as the GDR's parliament, the occasion captured the new role he'd found to play as a gray-templed diplomat-at-large from Planet Harry. Once, he'd been an official emissary of the United States government and JFK's Peace Corps. Now he was a world-famous American who was also beloved for battling American racism at home and opposing American militarism abroad. At East Berlin's Palast der Republik, he took the stage under a banner reading "Down with NATO Missile Decision," and decried the move by the United States to install Pershing II missiles in Germany's west. He also explained, as thousands of blue-shirted members of the Free German Youth sang along to

"Island in the Sun," that his set's highlight was about an island that the United States, that same week in 1983, had just invaded because its socialist leader, Maurice Bishop, had voiced affinity for Moscow. He dedicated the rendition to "the hope that the people of Grenada will one day be free."

If all of that makes it sound like Harry was devoted to spewing Soviet agitprop on such occasions, he took care not to toe party lines. In East Berlin, he loudly and publicly embraced an outré West German rock star, Udo Lindenberg, who was famous for ridiculing the GDR's head of state. "Oh Erich, why are you such a stubborn mate?" went the fedora-wearing singer's sarcastic dare to East Germany's communist leader, Erich Honecker. "Why don't you let me sing in the workers' and peasants' state?" Not long before Harry's visit, Lindenberg also criticized NATO's role in spurring a mad arms race—and Honecker's minions allowed him to join the bill of Harry's historic show in Mitte. When Lindenberg took the Palast der Republik's stage, he also decried Moscow's deployment of SS-20 missiles trained on the west. In Deutschland's slow march toward tearing down the wall and reunifying its denizens east and west, this was a key moment. Harry would engage similarly with other governments unfriendly to the United States during the Cold War. He may have been a critic, often ardent, of American foreign policy. But he wasn't an ardent Stalinist, like his mentor Paul Robeson, who cozied up to the USSR and lost his passport and his health as a consequence. And this was a different moment. Across the 1970s and '80s, the causes Harry espoused—for nuclear disarmament, and against hunger and racism—concurred with his stature as a *bien-pensant* ambassador for UNICEF.

As a proud son of the Caribbean, Harry had watched with admiring fascination when Fidel Castro and his band of guerrillas seized Havana in 1959. He was moved by Castro's promise not merely to change Cuba's status as a de facto colony of America's military and its mobsters, but to build a new society wherein the descendants of peasants and slaves might enjoy certain benefits of modernity—good health care and schools, basic nutrition, literacy—that Harry's kin in Jamaica never had. When he and Julie landed in Havana for the first time, in 1974, they didn't know they'd meet Fidel for more than a photo op. But after checking into their room in the Hotel Riviera by Havana's seafront, they received a call from the lobby. The comandante had arrived, they were told, and wanted to see them. Harry had just emerged from the shower; he answered his room's door in his boxers, and was led to a room across the hall. It was the start, for these two tall and verbose Caribbean men, of a long and significant friendship.

The comandante's loathing for *yanqui* aggression toward Cuba—and the government that tried hundreds of times to have him assassinated—was matched only by his love for

American baseball and American literature and films. He also loved American pop from the era that matched the 1940s and '50s vintage of the Buicks that still rumble down Havana's streets, when he'd spent time in the U.S. as a young man, like many sons of Cuban privilege. Like Harry, Fidel had grown up in a corner of the Caribbean—Cuba's rural Oriente province—devoted to agriculture. His Galician parents belonged not to the island's class of peasants who'd cut cane and harvested its fruits, like Harry's forebears in Jamaica, but its landowners. But his affinity for the island work songs that inspired Harry's early hits ran deep. So did his admiration for the culture and political movements of Black Americans: Fidel made a point, whenever he was in New York to visit the UN, of staying at Harlem's Hotel Theresa. Dressed in his customary fatigues, he was thrilled to meet this eminence of Harlem and of civil rights who'd flouted the U.S. embargo on Cuba to come see him. He was even more charmed by Julie, whose politics befit an alumna of the Little Red School House, and whose love for Cuban culture reached back to her days in Katherine Dunham's company studying Afro-Caribbean dance.

Fidel Castro was famous, per a popular joke on this musical island, for being the only Cuban who didn't love to dance. But he did love to talk. And across his half century in power, one of the comandante's favorite pastimes, when dignitaries and celebrities he thought might be sympathetic to his cause came to visit, was to engage them—never mind his packed schedule and many duties—in conversations as long as his hours-long speeches. This was his tack with Harry and Julie, who he insisted join him in his car, after they'd already spent hours together at the hotel, so that he might give them a personal tour of Havana's sights and then share, in his cigars-and-rum-soaked hospitality, a lofty debate about the fate of capitalism and mankind over dinner. This, for these dyed-in-the-wool lefties, was heaven. They returned just a few months later, this time with Sidney Poitier and Sidney's soon-to-be-wife, Joanna Shimkus, in tow. Sidney was charmed by Fidel's encyclopedic knowledge of his movies and sympathetic to his cause, but suspicious of his politics. He didn't return. But Harry and Julie did, for the annual film festival and otherwise, year after year.

In 1982, Harry collaborated with the Cuban director Orlando Rojas on a film that evinces the reflective mood that Cuba brought out in Harry. *A veces miro mi vida (Sometimes I Look at My Life)* is built from interview footage of Harry waxing expansive, under swaying Havana palms, about his journey's beats and the pain he still felt at his hero Paul Robeson's sad death in 1976. It's intercut with shots of Harry performing in Havana and with extended clips from his movies that sometimes correspond, and sometimes don't, to his memories in voiceover. I first saw the film on a VCR tape at the Center for Cuban Studies in New York; it's unreleasable in the U.S. because of all the unlicensed Hollywood IP. But it's notable for the ways that Harry, recounting his life's full arc for the first time, highlights Cuba's effect on him. "You become the victim of your possessions," he says of his privileged American existence, "and being with people conscious of these things, coming to Cuba, has had the most powerful impact. I'm at my best in life [here]."

Later, as Harry and Julie's marriage began to founder, she often declined to accompany him on his travels. But she always went to Cuba, a socialist island whose problems were grave but whose virtues—in the peace of its streets and the schools and doctors the state furnished its people—were as attractive as Havana's rumba and rum. Harry and Julie made a point, over the years, of visiting with dissidents whose views they also conveyed to Castro. But mostly they reveled, as the comandante's guests, in hobnobbing with lefty intellectuals from across the hemisphere, from Gabriel García Márquez to Jorge Amado, for whom Havana served as a nexus across the decades of the Cold War. On one trip, accompanied by Julie's parents, they journeyed with a teary Fidel to the jail cell where, as a defiant young radical, he'd been imprisoned by the regime his revolution would depose in 1959. "History will absolve me," he'd proclaimed to the judge who'd jailed him in his youth. And now, he insisted to his friends, history had proved him right.

Their conversation would continue, at regular intervals, over the next thirty years—and win Harry the adoration of a new generation of Afro-Cubans on whose behalf he intervened with Castro, in 1999, to momentous effect. During lunch one day at the Hotel Nacional, Harry and Julie met a group of young Afro-Cubans in baggy clothes who invited them to attend a boisterous concert, that night, that they were performing with fellow members of a small but energetic scene of young *Habaneros* devoted to lending a home-grown take, rapping in rapid-fire Cuban Spanish, on hip-hop. Impressed by their energy and passion, Harry was disappointed to hear their community was more often shunned than supported by Cuba's powers that be. Harry asked Fidel at lunch the next day if he was aware of this scene's existence and its repression. Fidel wasn't. In fact, he barely knew what hip-hop was. But after Harry explained that hip-hop was a Black music created by impoverished urban youth that had grown popular among young Americans of all backgrounds and was a crucial venue for critiquing the society's ills, Castro's interest was piqued. He asked Harry to accompany him on his rounds that afternoon—a graduation speech for medical students, a dinner for Cuba's prima ballerina, Alicia Alonso—and continued to pepper him with questions. His minister of culture, Abel Prieto, was a long-haired hippie who'd helped lend the once-counter-cultural sounds of *nueva trova*—singer-songwriters like Silvio Rodríguez and Pablo Milanés, Cuba's analogues to Bob Dylan and Joni Mitchell—the support of the Cuban state. Prieto was as ignorant of rap as his boss was, but just as open to hearing, from their visiting eminence of folk music, why it mattered.

The by now seventy-something Harry was in fact something of an authority on the topic: among his foremost credits as a producer of films was a seminal 1984 feature, *Beat Street*, about the creativity under duress of Black and Puerto Rican kids in the Bronx. Their vibrant subculture's exponents had by then become familiar on Manhattan's subway platforms and downtown clubs but weren't yet fixtures on MTV or in record shops worldwide. From the vantage of forty years later, a span during which the aesthetics and "elements" of hip-hop—breakdancing, graffiti, DJing, and most especially rap—conquered pop, it's easy to forget the origins of an idiom that became, and remains in the 2020s, a lingua franca of youth culture everywhere. But *Beat Street*, a film Harry produced with partners in Hollywood after he bought a gritty script by the music journalist Steven Hager, was an important marker in the mainstreaming of a genre whose key progenitors in the housing projects of the Bronx—those kids of Jamaican immigrants who first seized on mixing beats and rapping over their breaks—shared his heritage and cultural DNA. By the late 1990s, hip-hop's Cuban moment was arriving alongside visits to the island from a generation of politically minded rappers from America. For the likes of Common and Mos Def, those staples of dorm-room soundtracks for those of us who were undergrads at the time, it became a kind of sacred rite to come to Havana to commune with Black American dissidents in exile, including Assata Shakur, who'd settled in Cuba after fleeing the States.

When I landed in Havana in the early 2000s to work on a book about the state of its *revolución* at a time when its leaders were old men, and many of their grandkids had grown deeply skeptical of the chronic contradictions and shortages of one-party rule, the hip-hop scene was flourishing. A half-dozen groups regularly gigged around town, in palm-fringed vacant lots and at state-run clubs, with the help of loudspeakers and mics furnished by a new government office—the Cuban Rap Agency—within Abel Prieto's Ministry of Culture. At many of them, enthused attendees included Assata Shakur and her comrade Nehanda Abiodun, a Harlem-born veteran of the Black Liberation Army who'd helped liberate Assata from a New Jersey prison before landing in Cuba and becoming the *madrina* (godmother) of Cuban hip-hop. In the songs performed, the syncopations and speed of Cuban Spanish, so supremely matched to the unexcelled polyrhythms of the island's natal musics, didn't always mesh with the basic *"boom-boom-bap"* of their backing tracks' rudimentary beats. But the energy and sense of catharsis was palpable for young *Habaneros* who bobbed their heads and yelled along to lyrics that gave amplified voice to long-simmering Afro-Cuban frustrations with a government that claimed to have eliminated racism long ago, but whose police routinely harassed Cubans with darker complexions. One such anthem, by a group called Clan 537, bespoke that dynamic with an allegory, set in school, with which Harry—himself once a black boy viewed as a delinquent by his teachers—would have resonated deeply. *"Quién tiró la tiza?"* it went: *Who threw the chalk?* The reply, in call-and-response style, was sarcastic: *"El negro, eso!" The black boy,* of course.

When the Roots came down to play a raucous show at one of the city's biggest venues in the spring of 2004, I sat on a stoop in the city's leafy Vedado district with Questlove and members of the Cuban group behind "Quién Tiró La Tiza?" Clan 537 and EPG & B were a dreadlocked crew of cousins who lived with their extended family in a crumbling mansion abandoned by members of the upper crust after Fidel's revolution in 1959, and handed over to a retinue impoverished Afro-Cubans: people who'd been helped hugely by the revolution but who also, now, nurtured deep frustrations with its current state. When a member of the Roots' own retinue asked them who they had to thank for the speakers plugged in on the sidewalk outside, furnishing the score to the night's party, they answered: "Harry Belafonte!"

The recording career of the young Cubans' ally, after his old contract with RCA expired not long after the last hurrah that was *Calypso Carnival* in 1971, had slowed considerably. But an agreement later that decade to return to the studio with Columbia Records yielded one of the rare songs to endure that he penned himself—albeit with inspiration from folkloric sources. A notebook I found in his papers at the Schomburg suggests that Harry first jotted the lyrics that would become "Turn the World Around" at his and Julie's upstate retreat in Chatham, New York, in 1975. But its source material, which he adapted to pop-friendly choral form with the help of arranger Bob Freedman, was owed to a storyteller he'd met in Guinea, West Africa, who'd told Harry about the elemental sources—fire, water, mountain/earth—for his people's strength. "We come from the fire / Living in the fire," go the song's first lines, before reminding all humans who want to change their lot, or their world, of the import of returning to their roots: "Go back to the fire / Turn the world around." The song is a joyous major-key affirmation of life in 5/4 time. It runs through similar call-and-response odes to the import of returning to the source, and to roots more earthy and aqueous, before underscoring the need for self-knowledge and mutual recognition—for discovering who we are, as its lyric goes, to see each other clearly.

Almost pidgin-like in its simplicity, "Turn the World Around" was catchy enough on an eponymous LP that Columbia released in Europe in 1977. But it was immortalized thanks to an invitation Harry received from Jim Henson the next year to guest-star on an episode of *The Muppet Show*.

Henson was the genius puppeteer whose creations conquered kids' TV in the seventies, most notably via their presence on a show—*Sesame Street*—that depicted an urban world as diverse as a real New York neighborhood. With its mission to use TV's addictive qualities not to rot kids' brains but teach them their ABC's, *Sesame Street* changed American culture by changing American TV: with its kids and Muppets and grown-ups of all colors living and learning together, it brought to the mainstream the same multicultural vision as Harry's old network specials. Jim Henson had lent his talents to the show at the invitation of *Sesame Street*'s visionary founder, Joan Ganz Cooney. Henson was proud of Big Bird and Cookie Monster's ascent to omnipresence in the minds of preschoolers everywhere. But he was also determined to lend his unique sensibility and puppets to more adult forms of pathos and humor. So in 1976, Henson launched *The Muppet Show*.

Taped in England with support from the ITV network there, after America's flagships passed on it, the show—which quickly became a hit and would air for five seasons before folding in 1981—was distributed via syndication worldwide. Set in an old vaudeville theater where Kermit the Frog is a melancholic but earnest showrunner whose hands are more than full trying to stage a weekly variety show with the likes of Miss Piggy and Fozzie Bear, the show also quickly became a destination for famous human entertainers—from John Denver to Rita Moreno and Debbie Harry—who loved trading jokes and charms with Henson's Muppets. Usually for these gigs, Henson's team of writers and puppeteers created sketches and musical numbers for their guests to slot into. But for Harry, who came to the gig with his own strong ideas about how his own work and recent records might jibe with the show, Henson made an exception.

They collaborated closely on an episode that first aired in the U.S. on February 19, 1979, which Henson would recall as his favorite in the series. With the show built around Fozzie Bear's scrambling to write a script for what's occurring, its musical numbers included a rendition of "The Banana Boat Song," aboard ship, wherein Fozzie Bear struggles to sing along; a raucous drum battle between Harry and Animal, which leaves both combatants passed out on their skins; and, for its finale, a performance of "Turn the World

Around." Harry is dressed in a pirate's shirt with puff-sleeves and deep V-neck, a talking drum under his arm. He harmonizes with a chorus of bespoke Muppets, specially built for the occasion, who resemble dancing African masks, based on Baule and Chokwe forms that Henson's team had tried to mimic in ways that paid homage rather than give offense. Deeply sonorous or chirpy of voice, with grassy manes of hair flopping over mahogany features, the Muppets lend Harry's delivery, which here as ever risks a surfeit of sanctimony and sentiment, an aspect at once playful and profound.

As the song plays over the end credits, even Statler and Waldorf, *The Muppet Show*'s resident crotchety critics, join in rather than make their usual snarky cracks. In joining Harry's sage words to the Muppets' silly mien, their collaboration modeled a love for storytelling and humor and the human family that embodied his and Henson's shared belief in how culture engenders social change. After Henson died in 1990 of a freak infection, far too young, his memorial service was held in Manhattan, at St. John the Divine. Harry spoke with admiration of his friend's cherished belief in, as he put it, "the ability to love and to care and to find greatness in difference." And then he sang Henson's favorite song: "Turn the World Around."

26

Returning to the source that was Africa had been a focus for Harry since long before "Turn the World Around." But in the 1980s and '90s, his focus on the continent came to animate his foremost achievements and endeavors in the realms of both music and politics, and in finding history-making ways to join them. To be sure, sundry business schemes and extracurricular ventures also occupied his life's third act. He launched one such in Aruba, with his gambling buddy Roger Moore. The ill-fated plan to purchase and develop a fabulous resort with the James Bond of the 1970s and 1980s, on a flamingo-ringed islet in the Dutch Antilles, didn't work out. But he also undertook UNICEF-sponsored junkets to Africa, with Moore and fellow UNI-CEF goodwill ambassadors like Audrey Hepburn, and an ambitious scheme he launched with Jamaica's socialist prime minister, Michael Manley, to organize a global festival of diasporic arts in Jamaica whose name—Djoliba—recalled the mouth of the Niger River from which many enslaved Africans were brought to the Caribbean. That festival didn't work out, but other attempts to change how America and Americans engaged the continent, in an era when he also cofounded TransAfrica—the first lobbying group in Washington dedicated to African issues—came to fruition.

In the 1980s, two developments on opposite ends of the continent changed the world's perception of Africa: the famine that gripped the continent's northeastern horn in the decade's early years and the movement to end apartheid, in South Africa, that became a global cause célèbre. Harry played notable roles in shaping the course of both.

He wasn't the only global citizen, or pop musician, to be moved to tears by the story that reached the world, in October of 1984, with images of skeletally malnourished children in a refugee camp in Ethiopia. The footage, captured by a Kenyan photojournalist named Mohamed Amin, was included in a story on BBC News and then, days later, in a broadcast on NBC that Harry glimpsed in New York. The facts the images told—that an ongoing famine in East Africa threatened to kill some eight million children unless the world acted—inspired what may remain history's largest humanitarian relief effort. In the U.K., where a third of adults were said to have seen that initial BBC report, among those moved to act was the Irish punk rocker and songwriter Bob Geldof. The hastily written and recorded song that Geldof released with a supergroup of his rocker pals to raise money for famine relief, "Do They Know It's Christmas?," hit stores just before the holidays, and sold millions. Harry was inspired by Geldof's example—his "benefit record" remained for many years the fastest-selling single in U.K. history. He seized on the idea of doing something similar here, leveraging the power of America's musical celebrities for Africa's starving young.

What happened in the recording studio in Los Angeles, where Harry eventually gathered an astonishing cohort of those musical celebrities, was detailed in a 2024 Netflix documentary called *The Greatest Night in Pop*. "We Are the World" was the product of Harry's vision and the persistence with which he called the talent manager and industry insider Ken Kragen, whose roster of clients included many of the stars whom he regarded as essential. Over dinner at a restaurant on Melrose Place, Harry and his daughter Shari, who lived in LA and was then enjoying much success as a model, convinced Kragen to lean on the client of his—Lionel Richie—who the Belafontes thought might be ideal, assuming they could convene a critical mass of stars to the cause, to write a tune for them to sing. Kragen got Richie to agree, and the ex-Commodores front man quickly came up with a basal phrase and melody ("We are the world, we are the children . . .") that he then proceeded, with the fellow Motown alum who was now the world's biggest star, to turn into a song.

Michael Jackson's *Thriller* had just broken Harry's long-standing record for weeks spent atop *Billboard*'s album charts. Jackson's reputation for eccentricity and diva-dom was growing as outsize as his success. But he took the cause behind "We Are the World," and of writing a song for it, seriously indeed. With Michael's own producer of eminence, Quincy Jones, now also aboard to shepherd its recording, the yeses kept coming. And with them a plan was hatched to take advantage of the night in January when the industry's leading lights would all be in LA for the American Music Awards, to hustle them, after the show's end, to an all-night session in a room at nearby A&M Studios by whose entrance Quincy Jones taped a sign reading, "Check your ego at the door."

Arriving to take part, and to follow Jones's advice as Jackson and Richie taught everyone the song, were Bruce Springsteen and Tina Turner; Dionne Warwick and Bob Dylan; Willie Nelson and Cyndi Lauper; Billy Joel and

Kenny Rogers and Huey Lewis. Stevie Wonder greeted everyone with a promise that if they didn't wrap recording in one take, he and Ray Charles would drive everybody home. Harry and other stars, including Waylon Jennings and Sheila E., served by singing backup rather than lead. "We Are the World" went on to sell some 20 million units, making it the bestselling single in history; it raised $100 million for famine relief; and it encouraged Bob Geldof and company to produce a pair of simultaneous concerts on two continents that they called Live Aid, a broadcast that raised millions more.

In many ways, the work of the organization Harry had set up to release the recording, USA for Africa, was only beginning. It turns out that figuring out how best to spend $100 million on medical supplies and tents and equipment for drilling wells and purifying water and other necessities, and getting the goods purchased halfway around the world by cargo plane and other means, wasn't easy. Neither, as Harry quickly learned, was negotiating with the despotic rulers of Sudan and Ethiopia and their respective cronies and foes, who were manipulating the famine's course to their own ends, to get aid where it needed to go. Harry and Julie personally escorted USA for Africa's first two 747s full of goods from Belgium to Khartoum, alongside Ken Kragen and Marlon Jackson, Michael's least-famous sibling.

It wasn't hard, for critics who clocked the naivete at the core of the "famine relief," to point up the bleeding-heart politics that animated the cause's celebrity exponents. Mohamed Amin's images may have moved many to action, but humanitarianism, absent a deeper analysis of the context or causes of the suffering being assuaged, is a kind of anti-politics. There's a reason, forty years later and at a time when progressive young people recoil from "savior narratives" and dance to Nigerian Afrobeats on weekends, that news of a new musical about Live Aid opening in London, in 2025, was met with disdain: do we really need a musical, asked a column in *The Guardian*, about an aid effort that defined Africa as "a place beset by dependency and full of people who lack agency"? Such critiques were also around in the eighties. Harry was sympathetic to them. But his reply, to them and perhaps to his own questions about what had brought him to Ethiopia, also bear credence: saving thousands of lives and improving countless others, as their efforts no doubt did, was important. The scale of the suffering he and Julie witnessed, in the camps they visited, left a mark. So did the doctors and aid workers who told him that the only way to engage its enormity was to focus not on the crowd but on whichever individual, sitting before them, they sought to heal. And he returned with humbling memories of being asked by a group of Irish nuns, around a campfire in

Ethiopia's mountains, surrounded by tents of the hungry and ill they'd come to help, to sing them all his beloved version of "Danny Boy."

If that scene brought home, for Harry, his folk repertoire's reach across time and space and in engendering a sense of human family, there's a scene in the documentary that also underscored his import to his musical peers. When all of these eminences of music needed a tune to warm up with, one they all knew, the song they turned to wasn't, say, a Dylan classic. They didn't sing "Blowin' in the Wind." They sang "Day O". A blushing Harry swayed in the back of the room. All of them—Dylan and Wonder and Warwick and Springsteen, with M.J. and Willie and Cyndi Lauper—sang along. The vibe was set, under the aegis of Harry B, who waxed history's first million-selling record, until daylight came and they all got to go home.

27

In June 1986, TransAfrica and its allies on college campuses and in the movement to make South Africa's racist government an international pariah won a historic victory in Congress. The Comprehensive Anti-Apartheid Act passed the Senate and the House by large margins—and with enough votes to override Ronald Reagan's veto of the economic sanctions the bill entailed. Reagan, like every American president since 1948, had no issue with blue-chip American companies like Coca-Cola and GM doing business with Pretoria. Apartheid's fiercest foes, and a burgeoning campaign on college campuses to get America's universities to divest from South Africa, saw furnishing goods and services to the country as propping up its ruling National Party. And now that economic sanctions on the regime were American law, the international movement to end apartheid and free Nelson Mandela picked up steam. Harry, eager to help get a cause he'd backed since 1959 over the line, moved to bring new attention to Mandela's story and the glories of his nation's culture.

Harry made an impassioned attempt to produce a TV miniseries on Mandela's life that resulted in a Hollywood drama that caused him to fall out, once more, with his choice to play Madiba—Sidney Poitier—and to fall out for the first time with another immediate peer who, thanks to the huge popularity of *The Cosby Show*, was TV's biggest star. The rupture with Sidney, whom Harry had cast alongside Marlon Brando and Jane Fonda at a time when movie stars of that level never deigned to work in TV, derived from a seemingly simple reason: he didn't like the script. The project's other momentum killer was a disagreement over who'd won rights to make it.

Having negotiated with Mandela's lawyer and his complicated wife, Winnie, Harry had won her signature and Madiba's blessing by sending funds to a nonprofit she controlled, which is why he was shocked to learn that Winnie Mandela had apparently sold her husband's life rights twice—the second time to Bill Cosby's wife, Camille, who had her own designs on adapting Mandela's story. Harry's lawyers, waving his contract, which predated hers, eventually got the

Cosbys to stand down. But the resultant bad blood, not least with the network where Cosby was king—NBC—doomed Harry's dream of placing a Mandela miniseries on American TV. More successful was a massive concert he helped host at London's Wembley Stadium to hail Mandela's seventieth birthday in June 1988, in which stars ranging from Sting to Dire Straits and a young Tracy Chapman gathered under a banner demanding FREE NELSON MANDELA. Broadcast to sixty-seven countries, the last and biggest of the big political-benefit concerts that Live Aid made a major part of pop culture in the 1980s was seen by 600 million people.

That same spring, Tim Burton's campy film *Beetlejuice*, which became another pop icon of the decade, was a surprise hit in U.S. theaters—and brought Harry's "Day O" to a new generation. In the movie's most memorable scene, a ghost-possessed Catherine O'Hara lip-synchs Harry's lyrics, in her haunted dining room and with Winona Ryder looking on as a mirthful goth, playing the song for laughs that somehow register as born not of ridicule but admiration. After the film hit, Harry agreed to appear in a *Beetlejuice*-themed music video for his own song, briefly a fixture on MTV, that found him shaking his rear by an oilcan fire. If that video represented a good-natured if beseeching-feeling attempt to stay in American culture's eye, more meaningful to Harry was a new musical project—his last-ever studio album—to whose promotion and release he devoted much of 1988, and which aimed both to highlight the plight of South Africa's people and to hail their own culture's riches.

Harry's concept for *Paradise in Gazankulu* was to create, with an all-star cast of South Africa's leading practitioners of mbaqanga and township jazz, an album of original anti-apartheid songs. As a devoted ally of Mandela's African National Congress and the UN-sanctioned cultural boycott on the country, as well as a notorious foe of its government, traveling to South Africa himself was out of the question. He sent his keyboardist Richard Cummings and the songwriter Jake Holmes in his stead to lay down as many tracks as they could with Johannesburg's top players, and to meet with eminent writers like Nadine Gordimer and Athol Fugard while they were there to absorb inspiration for their record's lyrics. The resulting album was buoyant and replete with catchy beats. It was also not nearly as successful, either as art or as commerce, as another album made by similar means around the same time, Paul Simon's *Graceland*, which has endured as a classic.

Paul Simon's own fascination with South African pop, its resonance with doo-wop and other styles he'd grown up on, but also its differences, was sparked by a cassette he'd been slipped by a friend, called *Gum Boots No. 2: Accordion Jive Hits,* that entranced him on drives from Manhattan to Montauk. When he began contemplating traveling to Johannesburg to record with some of the same great musicians Harry's collaborators were also talking with there, he asked Harry what he thought. Harry strongly urged him to seek the blessing of the ANC's leader in exile, Oliver Tambo, in London. Simon didn't listen. He took the advice of Quincy Jones, who urged him to go ahead, instead. The resulting album was born of the tapes he brought home from JoBurg, laid down by the likes of Ladysmith Black Mambazo and the Boyoyo Boys, and over which he proceeded to pen some of the best songs he ever wrote. When *Graceland* landed in 1986, the album at first confounded the cognoscenti: What were apartheid's foes to make of Simon's poems of urbane ennui and First World problems—his elegies to spoiled girls and cinematographers' parties and boys in bubbles and the bodegas on upper Broadway—set to glorious Zulu harmonies and mbaqanga beats? But the undeniable brilliance of the songs, and the grace with which Simon celebrated his collaborators, won out. The concert for Mandela in Wembley Stadium may have represented a landmark in the emergence of a surging consensus among the cultured classes of the global north that apartheid had to go. But just as important to the global surge of interest in that cause and in the country's sublime music was Simon's global tour in support of *Graceland*—concerts featuring the living gods of South African culture, Hugh Masekela and Miriam Makeba, where exultant throngs from Australia to Zimbabwe and across the U.S. and Europe, danced to Zulu beats. When a version of that show hit New York's Central Park in 1991, tens of thousands sang along, as the mighty guitarist Ray Phiri led Simon's band, to "I Know What I Know" and "You Can Call Me Al."

Graceland hit in ways that *Paradise in Gazankulu* couldn't. Simon was among the foremost lyricists of his or any generation. Harry's collaborator on *Paradise in Gazankulu*, Jake Holmes, spent much of his career writing jingles. Most of the album's songs—including an ode to the anti-apartheid movement called "We Are the Wave," and another to its cities' charms and its sorrow ("Capetown, I'm drowning in your beauty / But my heart is feeling sad")—are so unsubtle as to verge on agitprop. The title track is a notable exception: it's a sarcastic and layered ode to life in one of the Bantustans, or ethnic homelands, built by the apartheid regime for South Africa's first nations. Still, *Paradise* was an ambitious and well-received project that also added to Harry's late-career repertoire a song that joined his early love for the carnival musics of the Caribbean to his more recent preoccupations with geopolitics and engendering world peace. You can find a video on YouTube of Harry with a crack band of African musicians in 1988 performing "Global Carnival" to a huge and joyous crowd in the same stadium in Zimbabwe where Paul Simon had brought his *Graceland* tour. That song's vision of the warring peoples of the world uniting on the carnival street ("Israel and Palestine / forming up a conga line") may sound naive. But Harry's performance exemplified the elder-statesman role he had by then come to play in the global movement against apartheid, which became a synecdoche for combating ethnic strife everywhere.

When Nelson Mandela was at last released from prison in February 1990, Harry received a call from Oliver Tambo and the ANC to let him know that they wanted him to be in charge of hosting Mandela's visit to the United States. After a concert in London's Wembley Stadium in April toasting his freedom, the leader known as Madiba raised his fist to a euphoric crowd. And then he set off to greet his legion of admirers and friends across the Atlantic on an eleven-day tour of the United States. Having declined George H. W. Bush's invitation to visit Washington in an official capacity as South Africa's soon-to-be head of state, Mandela, the ANC insisted, was instead coming as a private citizen who wished to offer appreciation and thanks to the countless American individuals and organizations— President Bush and the Republican Party not among them— who'd publicly supported his struggle.

First on that list was Harry Belafonte and TransAfrica

and the ANC's allies in the Congressional Black Caucus. With the Secret Service declining to handle security, the Mandela welcome committee also rejected their urging that big public events and open-air venues during his visit be kept to a minimum. With responsibility for his safety falling instead to the State Department and local police forces whose officers would work serious overtime wrangling outsize but deliriously happy crowds, other diplomatic aspects of preparation for Mandela's visit fell to Harry—including an urgent effort, after the Jewish Defense League raised alarms about Mandela's comradeship with Yasser Arafat, to assuage fears that he was anti-Semitic, which was achieved with the help of a summit Harry helped broker in Geneva between Mandela and American Jewish leaders.

With his colleagues at TransAfrica and an NAACP-affiliated lawyer named Roger Wilkins, Harry helped coordinate Mandela's itinerary and field innumerable queries from parties who wanted to be included, to make decisions, and to raise funds in accordance with the ANC's strict wish that no money be accepted from any company that did business in South Africa. The ANC also stipulated that Mandela would visit only locales and organizations that had backed apartheid's downfall. The plane their traveling party would use was furnished by a New York real estate huckster who would falsely claim, decades later after he became a politi-

cian, that he'd loaned it for free. In fact, Donald Trump's avi-
ation start-up accepted $130,000 for the use of a 727 in his
fleet. Aboard that 727, Harry and Julie would accompany
Nelson and Winnie and their entourage, each leg of the way,
to greet throngs of well-wishers and the sundry mayors and
bigwigs and celebrities who all craved a moment with a man
whose cause Harry had held dear for decades but whom he
didn't meet until Mandela stepped off the plane that June at
JFK Airport.

"Harry boy!" is how Mandela greeted him on the tarmac
before they headed to their first assignation at a high school
in Brooklyn and on to a ticker-tape parade in Manhattan
and an evening rally at Yankee Stadium. Harry's own con-
nection with Madiba, whom he'd long regarded as a personal
hero, was deep. Their admiration was mutual. Mandela, a
devoted student of America's civil rights era, grilled Harry
with questions about how Dr. King had confronted certain
conundrums and turning points. Their tour to cities Harry
had once visited with Martin also included an obligatory
stop in Atlanta, where Mandela laid a wreath by Martin's
tomb. "In those eleven days, I watched saints become devils
and devils become saints," Harry later wrote. "Everyone
from the President on down wanted to touch Mandela's garment, and no one wanted to take no for an answer."

In Washington, D.C., it fell to Harry to inform Mayor

Marion Barry, an old SNCCer who was by then embroiled in scandal after having been indicted and photographed smoking crack cocaine, that he would not be photographed with Mandela or allowed to shake his hand. In California, the tour's last stop before the great man departed America wasn't in San Francisco, reportedly on account of an exhibition at its de Young Fine Arts Museum sponsored by an oil company—Royal Dutch Shell—that did big business in South Africa. Instead he greeted some 60,000 people across the bay at the Oakland Coliseum, in the hometown of the Black Panthers and of the ANC's foremost ally in Congress, Ron Dellums. "Despite my seventy-one years, at the end of this visit I feel like a young man of thirty-five," Mandela said, not far from docks where longshoremen had refused to unload goods from South Africa. "I feel like an old battery that has been recharged. And if I feel so young, it is the people of the United States of America that are responsible for this." At Oakland's airport nearby, Harry and Julie bade farewell to Winnie and Nelson. As their plane took off over the still-full Coliseum and waggled its wings, the exultant crowd still gathered there went wild—for Nelson Mandela, and against racism.

28

As he pushed through his seventh decade and then—after a prostate cancer scare at sixty-nine—into his eighth, Harry's life didn't want for incidents. Not a few of them involved being recognized for what he'd done before. "You know you're getting old," he said, "when you find yourself on the 'lifetime achievement' circuit." The valedictory phase contained its pleasures—few men who looked so good in a suit have so loved extemporizing an acceptance speech for this or that honor by reflecting on the state of the republic and world. But he was also a man for whom accepting adulation could as often impel feelings of ire—at himself for not measuring up to praise, at his society for giving it—as contentment.

He became well known, whenever he appeared on the

radio or TV, for intemperate utterances. He was the crotchety radical who called George W. Bush "the greatest terrorist in the world" and Colin Powell "a house slave" for serving his White House. He traduced Beyoncé and Jay-Z for not doing more for the Black community and social justice and despaired of America's lack of progress since the civil rights years and in an era when, as he would tell *The New York Times* in 2017, "the Supreme Court just reversed voting rights, and the police are shooting us down dead in the streets." But what occupied him just as much, as he began to travel less and to reflect ever more on the arc of a life he'd soon move to recount himself, were more personal matters: the home he'd made or hadn't made for his family; the roots and results of the anger that drove his success but harmed his relationships; his marriage with Julie which hadn't, for many years, been a happy one.

For many people, introspection in old age translates largely to acceptance—with one's lot and one's mate, with one's flaws and one's decisions and one's people. In Harry's case, senescence seems only to have deepened his resolve to confront, with actions rather than regret, the contradictions that made him. Fortunately for him, the therapist who'd helped him do this for decades survived into his nineties, too. He described Dr. Neubauer, whom he spoke with at least once a week for fifty years and often more than that, as the person who knew him best. Neubauer's own career had seen him gain prominence for his work with children. Today he's remembered for leading controversial long-term studies on the psychological development of twins secretly separated at birth. But he also wrote influential papers on how kids' psyches could be impacted as much by absent fathers as absent moms. Harry's mother, in his case, had long since emerged, in his work with Dr. Neubauer, as the source of traits and struggles ranging from his rage at injustice to his stymied needs for love. Millie's death was always going to be a blow. But the manner of her passing evinced all the ways that he'd felt trapped by her psyche's limits since boyhood.

In the one-room flat in Harlem where she spent her last years, with a shared bathroom down the hall, refusing all but minimal help and Harry's every offer to move her some place better, she returned to the wrathful self-pity she knew. Their strained dynamic was distilled in the last conversation he had with her. He'd just returned from a visit to Jamaica, with a request from Millie's own dying mum, that she go see Jane Love in Saint Ann one last time. Millie insisted it wasn't possible. She said she had nothing to wear. By then she had renounced her family, whose members' shortcomings she blamed for all her sorrows, in favor of Jesus.

Experiencing heart trouble, she checked into a hospital under a fake name, her old habit to evade the authorities, and when she expired there, he had no idea where she was. With no next of kin listed and no one to claim her, the city carted her off to the potter's field, on Hart Island off the Bronx, that's long served as New York's repository for its indigent and luckless. It took several days before Harry and his sister Shirley to figure out where she was—and then to have her body disinterred and moved to a proper plot in Queens, a grim denouement to the life of a woman Harry had called the most selfish person he'd ever met the last time they spoke.

The death of Millie's second son, by whose grave she was eventually buried at Woodlawn Cemetery in the Bronx, nearly matched hers for sadness. Harry's little brother Dennis, whom he'd resented having to care for when they were boys, but whose abandonment in Jamaica by their parents left Harry with deep feelings of guilt and Dennis with other scars, suffered from mental illness as an adult. A lover of movies who had a hard time engaging people, Dennis held down a job for years, which Harry got him, that suited his affinities. He oversaw a warehouse where United Artists stored its films and where he spent much of his time drafting script after awful script, often knockoffs on westerns and other flicks he loved, that invariably starred his brother. This expression of Dennis's cinephilia was benign enough. It was only after he died in his forties—he collapsed at a restaurant in the Bronx; Harry went to identify the body—that his apartment was found to contain reels upon reels of original prints, stuffed into every cabinet and cranny, that he'd pilfered from work.

—

If these were sources of intimate pain and patterns to avoid, the bond he later formed with his little sister, Shirley, who became a beloved presence in his and Julie's home after they extracted her from the church, was a source of hope. So was the peaceful détente he gained with his long-estranged father, whose own maturation and successful second marriage Harry admired—not least as he struggled, at times, to maintain happy ties with his own kids. On both David and his sister, Gina, his absences and his anger left their marks. Flying them out to Caesars Palace to eat room service on vacation, Harry would later reflect, was no substitute for all the dinners he missed on West End Avenue. The guilt he felt fed the ways he also came to blame himself, in ways his kids roundly rejected, for their youthful trials. David dropped out of college and struggled to find his feet as a young man. Gina, who'd studied theater at SUNY Purchase, moved to LA to try to make it as an actor on TV. Harry wondered if the entitlement they felt, and the weight of his surname, had nudged them toward a capricious business—show business— where making a name for themselves would always be difficult. He wondered if the privilege he'd lent them had hindered as much as helped their paths.

His daughter Shari, born just as Harry and her mother were separating back in 1954, also pursued a career in Hollywood. For a time in the eighties, she was an in-demand model and successful presence on TV. But as the limelight faded and Shari strove to keep it on herself, and earn a living—by, for example, pitching SlimFast and posing for *Playboy*—her attempts to transition into producing met as much frustration as success. Harry, in turn, bristled at Shari's prevailing on him to attach himself to her projects he didn't like. But their relationship improved as they both aged (and as Shari's later roles on shows like Tyler Perry's *Sistas* and Apple's *Morning Show* kept her working through middle age). For many years, the most copacetic of his relationships with his kids was with Shari's older sister, Adrienne, the daughter he'd been most present for in her early years, and who then was raised mostly by Marguerite and found a stable life, far from Manhattan or Hollywood, after following in her mother's path to attend a historically Black college down South.

Adrienne settled near where she went to school, in West Virginia, where she worked as a counselor and now runs her own foundation after peacefully raising two biracial kids in this old bastion of Jim Crow, to Harry's wonder, with her white husband from Missouri. At family gatherings, Adrienne is the genial presence who's bemused by her siblings who belong to the "show business crowd." When her and Shari's mother Marguerite died suddenly of a pulmonary embolism, at seventy-four, all of their siblings dropped everything to support them and attend her funeral. For Harry, it meant a great deal to see his grown children, in this blended family, remain close to each other and come together for family occasions happy and sad. They also accepted into their fold, with grace and in friendship and not long before Harry passed, another brother whose existence they only learned of decades after his birth, to a long-ago consort of their dad's in Vancouver. In later years, Harry's relationship with David worsened. But he rejoiced with all his kids in his son's third wedding, to a Danish TV presenter and model, Malena Mathiesen, with whom David would have two kids, named Sarafina and Amadeus, whose *farfar* Harry loved attending their school plays in New York.

If Harry at times regretted his kids' being drawn to what he called "show business and its sorrows," there was only one person to blame for his progeny's affliction. As he passed late retirement age, he may have stepped back from acting. But the lingering bug made him accept an invitation from his friend Robert Altman to appear in a film as a gangster.

Kansas City was Altman's 1996 ode to the mob-run cow town where he grew up, drenched in 1930s-era jazz played by a new era's leading jazz lights—Joshua Redman channels Harry's old chum Lester Young. Harry plays a scowling crime boss with slicked-back hair. It's not a film that's lasted, in Altman's much-admired oeuvre, like *Nashville*. But Harry's admired turn as the gangster Seldom Seen, whose dark swagger and violent air he said he modeled on his uncle Lenny, won him awards. His daughter Gina joined him on set as his acting coach, for this film and others— including a documentary on his life, an intimate endeavor through which he revisited characters from his past in other ways, which she produced a decade later.

During this period, Harry also gained the satisfaction of seeing the grand anthology of Black music, which he'd begun work on decades earlier but was shelved in 1971, unearthed from RCA's vaults after the company was acquired, in the eighties, by the German conglomerate BMG.

It took RCA's new corporate owners a dozen years to grasp what was on the million-plus tapes of master recordings, in sundry formats and sizes, housed in a huge underground storage facility first built by the military under a mountain in Pennsylvania. The archive's new owners created a database to make this trove searchable. But for Alex Miller, an executive at BMG who was tasked in 1998 with

combing RCA's archives to find music to release on a bou-
tique label he ran called Buddha Records, it wasn't always
easy to tell what was what—a tape might be marked "FS" for
Frank Sinatra or "EP" for Elvis Presley, with its date of creation the only clue, short of pulling out the tape and playing it,
as to what such initials stood for. In Miller's first months of
poking around, he uncovered amazing treasures, like a recording of Fats Waller performing live in 1938. And Miller
told me that it was by entering now-passé words like "Negro"
that he happened into a stunning array of tapes featuring
some voices he knew—Sonny Terry's, Bessie Jones's, Harry
Belafonte's—along with many that he didn't, all labeled "The
Anthology of Negro Folk Music." Most perplexing and rich,
on these tapes from the 1950s and '60s, was the presence of
African drumming. Eventually, with the help of old-timers
at RCA and notes from the sessions, Miller figured out what
they were. He called Harry, who still retained rights to the
masters. A few weeks later, Harry called back. The owner of
the gravelly voice on Miller's phone didn't identify himself,
but he knew who it was: "So you've found the anthology."

The music on the tapes was astonishing to Miller and his
colleagues not merely for its quality—RCA's engineers and
Belafonte's distinguished choral arranger, Leonard De Paur,
had lent the project's sessions at Webster Hall a Broadway-
ready gloss. Stunning, too, was the range of material given

the Fisk Jubilee Singers–style treatment by the talents they assembled: Ashanti war chants and minstrel songs from the Civil War era; folk tunes from Georgia's Sea Islands; Creole dances from Congo Square in New Orleans. The endeavor recorded on the tapes, as Harry said, was "not a weekend project." David Belafonte, who was working at the time as a sound engineer and producer at Belafonte Enterprises in New York, supervised these tapes' remastering and their preparation for release with Alex Miller, who procured a letter from Henry Louis Gates Jr. attesting to the project's worth for his German bosses at BMG to get them to sign off on its release. He described collaborating with the Belafontes to release the magnum opus of his mother's favorite-ever singer as the highlight of a distinguished career.

When the box set he put together with the Belafontes was finally released, the anthology was called *The Long Road to Freedom*. It included five CDs rather than its originally mooted LPs and came with a 140-page hardcover book, lavishly produced and designed, for which Miller got International Paper, on whose finest stock it was printed, to foot the bill. It included a moving introduction by Harry on the anthology's aims and his collaboration with George Marek, alongside an extended if unevenly edited set of essays by the scholar Mari Evans on the "African-matrixed" traits of gospel and blues and ring shouts. Originally slated for release in

2000, the box set's street date was pushed back a year to allow for the inclusion of archival images—including beautiful photos of its original sessions by Roy DeCarava—which Miller had rescued from another RCA-leased warehouse, this one in Queens, just before the facility's owner binned them. It was finally released on September 11, 2001.

This inauspicious date wasn't the only reason it sold more like a gorgeous artifact for connoisseurs than the mass-market heirloom that Harry and Mr. Marek, with the help of *Reader's Digest*, had once hoped it could become. But the project's contents and aims grow only more impressive when one considers they were hatched before many scholars had tried to connect the varied traditions Harry and his collaborators sought to join. And when describing the anthology to journalists, Harry wasn't shy to assert how those contents and aims also tied together his own life's strands. He insisted, as he had done for decades, on the centrality of Black culture to American history, and on connecting Black Americans to a larger diaspora. "Look at the beauty of this music, listen to these voices," he told an interviewer from Harvard's *Transition* magazine. "And if you like what you hear, if you are moved by what you hear, doesn't that make you want to know more about how this music came to be?"

29

If the box set that would seal Harry's legacy never sold like the name-making albums that launched him, the media moment it occasioned was one in which his story overlapped with history once more. On the morning of September 11, he visited the set of the *Today* show at Rockefeller Center in midtown Manhattan. His chat there with Katie Couric began sunnily enough, as he recounted how the anthology had come to be and she congratulated him on its release. Then their conversation took a turn, as Harry's media appearances tended to in those days, toward more tendentious topics—including his displeasure with the blithe approach of the United States toward resentments that its policies were causing in the Middle East.

At a just-concluded UN World Conference Against Racism in South Africa as a delegate from UNICEF, he'd made headlines by avowing the gathering's decision to condemn Israel's treatment of Palestinians. Couric politely prompted him to clarify his position, which he did by confirming his view that "the United States, which dominates so much of the world order, . . . has a responsibility to lead the world to a new level of thought—or at least open up debate, so that new information can come into the discourse, to be able to shape policies that [take] us out of the abyss of violence, killing, anger, rage. And I think we should be less arrogant about how we spend our resources." She extolled the anthology once more, as an obligatory product shot of the box set filled the frame, its cover bedecked with a handsome painting by Charles White of Lead Belly, from Harry's own collection, strumming his guitar for a child. The camera cuts, at 8:45 a.m., to an exterior view on Rockefeller Plaza. A man in the foreground looks back over his shoulder and up into the sky. The first plane, screeching south over Manhattan toward the World Trade Center, is moments from engulfing the North Tower in flame.

A few weeks later, in this shell-shocked city just beginning to reckon with what had occurred and where its fallout might lead, Harry was named the UN Association of New York's Humanitarian of the Year. At the ceremony, the night's host later told me, UN Secretary-General Kofi Annan joined him onstage—and broke the ice by singing a song with him which, Annan said, he'd first heard as a boy in Ghana and turned to whenever he needed solace. "Day O!" they began. Annan, like everyone else in attendance, knew every word.

Harry's last concerts, in 2004, more often took place at universities than casinos (and he'd also finally given up gambling, after decades of talking with his shrink about why he felt so compelled to flirt with returning, in the pit at Caesars Palace, to his impoverished roots). At seventy-seven, he could still command a stage and was, in Europe at least, still a major draw: the 10,000 people who turned out to see him in Hamburg's biggest hall that summer proved that nearly fifty years after he'd first performed in postwar Berlin, as he observed in *My Song*, Germany retained his strongest and most loyal audience. But his voice, afflicted by chronic laryngitis and never-healed injuries to his vocal cords, was now permanently hoarse. It was time to stop singing his songs.

It was also time, as it happened, to end a long marriage that had grown unwell, and to create the happy third one that followed. Seventy-seven isn't an age when most men contemplate divorce. But Harry and Julie both had come to feel by then, notwithstanding their deep bonds as co-parents and activists and public figures, that, as Harry put it, "love had left the room." Or rather the twenty-one rooms of the grand apartment they'd shared for almost five decades but to whose opposite wings they'd now often retreat, after dinner or as often now before it, in bitterness and drink. They'd spent decades turning their home, with its red walls hung with photos of their luminary friends and art from their travels, into a stage for history being made. They were referred to by their own grown kids as sparring partners; they "substituted politics for passion, and then confused the two," as Harry put it. Another factor, perhaps, was their mutual enabling of addictive habits. By the time they split, Julie's alcoholism had worsened to the point where her kids were considering an intervention.

Her divorce, Julie's daughter Gina later told me, saddened Julie deeply. To be Mrs. Harry Belafonte, she'd given up a lot: no longer playing that role, at this point in her life, wasn't part of the plan. But either way, and financial consequences notwithstanding, the divorce she and Harry attained was, for Harry at least, not a choice but a necessity in whose aftermath Julie would also land squarely on her feet. Becoming a documentary filmmaker in her seventies, she also grew grateful for the kind woman with whom Harry had taken up before their split, and who would care for her comrade and husband of forty-seven years in his dotage.

Harry had first come know Pamela Frank in the eighties through their shared social circle and her engagement, as both a photographer and a patron of the arts, with the movement against apartheid: Pam had prevailed on Harry, back in 1986, to help her bring a South African play called *Asinamali!* to Broadway. Years later, as his marriage was unraveling and their friendship evolved into something else, she loved reminding him that in fact the first time they'd met was decades before. Pam recounted the story to me with delight, at lunch near their apartment years later, after pulling out an iPhone whose plastic case, she acknowledged with a laugh, she'd found on the Internet: it was imprinted with photos of Harry in his pomp. The image she wanted to show me, though, was a black-and-white shot she pulled up on the screen of the star who became her husband, looking glamorous and pensive in an airport in the Bahamas, that she'd taken there in 1963.

At the time, Pam was an undergrad at Syracuse who'd gone to the Bahamas for spring break. She was traveling with her best friend, a young woman called Neilia Hunter who, on the beach there a few days before, had met a young politician from Delaware—Joe Biden—who became her husband. Nine years later, just after Biden was first elected to the U.S. Senate in 1972, Neilia died in a tragic car crash. For her college bestie Pam, their trip was a poignant memory. It also yielded her glancing encounter with Harry, which occurred when she'd found herself behind him in line at the airport—he was en route to visit Sidney Poitier on Cat Island—and asked if she could take his picture. When they reconnected years later, she beamed as she did when she recounted the tale to me.

Luckily for him, this woman fate put in his path became a cherished partner whose own family—Pam had two kids from a previous marriage—he also loved and admired. Theirs was a relationship of pacific acceptance and care of which Dr. Neubauer, among others in their circle, keenly approved. They were on a Hawaiian vacation, at Carlos Santana's house in Kauai, when they decided to plan a wedding whose guest list would be comprised solely of family and a few friends. Only when they decided to expand that list slightly, by inviting Harry's long-suffering therapist, did they learn that Dr. Neubauer had passed. They fondly joked that he'd signed off, at least where this patient was concerned, after completing his job. Harry's last marriage was one, as his daughter Gina would say at his memorial, after acknowledging her and Pam's rocky start, that she credited not merely with helping heal many of the broken parts within him, but with "helping you realize that love is real, and can be trusted."

As Harry began a slow retreat from public life, Pam also

helped him begin documenting the life story that he'd long threatened to write out but never had. To that point, all he had managed to write down were a few stray lines: he was a lover of words and stories who could talk for hours, but who never wrote much. But now in need of money, and with intimations of his mortality growing louder, he acquiesced to hiring a writer, the veteran *Vanity Fair* correspondent Michael Shnayerson, to help. He chose Shnayerson for the gig, the latter told me, for reasons more political than literary: Shnayerson's previous books included an account of a group of brave West Virginians' battle against the depredations of Big Coal that was right up Harry's street, and accorded with his daughter Adrienne's husband's work there with the United Mine Workers. The result of the months of afternoons Shnayerson spent interviewing Harry at his and Pam's apartment off 72nd Street was his memoir, *My Song*.

A documentary about his life appeared the same year, *Sing Your Song*. Both projects were framed in relation to a bit of advice from Paul Robeson that became his watchword: "Get them to sing your song, and they'll want to know who you are." The impetus and funding for *Sing Your Song* came from a Canadian producer and music industry impresario—Michael Cohl was a chairman of the Live Nation conglomerate—whose first choice to direct the film didn't work out.

Cohl granted Harry and Gina, a producer on the project,

freedom to tell his story as they wished. The resulting film, which began with a visit to his youthful haunts in Harlem with a camera crew in 2005, and took six years to complete, covered much of the same ground as his memoir. But it also focused on his work as an activist—especially in working with and for incarcerated youth, and in a mentorship and movement-building organization that he called The Gathering for Justice—that enlivened those years. Shaped into a narrative by the veteran film editor who became *Sing Your Song*'s director, Susanne Rostock, it opened Sundance and played to particularly thrilled audiences in Europe, where in the winter of 2011 I caught up with Harry before the German premiere at the Berlin Film Festival.

There at the elegant Hotel Adlon by the Brandenburg Gate, Harry was in ebullient yet forceful form. He was especially pleased to be sharing the film in that city, freighted with history's weight, whose transformations since the fifties he'd seen up close. Another bit of history he'd played a role in shaping was the recent ascent to the White House of a president—Barack Obama—whose father he'd helped bring to the U.S. from Kenya in the sixties, and in whose mien and grace, and wild popularity among American liberals, one sensed a strong echo of Belafonte's own. Harry voiced great pride in Obama's ascent. He also felt great relief at his administration's supplanting what he saw as the villainy of

George W. Bush. But ever the radical, he'd also quickly grown frustrated at Obama's moderate policies. There by the Brandenburg Gate, on a frigid February day, he told me why: "I don't know if he's got a rabbit in the hat, that he'll pull out at some point, startle all of us," Harry rasped. "But there has been no indication whatsoever that there is a rabbit in the hat. There's been no indication that he even has a hat. So I treat him like I would treat anybody who sits in the seat of power. You push them as much as you can, awaken social consciousness, and try and go out there and make him do things."

30

Longevity, as Dr. King said, has its place. King wasn't there to see it, but after 1968, Harry had to face the descent from the mountaintop their movement had climbed—the victories they won and the "beloved community" they made; the stake that King's dream gained in mainstream American culture. Defining a movement's core aims and beliefs can feel even harder after the euphoria of its initial success. And Harry lived long enough to spend not years but decades on the lifetime-achievement-award circuit—and thus take part in celebrating and quarreling over the more radical legacies of a movement that was ongoing more than fifty years after his friend's demise.

Harry continued to pour himself into cause after cause. In his old age, he started—or as often helped his kids start—

new organizations and projects predicated on growing what they all called The Movement. "All of us see the world as it exists," he wrote of his heroes in *My Song*. "Fewer envision what it might look like if made to change; and fewer still try to put together the people and ideas that will make change happen." To the several younger generations of activists and ex-gang-members and performers-with-a-conscience who called him "Mr. B" and sought lessons at his feet, he was a visionary himself. And a wholly uncompromising one, at that, who insisted until the end that "when Black people began to be anointed by the trinkets of this capitalist society and began to become big-time players and began to become heads of corporations, they became players in the game of our own demise."

The targets of that remark were many people—America's Black CEOs and Black politicians and Black power-brokers—who saw their positions as a direct result of, and testament to, the success of the civil rights movement. But to go back to what Henry Louis Gates Jr. observed, Harry was radical long before it was chic, and remained so long after it wasn't. If anything, he grew more so as his voice grew raspier and, with each passing year, felt less compunction about expressing his distaste for shmoozing the elite upon whose funds activists for social justice were, to his mind, too dependent. He much preferred taking the subway to meet with members of New York's Service Employees International Union,

SEIU 1199, with whose nurses and health aides he led a project meant to help working people enrich and narrate their lives through the arts, called Bread and Roses. When this old lefty did deign to mix with the "donor class," it was often to upbraid the spineless politics of too many of the Black politicians he'd once worked hard to get into office. Proclaiming philanthropy to be a big part of the problem, he also decried an era, recalled *New York Times* columnist Charles Blow, wherein "we've become a shadow of need rather than a vision of power."

That same sentiment animated an organization Harry founded in 2005 after he turned on a TV in a hotel room in Washington and glimpsed footage of a five-year old girl in Florida being handcuffed by police after growing unruly at school. Enraged by what he'd seen, and the larger criminalization of young people of color, he convened a meeting of old civil rights comrades and activists of eminence, called the Gathering of the Elders, to discuss what to do. He was disappointed by his wizened peers' reluctance, ensconced as they were in their own organizations and ways, to launch a new collective effort to combat the prison-industrial complex that had become "the New Jim Crow." So he resolved instead to meet and to organize with the people—incarcerated youth and their families—most impacted by an iniquitous system. With an LA-based lawyer named Connie Rice and a young activist called Carmen Perez, who became their group's director, he launched The Gathering for Justice as a series of summits involving ex-inmates and gang members and "peacemakers" across the country. Ten years later, in 2015 and with the organization's varied projects going strong, an anniversary gala was held at Harlem's Apollo Theater to raise funds for a new initiative called the Justice League, dedicated to orchestrating actions to protest police violence and brutality. They had just gotten NBA stars like LeBron James to warm up at Brooklyn's Barclays Center in a T-shirt they made—I CAN'T BREATHE, it said—to decry the death by asphyxiation of a New York man, Eric Garner, whose murder by police helped spark the #BlackLivesMatter movement.

The Apollo was the site, too, for Harry's ninety-third birthday. From the audience, I watched Common and Sheila E. wish him well—and an ailing Mighty Sparrow, the calypso great, who came from Trinidad to sing "Jean and Dinah" and make nice with a beloved onetime pretender to his throne. Harry rose on his cane to acknowledge the assembly as they celebrated the renaming of a Harlem branch of the New York Public Library in his honor, and to sway along as a beatboxing Doug E. Fresh accompanied Usher in a joyous rendition of a Stevie Wonder–styled "Happy Birthday" punctuated by a few choruses of "Day O." By the time of Harry's ninety-fifth, held at Town Hall in midtown, savvy attendees knew not to expect the man himself to turn up. The birthday party doubled as a fundraiser for the nonprofit Sankofa.org, which Harry and his daughter Gina had founded while working together on *Sing Your Song* to connect artists and entertainers with grassroots work for social justice and against violence. Among the group's affiliates and friends who serenaded Mr. B that night were Alicia Keys and John Legend and Common. Danny Glover and Alfre Woodard and Michael Moore offered tributes. Bill T. Jones danced.

With Harry's kids now establishing foundations predicated on furthering his legacy—David also had one—Harry made sure that part of that legacy, by the end, included his fierce opposition to a fellow New Yorker whose ascent to high office appalled him. On the eve of Donald Trump's fateful first election to the presidency in November 2016, Harry published an op-ed in *The New York Times* to place what was at stake in historical context. He invoked Langston Hughes—"America never was America to me, and yet I swear this oath—America will be!"—and recalled how the country in which Hughes wrote those lines, when Harry was eight years old, was a nation ruled by racist violence. He recounted the mighty movements it had taken to upend that system; to defeat Jim Crow and win voting rights for all; to gain full rights for women and to fight "to let people of all

genders and sexual orientations stand in the light." He jux-
taposed Hughes's vision of America as a noble aspiration to
seek to that of a candidate who saw the nation's greatness as
"some heavy, dead thing that we must reacquire," who "with
his simple, mean, boy's heart . . . wants us to follow him blind
into a restoration that is not possible and could not be endured if it were." Trump had promised, if elected, to "blow
up" Washington. Harry warned that "what old men know is
that things blown up—customs, folkways, social compacts,
human bodies—cannot so easily be put right."

It was a few weeks after Trump won that first time that
Harry sat down at Riverside Church with Noam Chomsky
and Amy Goodman from *Democracy Now!* "I thought I had
seen it all and done it all," he said, "only to find out that,
at eighty-nine, I knew nothing." He'd been so cheered, he
said, by young people's support for the campaign of Bernie
Sanders—only to be thrown back to facing down the darkest
demons of a country where "the Ku Klux Klan, for some of
us, is a constant." He served, the day after a sad inaugura-
tion, as an honorary cochair of the Women's March in Washington. Some months later, at the Carnegie Museum of Art
in Pittsburgh, he gave his last public talk. He was uncertain
on his feet but firm in his horror at what had befallen us.
"The country made a mistake," he told the assembled. "And
I think the next mistake might very well be the gas chamber.

And what happened to Jews [under] Hitler is not too far from our door."

Gas chambers may not have been among the ugly fruits of Trump's first term, but on the eve of his defeat in 2020, Harry wrote another op-ed for the *Times* to voice his indignation at Trump's courting the Black vote after four years during which the he'd sought to roll back civil rights and praised vile racists as "good people"; watched Black people die at shocking rates from Covid-19; and loosed the military on backers of #BlackLivesMatter. "We have learned exactly how much we have to lose," he wrote, "and we will not be bought off by the empty promises of the flimflam man."

Harry didn't live long enough to see the flimflam man's lies return him to power. On April 25, 2023, weeks after his ninety-sixth birthday, Harry died at home on 72nd Street. The cause was congestive heart failure. He'd been declining, by then, for some time. Their last time out in public, Pam told me, was for that celebration of his ninety-third birthday at the Apollo on March 1, 2020. The ensuing years of COVID-19, as the world shut down and then slowly opened back up, coincided with his retreating from it and not emerging again. His balance was already faulty; now his vision, already gone in one eye, was claimed by glaucoma in the other. He spent his days listening to music and to Pam, reading him the newspaper or books. He was able, with the help of a device that described what was happening on screen, to watch TV. He spoke often, she told me, about his gratitude— for the life he'd lived, the doors he'd walked through and knocked down, for where he'd ended up. Some weeks before he died, his daughters Adrienne and Gina came to say goodbye. And then, he told Pam as he entered hospice at home, he didn't want to see anyone else. There was, at the end, no death rattle or upset. There was Pam holding his hand, and his last peaceful breaths.

———

Among his last wishes, conveyed to his kin, was that no big memorial be held in his honor. But Harry's kids are as headstrong as he was. The next year, on what would have been his ninety-seventh birthday, I filed into Riverside Church and, with a thronging crowd, shuffled past where Bernie Sanders was checking his phone and Whoopi Goldberg and Bill de Blasio walked past a silver-maned Angela Davis, resplendent in a red-checked scarf, to join 1,500 other celebrants of his gigantic life. The assembled rose, in their kente cloth or suits, and a troupe of African drummers led his kin down the aisle. The dais was warmed, for his eulogists, by harmonies from Sweet Honey in the Rock. And then the night's speakers, for the next three hours, attached themselves in memories and praise to a man who, as the rapper

Chuck D of Public Enemy fame put it, "who taught all of us to turn 'me into we.'"

There were his last aged comrades from campaigns with King's SCLC and SNCC; his sister Angela Davis and his protégé Carmen Perez, her fellow prison abolitionist; his friend Kenneth Cole, with whom he worked on AIDS research. Spike Lee offered a succinct homily, borrowed from sports: "Harry was the GOAT." His adoring grandkids evoked images of warm hugs and cleaning chicken bones with his teeth. His daughter Gina, who'd pulled this gathering together, recalled how she'd won his attention in professional contexts where she called him Harry in ways she never did when calling him Dad, and turned away from public accomplishments to give thanks for private ones. "Your journey in psychotherapy and your efforts to right the wrongs," she told him, "are inspiring to those around you." Whoopi Goldberg told us all: "Every time you see folks of color on television, remember: Harry put them there." She looked skyward: "Thanks, Harry."

Harry, as Auden once said of Yeats, had become his admirers. But it was hard not to feel that he also remained, in certain ways, beyond them. I was reminded of what Harry's friend Chris Blackwell, the Jamaican impresario who brought reggae music to the world, told me at his plush home on Jamaica's north coast, which became Harry's favorite place to contemplate life. "Just walking down the street with Harry, you felt inadequate," Blackwell said. That Harry also often felt inadequate to the tasks he set himself was key to his journey's trials and joys. "Sometimes I look at my life," he said in the film made in Cuba, "and I don't quite see who I am, or who I think I am. It's like I'm too many things." What got him through, he said, and let him meet each new experience with surety and vim, was that he'd realized early on how vital his quest to feel differently—to know who he was—could be to his life and his people.

He'd been born to a society that taught him that America's Indians were savages and that Africa wasn't home to his mighty ancestors but to Tarzan and apes. He did his damnedest to bury such stereotypes "not only because I considered it the correct thing to do, or because it was something that had to be proven to white people. I felt desperately that black people ourselves needed it. In so many places we knew nothing about ourselves, about our history. We didn't know who we were." There at Riverside Church, his mourners knew who Harry was, indeed—and knew who we were, too, because he'd shown us how to turn awareness of our past, and disquiet at our present, into cause not for paralysis or shame but for sustenance and song. Though dark was falling, daylight had come. It was time to go home.

Acknowledgments

4 pages [TK]

ACKNOWLEDGMENTS

Notes

CHAPTER 1

2 **"Warning:** Calypso Next": "Warning: Calypso Next New Beat; R.I.P. for R'n'R?," *Variety*, December 11, 1957, 1+.

2 **"proved that Americans"**: Harry Belafonte interviewed by Alex Miller in the companion book to *The Long Road to Freedom: An Anthology of Black Music* (Buddha Records/BMG, 2001), 21.

5 **"we carried ourselves"**: Harry Belafonte, author interview, September 9, 2010.

5 **"I think people"**: Johnny Carson as quoted by Henry Louis Gates Jr., "Belafonte's Balancing Act," *The New Yorker*, August 18, 1996. https://www.newyorker.com/magazine/1996/08/26/belafontes-balancing-act.

6 **"Perhaps in the end"**: Harry Belafonte with Michael Shnayerson, *My Song: A Memoir* (Knopf, 2011), 11.

6 **"first Negro matinée idol"**: Jack Hamilton, "The Storm Over Belafonte," *Look*, June 25, 1957.

7 **"a house slave"**: Harry Belafonte, interview by Ted Leitner on KFMB 760 AM, San Diego, CA, October 10, 2002: "In the days of slavery there were those slaves who lived on the plantation, and there were those slaves who lived in the house. You got the privilege of living in the house if you served the master . . . exactly the way the master intended to have you serve him. Colin Powell was permitted to come into the house of the master." As quoted in "Belafonte Won't Back Down from Powell Slave Reference," CNN, October 16, 2002. https://web.archive.org/web

NOTES

/20091225224441/http://archives.cnn.com/2002/US/10/15/bela
fonte.powell/

7 **"Have you seen"**: Odetta as quoted by Gates, "Belafonte's Balancing Act."

8 **"Belaphony"**: "Folk Singing: Sibyl with Guitar," *Time*, November 23, 1962. (Text by John McPhee but published without byline.)

8 **"Everything about him"**: Bob Dylan, *Chronicles: Volume One* (Simon & Schuster, 2004), 68.

9 **"the voices of others"**: Belafonte to Miller, *The Long Road to Freedom*, 21.

11 **"the best-looking"**: Barack Obama, *Dreams from My Father* (Crown, 2007), 51.

CHAPTER 2

13 **300,000 West Indians:** See Nancy Foner, ed. *Islands in the City: West Indian Migration to New York* (University of California Press, 2001); and Calvin Holder, "The Causes and Composition of West Indian Immigration to New York City, 1900–1952," *Afro-Americans in New York Life and History* 11, no. 2 (January 1987).

13 **"like a dark sea"**: Paule Marshall, *Brown Girl, Brownstones* (Random House, 1959), 2.

14 **"this man country"**: Marshall, *Brown Girl*, 13.

17 **"Of the 12.5 million"**: The invaluable database of the Slave Voyages Project is now hosted at Rice University and freely accessible via www.slavevoyages.org. Philip D. Curtin's seminal text in the field is *The Atlantic Slave Trade: A Census* (University of Wisconsin Press, 1972).

18 **"a modern life"**: C. L. R. James, "Appendix: From Toussaint L'Ouverture to Fidel Castro," in *The Black Jacobins: Toussaint L'Ouverture and the San Domingo Revolution* (Vintage, 1963), 391. For a contemporary exploration of James's arguments, and the Caribbean's broader influence on modern world culture, see Joshua Jelly-Schapiro, *Island People: The Caribbean and the World* (Knopf, 2016), 3-15.

19 **"formerly colonial coloured peoples"**: James, "Appendix," 410.

20 **"buckra, buckra"**: Vincent Brown, *The Reaper's Garden* (Harvard University Press, 2008), 1.

20 **Tacky's Revolt:** See Vincent Brown, *Tacky's Revolt: The Story of an Atlantic Slave War* (Harvard University Press, 2022) and Tom Zoellner, *Island on Fire: the Revolt that Ended Slavery in the British Empire* (Harvard University Press, 2022).

20 **"a state of rebellion"**: Joshua Jelly-Schapiro, "Back in the Day-O: Harry Belafonte on His New Memoir, *My Song*," *New York*, October 6, 2011. https://nymag.com/arts/books/features/harry-belafonte-2011-10/.

24 **"Africa for the Africans"**: See Colin Grant, *Negro with a Hat: The Rise and Fall of Marcus Garvey* (Oxford University Press, 2008); and Marcus Garvey, *The Philosophy and Opinions of Marcus Garvey: Or, Africa for the Africans*, ed. Amy Jacques Garvey (Africa World Press, 1987), 1923.

25 **"sex was a powerful thing"**: Harry Belafonte with Michael Shnayerson, *My Song: A Memoir* (Knopf, 2011), 23.

CHAPTER 3

28 **"great white fleet"**: See Joshua Jelly-Schapiro, "¡Bananas!" in *Unfathomable City: A New Orleans Atlas*, ed. Rebecca Solnit and Rebecca Snedeker, (University of California Press, 2014), 73-81.

29 **"an environment that sang"**: Belafonte as quoted by Jeanne Van Holmes, "Belafonte Gives It All He's Got," *The Saturday Evening Post,* April 20, 1957.

29 **"white and blue-eyed"**: Harry Belafonte with Michael Shnayerson, *My Song: A Memoir* (Knopf, 2011), 33.

31 **"Third World Superstar"**: https://afropop.org/articles/the-international-bob-marley.

31 **"Slave driver"**: Bob Marley, "Slave Driver," *Catch a Fire* (Island LP 9241, 1973).

32 **"Look to the east"**: See Rex Nettleford, M. G. Smith, and Roy Aguier, *The Rastafarians in Kingston, Jamaica* (University of the West Indies Press, 1967), 5.

33 **"fishmongers were the best"**: Belafonte, *My Song*, 40.

36 **"People from the Caribbean"**: Joshua Jelly-Schapiro, "Back in the Day-O: Harry Belafonte on His New Memoir, *My Song*," *New York*, October 6, 2011, https://nymag.com/arts/books/features/harry-belafonte-2011-10/.

38 **"Those class distinctions"**: Belafonte as quoted by Jeanne Van Holmes, "Belafonte Gives It All He's Got," *The Saturday Evening Post,* April 20, 1957.

39 **"deeply rooted certainty"**: Harry Belafonte with Michael Shnayerson, *My Song: A Memoir* (Knopf, 2011), 44.

42 **"diaspora in the flesh"**: Michael Eldridge, "Remains of the Day-O: A Conversation with Harry Belafonte," *Transition* 92 (2002), 117.

46 **Double V campaign:** The campaign was sparked by a letter from James G. Washington, a cafeteria worker in Wichita, Kansas, which *The Pittsburgh Courier* published on January 31, 1942—and quickly followed, in its ensuing weekly editions, with drawings to launch the campaign. See Pat Washburn, "The Pittsburg Courier's Double V Campaign in 1942," Association for Education in Journalism, Michigan State University, August 1981, https://files.eric.ed.gov/fulltext/ED205956.pdf.

CHAPTER 5

50 **"my first friend":** Harry Belafonte with Michael Shnayerson, *My Song: A Memoir* (Knopf, 2011), 59.
51 **"I couldn't understand it":** Poitier as quoted by Arnold Shaw in *Belafonte: An Unauthorized Biography* (Chilton Company, 1960), 26.
51 **"I firmly believe":** Poitier as quoted by Henry Louis Gates Jr., "Belafonte's Balancing Act," *The New Yorker,* August 18, 1996, https://www.newyorker.com/magazine/1996/08/26/belafontes-balancing-act.
54 **Since the 1920s:** On Robeson's larger life and legacies, see Martin Duberman, *Paul Robeson: A Biography* (New Press, 1995).
54 **"something grand and wonderful":** Belafonte, *My Song,* 62.

CHAPTER 6

58 **"political theater":** See Erwin Piscator, *The Political Theatre: A History, 1914-1929,* trans. Hugh Rorrison (Avon Books, 1978).
59 **"a big kid":** Marguerite Belafonte as quoted by Arnold Shaw in *Belafonte: An Unauthorized Biography* (Chilton Company, 1960), 46.
63 **"impressed me also":** Eleanor Roosevelt, My Day, United Feature Syndicate, May 21, 1948. Viewable online via the Eleanor Roosevelt Papers Project, George Washington University, https://erpapers.columbian.gwu.edu/my-day.
64 **notices in *DownBeat*:** "Unknown Belafonte Just Sang Self Into Roost Job," *DownBeat,* March 11, 1949, 12.
65 **"I became subservient":** Harry Belafonte, interviewed by Charles Werth on KRHM 94.7 FM Los Angeles, c. 1958, as quoted by Shaw, *Belafonte,* 61.
65 **unheralded sides:** Belafonte's first-ever commercial recording was for Monte Kay's Roost label, in early 1949—he sang "Lean on Me" and his

own composition, "Recognition," with Howard McGhee and His Orchestra (Roost 501, 78-rpm single). For Capitol in June 1949, Belafonte recorded eight songs with the Pete Rugolo Orchestra; four of these—"Close Your Eyes," "Sometimes I Feel Like a Motherless Child," "I Still Get a Thrill," and "Deep as the River"—were also released by the label, once his star had risen in 1955, as a 7-inch EP, *Close Your Eyes* (Capitol EAP 1-619).

65 **"exploiting the feelings"**: Monte Kay as quoted by Shaw, *Belafonte*, 71.

66 **became important**: See Shaw, *Belafonte*, 74-82, and Colin Escott's companion book to the five-CD box set *Island in the Sun* (Harry Belafonte, Bear Family Records BCD 16262, 2002), "The Sage," 6-8. Text reproduced on Rock's Back Pages: https://www-rocksbackpages-com.proxy.library.nyu.edu/Library/Article/harry-belafonte-iisland-in-the-suni.

66 **"difficult to sustain"**: Joe Smith, *Off the record interview with Harry Belafonte*, August 22, 1987, The Joe Smith Collection (1986–1988), Library of Congress. Audio: https://www.loc.gov/item/jsmith000093/.

67 **"old, weird America"**: Greil Marcus describing the world figured by Harry Smith's *Anthology of American Folk Music*, in *Invisible Republic: Bob Dylan's Basement Tapes* (Henry Holt, 1987), 89. A later edition of the book was published with the title *Old, Weird America* (Picador, 2011).

CHAPTER 7

69 **John Lomax and his son Alan**: See John Szwed, *Alan Lomax: The Man Who Recorded the World* (Viking, 2010), 31-58.

69 **concept of "folklore"**: William John Thoms's first use of the term "Folk-lore" appeared in a letter, composed under the pen name Ambrose Merton, published on August 22, 1846, in *The Athenæum*, the prominent British journal in which Thoms's regular column Folk-lore would subsequently appear.

000 **Seeger, the privileged son**: See David King Dunaway, *How Can I Keep From Singing?: The Ballad of Pete Seeger* (Random House, 2008) and Ann Pescatello, *Charles Seeger: A Life in American Music* (University of Pittsburgh Press, 1982).

71 **the Congress of Industrial Organizations**: On the CIO's entwinements with American culture in the 1930s and after, see Michael Denning, *The Popular Front: The Laboring of American Culture in the Twentieth Century* (Verso, 1996), 1-50.

71 **People's Songs:** Per the newsletter that announced the organization's founding on December 31, 1945, by Pete Seeger, Alan Lomax, and Lee Hays et al., People's Songs aimed to "create, promote, and distribute songs of labor and the American people." *People's Songs Newsletter, vol. 1, no. 1* (1945). See also Robbie Lieberman, *"My Song Is My Weapon": People's Songs, American Communism, and the Politics of Culture, 1930–1950* (University of Illinois Press, 1989), 67-84.

72 **folk revival's foremost:** On the roles of "the Village" in the folk revival and larger history of modern American music, see David Browne, *Talkin' Greenwich Village: The Heady Rise and Slow Fall of America's Bohemian Music Capital* (Da Capo, 2024); Ronald D. Cohen, *Rainbow Quest: The Folk Music Revival and American Society, 1940–1970* (University of Massachusetts Press, 2002); and Dave Van Ronk with Elijah Wald, *The Mayor of MacDougal Street* (Da Capo, 2013).

72 **the Yiddish-speaking son:** See Peter D. Goldsmith, *Making People's Music: Moe Asch and Folkways Records* (Smithsonian Institution Press, 1998).

74 **an agoraphobic connoisseur:** See David Suisman, "Listening to the City," *Smithsonian Folkways Magazine* Fall/Winter 2012; Benjamin Serby, "Tony Schwartz's New York Recordings: Sound, Place, and Civic Identity," Gotham Center for New York City History, July 13, 2017, https://www.gothamcenter.org/blog/tony-schwartzs-new-york-recordings-sound-place-and-civic-identity; and the Kitchen Sisters, "Tony Schwartz: 30,000 Recordings Later," produced for NPR's *Lost and Found Sound* and aired on *All Things Considered*, February 26, 2004, https://kitchensisters.org/present/tony-schwartz-30000-recordings-later/.

74 **Zulu-derived song:** On "Wimoweh" and the larger roles of Zulu music in global pop from the 1930s to the present, see Joe Boyd, *And the Roots of Rhythm Remain* (Ze Books, 2024), especially chapter 1, "Mbube," 17–78.

75 **"now a folk minstrel":** Goings on About Town, *The New Yorker*, October 27, 1951, 8. (Published without byline but written by Rogers E. M. Whitaker.)

75 **"It moves many to tears":** Barry Ulanov, "In Person: Harry Belafonte," *Metronome*, January 1952, 17. The full passage: "Harry has the most attractive package in the folk field . . . Combining his newly found stentorian tones with the unrestrained guitar of Craig Work, Harry moves and tears his way through a variety of songs—Negro and Brazilian Negro, American white and European—the best of music that man has made and hasn't signed, the best of the music of the primitive and the untutored. It moves many to tears, this presentation of our international folk heritage; it also makes much of a music that has been pret-

tied and fussed and turned tastelessly indoors in the past. Here, it has a beat and a boom and a fine representative quality, and it's here to stay this way, I think, and more power to it—if there can be any more power to it than what the new Belafonte gives it."

77 **"where folk music was heading":** Harry Belafonte with Michael Shnayerson, *My Song: A Memoir* (Knopf, 2011), 106.

79 **"He was an actor":** Maurice Zolotow, "Belafonte," *The American Weekly,* May 10, 1959.

CHAPTER 8

80 **series of singles:** Belafonte's first dates for RCA Victor, after being signed to the label by Dave Kapp, found him singing "Chiminey Smoke" and "A-Roving" (RCA Victor 47-4676, 7-inch 45-rpm single, 1952); "Man Smart (Woman Smarter)"—his first calypso—along with "Jerry (This Timber Got to Roll)," "Scarlet Ribbons," and "Shenandoah," all released on *Harry Belafonte Sings "Man Smart" and Other Folk Songs* (RCA Victor EPA 412, 7-inch 45-rpm EP). His fourth date for the label, on February 6, 1953, saw him record, at Dave Kapp's insistence, a Japanese song previously recorded by a solder-singer named Richard Bowers—"Gomen Nasai" reached #19 on *Billboard*'s singles chart (RCA Victor 47-5210, 7-inch, 45-rpm, 1953).

82 **Preminger was notorious:** Nathaniel Rich, "The Deceptive Director," *The New York Review of Books,* November 6, 2008. https://www.ny books.com/articles/2008/11/06/the-deceptive-director/. The notable biographies of Preminger discussed by Rich are Foster Hirsch, *Otto Preminger: The Man Who Would Be King* (Knopf, 2007) and Chris Fujiwara, *The World and Its Double: The Life and Work of Otto Preminger* (Faber and Faber, 2008). Preminger's own take on his life is Otto Preminger, *Preminger: An Auobiography* (Doubleday, 1977).

84 **"an opulent production":** "Carmen Jones," *Variety,* December 31, 1953.

84 **"a big musical shenanigan":** Bosley Crowther, "Updated Translation of Bizet Work Bows," *The New York Times,* October 29, 1954.

85 **"More than any movie":** James Baldwin, "On the Horizon: Life Straight in De Eye," *Commentary,* January 1955. Republished as "Carmen Jones: The Dark Is Light Enough," in Baldwin's *Notes of a Native Son* (Beacon Press, 1955).

000 **recording his first:** Peter Guralnick, *Last Train to Memphis: The Rise of Elvis Presley* (Little, Brown, 1994).

87 **"Although he is brown-skinned"**: Attaway as quoted by Arnold Shaw in *Belafonte: An Unauthorized Biography* (Chilton Company, 1960), 252.

87 **"At the present stage"**: Attaway as quoted by Shaw, *Belafonte*, 252.

88 **"not *too* black . . . "**: Harry Belafonte with Michael Shnayerson, *My Song: A Memoir* (Knopf, 2011), 146.

CHAPTER 9

93 **"mysteries of native rituals"**: Les Baxter, *Ritual of the Savage* (Capitol T288, 1951), liner notes. On exotica and marketing "adult music" in the 1950s, see Elijah Wald's *How The Beatles Destroyed Rock 'N' Roll* (Oxford University Press, 2009), especially chapter 14, "Big Records for Adults," 184–198.

94 **"any kind of music"**: Marek as quoted in "Music: The Compleat Diskman," *Time*, December 14, 1959. See also Marek's obituary: Bernard Holland, "George P. Marek, 84, Author and Ex-RCA Victor Official," *The New York Times*, January 8, 1987.

94 **"very much an intellectual"**: Belafonte to Michael Eldridge, "Remains of the Day-O: A Conversation with Harry Belafonte," *Transition* 92 (2002),125. Among Marek's own books are *The Good Housekeeping Guide to Musical Enjoyment* (Rinehart, 1949); *Puccini: A Biography* (Simon & Schuster, 1951); and *Gentle Genius: The Story of Felix Mendelssohn* (Funk & Wagnalls, 1972).

000 **"sell 60 million copies"**: Quincy Jones audio commentary on *Thriller: Special Edition* (Sony 2-504422, 2001, CD).

99 **"integrated trip through the West Indies"**: Bill Attaway, liner notes to *Calypso* (RCA Victor LPM-1248, 1956, LP).

100 **"jazz feeling"**: Tony Scott as quoted by Dom Cerulli, "Belafonte: Where Do We Go From Here?" *DownBeat*, April 4, 1957.

100 **Burgie was born in Brooklyn**: See Irving Burgie, *Day-O!!! The Autobiography of Irving Burgie* (Caribe Publishing, 2006).

102 **both by King Radio**: King Radio (aka Norman Span) first recorded "Man Smart (Woman Smarter)" in 1936 (Decca 17287, 10" 78rpm) and "Brown Skin Girl" in 1950 (Kiskedee 5006, 10" 78rpm). To hear his orignal version of "Man Smart,": https://www.youtube.com/watch?v=50nS2ldCXJk.

102 **"Miss Lou"**: See Mervyn Morris, *Miss Lou: Louise Bennett and Jamaican Culture* (Ian Randle Publishers, 2014); and Garnette Cadogan, "Mother of Us All," *The Caribbean Review of Books* 10 (November

2006). Among Bennett's cherished collections of poetry and tales are *Anancy Stories and Poems in Dialect* (The Gleaner Co. Ltd., 1944) and *Jamaica Labrish* (Sangster's, 1966).

103 **"Day Dah Light":** Louise Bennett, *Jamaican Folk Songs* (Folkways 6846, 1954; rereleased on CD and for digital download by Smithsonian Folkways in 2004), https://folkways.si.edu/louise-bennett/jamaican-folk-songs/caribbean-world/music/album/smithsonian. "Day Dah Light" was also included in the British scholar Tom Murray's book *Folk Songs of Jamaica* (Oxford University Press, 1952).

103 **Edric Connor:** Edric Connor and the Caribbeans, *Songs from Jamaica*, released on the Argo label in the U.K. (RG 33, 1954). See also Edric Connor's autobiography, *Horizons: The Life and Times of Edric Connor* (Ian Randle Publishers, 2006), with a foreword by George Lamming and introduction by Bridget Brereton and Gordon Rohlehr.

103 **"laugh at themselves":** Attaway, *Calypso* liner notes.

105 **"I took that song":** Belafonte to Gwen Ifill, *PBS News Hour*, November 14, 2011, https://www.pbs.org/video/pbs-newshour-harry-belafonte-reflects-on-life-as-a-singer-actor-and/.

CHAPTER 10

106 **"admit in court":** In 1960 in federal court in New York, a composer and ex-associate of Burgie's named Lionel Walters, who'd registered a U.S. copyright for an adapted version of "Iron Bar" in 1954, filed suit against Shari Music Publishing Corporation, Irving Burgie aka Lord Burgess, Radio Corporation of America (RCA-Victor Record Division), and Harry Belafonte for stealing his work—a suit (126 U.S.P.Q. 268 (S.D.N.Y. 1960)) that bore no fruit for Walters but in which Burgie stated that he'd borrowed the melody for "Jamaica Farewell" from the Jamaican folk song, also called "Iron Bar," upon which Walters's piece was also based. https://blogs.law.gwu.edu/mcir/case/walters-v-shari-music-publishing-corp/.

000 **"gets the royalties":** Irving Burgie, author interview, October 22, 2009. On Burgie's continuing control of his copyrights and dramatic-stage and audio-visual rights to his catalog, and the administrative agreement he signed with BMG Publishing Group in 2011, after BMG's acquisition of Cherry Lane Publishing in 2010, see press release from his lawyers, issued December 7, 2010: https://www.mclaughlinstern.com/mclaughlin-stern-client-irving-burgie-reacquires-copyrights-to-signature-songs-of-harry-belafonte/.

NOTES

107 **"not even calypso"**: Belafonte as quoted in "The Calypso Craze," *Newsweek*, February 27, 1957.

108 **"hysterical type of fervor"**: Harry Belafonte, letter to the *New York Mirror*, May 5, 1957, as quoted by Ronald D. Cohen, *Rainbow Quest: The Folk Music Revival and American Society, 1940–1970* (University of Massachusetts Press, 2002), 99.

108 **dominant fad:** See Michael Eldridge and Ray Funk's companion book to *Calypso Craze: 1956–57 and Beyond*, a six-CD box set (Bear Family Records BCD 16947 GK, 2014).

108 **calypso's putative hold:** See Michael Eldridge, "Bop Girl Goes Calypso: Containing Race and Youth Culture in Cold War America," *Anthurium: A Caribbean Studies Journal*, vol. 3, no. 2 (December 2005). https://anthurium.miami.edu/articles/46/files/submission/proof/46-1-83-1-10-20180919.pdf.

109 *Miss Calypso*: Maya Angelou, *Miss Calypso* (Liberty LRP 3028, 1956, LP).

109 **Geoffrey Holder:** See Geoffrey Holder, "That Fad from Trinidad," *New York Times Magazine*, April 21, 1957; and Shane Vogel, *Stolen Time: Black Fad Performance and the Calypso Craze* (University of Chicago Press, 2018), 132-162.

110 **King Solomon sang:** King Solomon, "Belafonte," *Calypso Kings and Pink Gin* LP (Cook 01185, 1957; rereleased on CD and for digital download by Smithsonian Folkways in 2012), https://folkways.si.edu/calypso-kings-and-pink-gin/caribbean-world/music/album/smithsonian.

111 **Emory Cook:** See Joshua Jelly-Schapiro, "Sounds of Our Times," *The Believer*, July 2013. https://www.thebeliever.net/sounds-of-our-times/.

111 **"No More Rocking and Rolling"**: Mighty Sparrow, "No More Rocking and Rolling," *King Sparrow's Calypso Carnival* LP (Cook 00920, 1959; rereleased on CD and for digital download by Smithsonian Folkways in 2012), https://folkways.si.edu/the-mighty-sparrow/king-sparrows-calypso-carnival/caribbean-world/music/album/smithsonian.

111 **made his name:** Woody Guthrie, *Dust Bowl Ballads*, vols. 1 and 2 (Victor P 27, P 28, ten-inch, 78 rpm, 1940). Guthrie's own tall-tale account of his backstory is *Bound For Glory* (Dutton, 1943). His biographers include Joe Klein, who wrote *Woody Guthrie: A Life* (Random House, 1980), and Ed Cray, whose book is *Ramblin Man: The Life and Times of Woody Guthrie* (W. W. Norton, 2004).

114 **"I need your help"**: Harry Belafonte with Michael Shnayerson, *My Song: A Memoir* (Knopf, 2011), 149.

114 **"wasn't nonviolent by nature"**: Belafonte, *My Song*, 150.

NOTES

115 **"where your anger comes from"**: Belafonte, *My Song*, 11.
116 **"I collapsed mentally"**: Belafonte as quoted by David Gelman, "Belafonte: Profile-IV," *New York Post*, April 18, 1957.
117 **"blocks and breakthroughs"**: Belafonte, *My Song*, 135.
118 **hold him "spellbound"**: Eleanor Harris, "The Stormy Success of Harry Belafonte," *Redbook*, May 1958, as quoted by Judith E. Smith, *Becoming Belafonte: Black Artist, Public Radical* (University of Texas Press, 2014), 129.
118 **"smallest decision on his own"**: Harris as quoted by Smith, *Becoming Belafonte*, 129.
119 **"from birth and love"**: See the exhibition's accompanying book by Edward Steichen et al., *The Family of Man* (The Museum of Modern Art with Simon & Schuster and the Maco Magazine Corporation, 1955).
119 **"supervising every facet"**: Lincoln Haynes, "Theater," *Pasadena (CA) Independent*, December 22, 1955, as quoted by Smith, *Becoming Belafonte*, 131.
120 **"illustrate the basic likeness"**: Alfred Duckett, "Backstage with Belafonte: Big Gamble Pays Off for Harry," *Chicago Daily Defender*, August 22, 1956.

CHAPTER 11

124 **"careful limits of good taste"**: "New Pix Code OKs Miscegenation, Drinking, Smuggling, If 'In Good Taste,'" *Variety*, September 15, 1954.
125 **"inflame Negro people"**: Geoffrey Shurlock to Harry Cohn of Columbia Studios, May 13, 1955; letter stored in *Island in the Sun* folder in the Motion Picture Association of America files, Margaret Herrick Library, Academy of Motion Picture Arts and Sciences, Los Angeles, as quoted by Judith E. Smith, *Becoming Belafonte: Black Artist, Public Radical* (University of Texas Press, 2014), 148.
125 **"We should get a lift"**: Zanuck at screenplay conference on October 25, 1955, recorded in *Island in the Sun* script materials in the Twentieth Century Fox Collection, University of Southern California Cinematic Arts Library, as quoted by Smith, *Becoming Belafonte*, 149.
126 **"an American lake"**: Lieutenant Commander Ephraim R. Mclean, Jr., "The Caribbean—An American Lake," *United States Naval Institute Proceedings*, July 1941, vol. 67, no. 7 https://www.usni.org/magazines/proceedings/1941/july/caribbean-american-lake. See also Harvey Neptune, *Caliban and the Yankees: Trinidad and the United States Occupation* (University of North Carolina Press, 2007).

127 **"Coca-Cola advertisements"**: Patrick Leigh Fermor, *The Traveler's Tree: A Journey Through the Caribbean Islands* (New York Review Classics, 2010), 50.

127 **fifty-five-gallon oilcans**: See Stephen Stuempfle, *The Steelband Movement: The Forging of a National Art in Trinidad and Tobago* (University of Pennsylvania Press, 1996), and Kim Johnson, *The Illustrated Story of Pan*, (2nd ed., Pangea, 2021).

128 **successfully sued**: In 1948, a federal judge in New York ordered Morey Amsterdam and associates to pay $150,000 to Lord Invader and Lionel Belasco for profiting from Invader's lyrics and Belasco's melody for "Rum and Coca-Cola"—but also allowed Amsterdam to retain the song's U.S. copyright (*Baron* v. *Leo Feist* 78 F. Supp. 686 (S.D.N.Y. 1948)). The plaintiffs' lawyer in the case wrote a boastful account of his role in winning this judgment in Louis Nizer, *My Life in Court* (Doubleday, 1961). See also the Music Copyright Infringement Resource, Columbia Law School and USC Gould School of Law: http://mcir.usc.edu/cases/1940-1949/Pages/baronfeist.html.

129 **"I'd like to ask you, sir"**: Harry Belafonte with Michael Shnayerson, *My Song: A Memoir* (Knopf, 2011), 163.

129 **"who and what I was"**: Belafonte in *A veces miro mi vida (Sometimes I Look at My Life)*, directed by Orlando Rojas (ICAIC, 1982).

129 **"decision of those I work for"**: Belafonte, *My Song*, 164.

130 **"fucking each other to death"**: Belafonte as quoted by Henry Louis Gates Jr., "Belafonte's Balancing Act," *The New Yorker,* August 18, 1996, https://www.newyorker.com/magazine/1996/08/26/belafontes-balancing-act.

130 **"men of remarkable gifts"**: *Calypso Dreams*, directed by Geoffrey Dunn and Michael Horne (Caribbean Tales Worldwide, 2003).

132 **"WEDS WHITE DANCER"**: "Belafonte Weds White Dancer," *Amsterdam News,* April 13, 1957.

CHAPTER 12

133 **"integrate her company"**: Julie Belafonte in conversation with Cindy Campbell, John Kane, and Gina Belafonte on WBAI 99.5 FM, New York, June 16, 2015, as quoted by Ian Zack, "Julie Robinson Belafonte, Dancer, Actress, and Activist, Is Dead at 95," *New York Times*, March 21, 2024.v

134 **first photo shoot**: Jack Hamilton, "The Storm Over Belafonte," *Look*, June 25, 1957.

134 **"Many Negroes are wondering"**: "Will Harry's Marriage Affect His Status as Matinee Idol?" *Amsterdam News,* April 20, 1957.

134 **"Why I Married Julie"**: Harry Belafonte, "Why I Married Julie," *Ebony,* July 1957. "I believe in integration," he began his piece, "and work for it with all my heart and soul. But I did not marry Julie to further the cause of integration. I married her because I was in love with her and she married me because she was in love with me."

134 **"interracial marriage hinders"**: Commentary alongside Belafonte, "Why I Married Julie."

135 **"complete say about the style"**: "Harry Belafonte Gets Own TV Hit," *Chicago Defender,* October 8, 1955.

135 **"an adequate representation"**: Charles Mercer, "TV Displays Timidity Toward Negro, Is View," *Racine (Wisconsin) Journal Times,* October 5, 1955, as quoted by Judith E. Smith, *Becoming Belafonte: Black Artist, Public Radical* (University of Texas Press, 2014), 127.

135 **"maintain artistic integrity"**: Alfred Duckett, "Backstage with Belafonte: Belafonte Tells Ideas About Race," *Chicago Daily Defender,* August 23, 1956.

135 **"most important sociological film"**: Hilda See, "The Dandridge Story: 'Island in the Sun' Defies Old Rule with Dot, Justin," *Chicago Daily Defender,* February 2, 1957.

135 **"It stinks"**: "A Word or Two from Mr. Belafonte," *New York Post,* July 10, 1957.

136 **"kicking ass and taking names"**: John O. Killens, *Youngblood* (Dial Press, 1955), 426.

138 **"a new way forward"**: Harry Belafonte, as guest columnist for Dorothy Kilgallen's The Voice of Broadway, "New Era A-Dawning for the Negro," *New York Journal-American,* October 24, 1957.

140 **"With his bestselling recordings"**: James Goldwasser for the Chris Calhoun Agency, "Overview" of the Harry Belafonte Archive sold to the Schomburg Center for Research in Black Culture, New York Public Library, March 2020.

140 **"an industry as vast"**: "The Negro Star in Television," *New York Herald Tribune TV and Radio Magazine,* June 24, 1956.

141 **write songs in New York:** Belafonte discusses his work with Lord Melody in *Calypso Dreams,* directed by Geoffrey Dunn and Michael Horne (Caribbean Tales Worldwide, 2003).

141 **"ethnic sources of all nations"**: "TV/Radio What's On: Singer Works for $500 After Turning Down 45Gs," *New York Daily News,* August 6, 1957.

141 **"a tremendous lift"**: John P. Shanley, "Belafonte with Allen," *New York Times,* November 10, 1958.

142 **"highest individual fee"**: "Harry Belafonte's Five-Year BBC-TV Deal Sets Record," *Variety*, December 24, 1958.

142 **"a portrait of Negro life"**: "An Evening with Harry Belafonte," *TV Guide*, December 5–11, 1959.

144 **Born in Alabama**: See Ian Jack, *Odetta: A Life in Music and Protest* (Beacon Press, 2020).

144 **"There are many singers"**: Harry Belafonte, liner notes *to Odetta, My Eyes Have Seen* (Vanguard VRS-9059, 1959).

145 **"as good an excuse"**: Cecil Smith, "Belafonte Show Fine Christmas Gift," *Los Angeles Times*, December 14, 1959.

145 **"truly delightful"**: "Tonight with Belafonte," *Variety*, December 16, 1959.

145 **"a fascinating hour"**: Harry Harris, "Belafonte Show Delights," *Philadelphia Inquirer*, December 11, 1958.

145 **"The Belafonte show was zenith"**: A. S. (Doc) Young, The Big Beat, *Los Angeles Sentinel*, December 17, 1959.

147 **DEAR DADDY:** Adrienne and Shari Belafonte to Harry Belafonte, Western Union Telegram, December 10, 1958. Harry Belafonte Papers, Sc MG 933, Schomburg Center for Research in Black Culture, Manuscripts, Archives, and Rare Books Division, New York Public Library.

147 **THE GREATEST HOUR:** Richard Ashby to Harry Belafonte, Western Union Telegram, December 11, 1958.

147 **HIGHLIGHT OF MY LIFE:** Charles White to Harry Belafonte, Western Union Telegram, December 11, 1958.

148 **THE ADULT MAGNIFICENCE:** Joan Blondell to Harry Belafonte, Western Union Telegram, December 10, 1958.

148 **MANY A MOON:** Mr. and Mrs. Billy Eckstine to Harry Belafonte, Western Union Telegram, December 10, 1958.

148 **LONG ROAD TO FULFILLMENT:** Sidney Poitier to Harry Belafonte, Western Union Telegram, December 11, 1958.

148 **HOLE IN THE HEAD:** Poitier to Belafonte, Western Union Telegram, December 10, 1958.

CHAPTER 13

150 **nationally syndicated column:** Eleanor Roosevelt, My Day, October 20, 1958 (United Feature Syndicate). Viewable online via the Eleanor Roosevelt Papers Project, George Washington University, https://www2.gwu.edu/~erpapers/myday/displaydocedits.cfm?_y=1958&_f=md004254.

NOTES

151 **"For all the passion"**: Harry Belafonte with Michael Shnayerson, *My Song: A Memoir* (Knopf, 2011), 225.

152 **"one number erases the next"**: Per Arnold Shaw in *Belafonte: An Unauthorized Biography* (Chilton Company, 1960), 272-273: "As an album, the *Blues* LP is disappointing not only in its choice of material but in its lack of pace and variety. There is a sameness of mood (self-pity) of dynamics (soft) and of tempo (slow), which give the album a suprising monotony for a Belafonte album. As a friendly critic has said: 'One number erases the next.'"

153 **Bob Bollard:** Joshua Jelly-Schapiro, "Sounds of Our Times," *The Believer*, July 2013.

153 **"with protest in it"**: Nat Hentoff, "The Faces of Belafonte," *The Reporter*, July 1959.

154 **"rallying cries for justice"**: Belafonte, *My Song*, 147.

155 *New York 19*: Tony Schwartz, *New York 19* (Folkways FW05558, 1954, LP; rereleased on CD and for digital download by Smithsonian Folkways in 2007), https://folkways.si.edu/tony-schwartz/new-york-19/documentary/album/smithsonian.

156 **"natural as a morning sunrise"**: A. S. (Doc) Young, The Big Beat, *Los Angeles Sentinel*, December 17, 1959.

157 **"you've crossed a line"**: Belafonte, *My Song*, 220.

157 **"To change the culture"**: Belafonte, *My Song*, 221.

CHAPTER 14

158 **"long march through the institutions"**: For Stuart Hall's influential arguments on culture's roles in shifting hegemonic ideas around inclusion and difference, see his oft-cited article "Gramsci's Relevance for the Study of Race and Ethnicity," *Journal of Communication Inquiry* 10, no. 5 (1986), and *Stuart Hall: Critical Dialogues in Cultural Studies*, Kuan-Hsing Chen and Kevin Morley, eds. (Routledge, 1996), 131-150. The phrase "long march through the institutions" was in fact coined by Rudi Dutschke, a key figure of the so-called New Left in Germany, around 1967 and in reference to the long march of Mao's Red Army in China.

000 **"Committee for the Defense"**: Minutes of board meeting of the Committee for the Defense of Martin Luther King, Jr., and the Struggle for Freedom in the South, convened at the home of Judge Hubert Delany, March 6, 1960. Harry Belafonte Papers, Sc MG 933, Schomburg Center for Research in Black Culture, Manuscripts, Archives and Rare Books Division, New York Public Library.

160 **"Thanks a lot":** Letter from Harry Belafonte and Sidney Poitier to Sammy Davis, Jr., May 5, 1960. Harry Belafonte Papers, Sc MG 933, Schomburg Center for Research in Black Culture, Manuscripts, Archives and Rare Books Division, New York Public Library.

161 **"cords of memory shall lengthen":** Letter from Martin Luther King, Jr., to Harry Belafonte, March 9, 1960. Harry Belafonte Papers, Sc MG 933, Schomburg Center for Research in Black Culture, Manuscripts, Archives and Rare Books Division, New York Public Library.

164 **"I'll be voting for Kennedy":** See Belafonte's campaign ad for Kennedy, as posted online by the John F. Kennedy Library Foundation, "IFP:135-F80-1M Harry Belafonte 1960 Campaign Spot": https://www.youtube.com/watch?v=C21r3qfRk4Y.

165 **"If you anoint him":** Harry Belafonte with Michael Shnayerson, *My Song: A Memoir* (Knopf, 2011), 218.

CHAPTER 15

169 **"the true nerve center":** Harry Belafonte with Michael Shnayerson, *My Song: A Memoir* (Knopf, 2011), 252.

170 **"Americans and men of all lands":** Typewritten draft of a telegram sent by Harry Belafonte et al. to John F. Kennedy, the White House , April 1962. Harry Belafonte Papers, Sc MG 933, Schomburg Center for Research in Black Culture, Manuscripts, Archives and Rare Books Division, New York Public Library.

171 **"hold you responsible":** Typewritten draft of a telegram sent by Harry Belafonte et al. to Robert F. Kennedy, the Department of Justice , April 1962. Harry Belafonte Papers, Sc MG 933, Schomburg Center for Research in Black Culture, Manuscripts, Archives and Rare Books Division, New York Public Library.

172 **"the effectiveness of the march":** Martin Luther King, Jr. to Harry Belafonte, Western Union Telegram, July 22, 1963. Harry Belafonte Papers, Sc MG 933, Schomburg Center for Research in Black Culture, Manuscripts, Archives, and Rare Books Division, New York Public Library.

174 **"I'll do it":** Poitier also tells this story in *Sing Your Song*, the 2011 documentary about Belafonte's life produced by Michael Cohl, Gina Belafonte et al., directed by Susanne Rostock (Thought Engine Media Group).

NOTES

CHAPTER 16

183 **"the clown in Frank's court"**: Harry Belafonte with Michael Shnayerson, *My Song: A Memoir* (Knopf, 2011), 179.

184 **"Martin's pedestal"**: Belafonte, *My Song*, 299.

184 **"I wanted to do everything"**: Belafonte, *My Song*, 322.

185 **"bigger. More complex"**: Belafonte, *My Song*, 322.

185 **"Of all the black kids"**: Belafonte, *My Song*, 312.

186 **"serving two families"**: David Belafonte as quoted by Belafonte, *My Song*, 347.

CHAPTER 17

188 **"There's so much anger"**: Baldwin as quoted by Harry Belafonte with Michael Shnayerson, *My Song: A Memoir* (Knopf, 2011), 266. Belafonte also described his recollections of meeting to Taylor Branch in Branch's interviews with him for his *America in the King Years* trilogy, March 6–7, 1985, archived in the Taylor Branch Papers, University of North Carolina, Chapel Hill, Southern Historical Collection, Louis Round Wilson Library, audiocassette box 73.

189 **"froth combined with naivete"**: Belafonte, *My Song*, 266.

190 **"we have a party"**: Robert F. Kennedy as quoted by Belafonte, *My Song*, 267.

190 **"What you're asking"**: Jerome Smith as quoted by Belafonte, *My Song*, 267.

191 **"kiss it goodbye"**: Jerome Smith, *Jet*, June 13, 1963, as quoted by Taylor Branch, *Parting the Waters: America in the King Years, 1954–1963* (Simon & Schuster, 1989), 810.

000 **"many accomplished people"**: Lorraine Hansberry as quoted by Branch, *Parting the Waters*, 810.

191 **"You may think"**: Belafonte, *My Song*, 269.

192 **"Robert Kennedy consults"**: Layhmond Robinson, "Robert Kennedy Consults Negroes Here About North," *New York Times*, May 25, 1963. The reporter to whom Baldwin leaked news of the meeting also wrote a follow-up story the next day: Layhmond Robinson, "Robert Kennedy Fails to Sway Negroes at Secret Talks Here," *New York Times*, May 26, 1963.

192 **"not using the great prestige"**: Baldwin as quoted by Robinson, "Robert Kennedy Consults."

193 **"what Bobby needed to hear"**: King as quoted by Belafonte, *My Song*, 270.

193 **reported another article:** Cabell Phillips, "Civil Rights Fight Is Put to Kennedy. Humphrey Sure of Success If President Is Vigorous," *New York Times,* May 25, 1963.

193 **"the violence in Birmingham":** Phillips, "Civil Rights Fight."

194 **"Our task and our obligation":** John F. Kennedy, "Televised Address to the Nation on Civil Rights," June 11, 1963. (https://www.jfklibrary .org/learn/about-jfk/historic-speeches/televised-address-to-the -nation-on-civil-rights)

CHAPTER 18

195 **"toward transformation and into history":** Rebecca Solnit, *Wanderlust: A History of Walking* (Viking, 2000), 64.

197 **"last chance to stage":** Harry Belafonte with Michael Shnayerson, *My Song: A Memoir* (Knopf, 2011), 270.

197 **"Are you telling us":** Belafonte, *My Song,* 272.

198 **the first volume:** Taylor Branch, *Parting the Waters: America in the King Years, 1954–1963* (Simon & Schuster, 1989), 834-838.

000 **Rustin's expulsion from King's inner circle:** On Bayard Rustin's harassment by the FBI and Hoover's allies in Congress, which also threatened to derail the March on Washington later that summer of 1963, see John D'Emilio, *Lost Prophet: Bayard Rustin and the Quest for Peace and Justice in America* (The Free Press, 2003), 345–349.

199 **"Not the least":** Letter from Jack O'Dell to Martin Luther King, Jr., June 12, 1963. Martin Luther King, Jr. Papers, 1950-1968, Martin Luther King Jr., Center for Nonviolent Social Change, Inc., Atlanta.

200 **"steered Martin away":** Belafonte, *My Song,* 274.

201 **"what it means":** Belafonte, *My Song,* 281.

000 **as FOIA requests:** David J. Garrow, *The FBI and Martin Luther King, Jr.* (W.W. Norton, 1981), 9–20, 122–182.

202 **Walking is interrupted falling:** Garnette Cadogan, "Black and Blue," *Freeman's: Arrival* (Grove, 2015), https://lithub.com/walking-while -black/.)

CHAPTER 19

203 **"not out of demagoguery":** Belafonte, *My Song,* 280.

203 **"power of celebrity":** Belafonte, *My Song,* 279.

204 **"pushing my friends":** Belafonte, *My Song,* 280.

NOTES

205 **"generally disliked":** FBI, "Summary of Interview with Jay Richard Kennedy," January 1957, Harry Belafonte papers, Sc MG 617, Schomburg Center for Research in Black Culture, Manuscripts, Archives, and Rare Books Division, the New York Public Library.

205 **"agent of the Peking government":** FBI, "Morse Nelson Report on Harry Belafonte," 1964, Harry Belafonte Papers, Sc MG 617, Schomburg Center for Research in Black Culture, Manuscripts, Archives, and Rare Books Division, New York Public Library.

206 **"living, breathing, snarling":** Belafonte, *My Song*, 284.

207 **"all public accommodations":** Title II of the Civil Rights Act of 1964, Pub. L. No. 88-352, 78 Stat. 241 (1964), codified as amended at 42 U.S.C. §§ 2000a–2000h-6 (2012). https://www.archives.gov/mile stone-documents/civil-rights-act.

213 **"he wasn't' right":** Belafonte, *My Song*, 304.

213 **"what we want":** Carmichael's first public proclamation of "Black power" as a slogan and cause occurred on June 16, 1966, in Greenwood, Mississippi, at a rally during James Meredith's March Against Fear. https://www.youtube.com/watch?v=2lAm2QhFqlo.

214 **"dumb and dangerous":** Belafonte, *My Song*, 308.

214 **"out of the islands":** Belafonte, *My Song*, 308.

CHAPTER 20

217 **"appealed to everybody":** Bob Dylan, *Chronicles: Volume One* (Simon & Schuster, 2004), 68.

219 *Come Back, Africa*: Lionel Rogosin Films, 1959. Restored by Milestone Films in 2012 and now available for streaming on the Criterion Channel: https://www.criterionchannel.com/come-back-africa.

222 *An Evening with Belafonte/Makeba*: RCA Victor LSP-3420, LP.

222 **"Ndodemnyama we Verwoerd":** Michela E. Vershbow, "The Sounds of Resistance: The Role of Music in South Africa's Anti-Apartheid Movement," *Inquiries* 2, no. 6, 2010, http://www.inquiriesjournal.com/arti cles/265/the-sounds-of-resistance-the-role-of-music-in-south -africas-anti-apartheid-movement.

223 **her solo albums:** Miriam Makeba, *Miriam Makeba* (RCA Victor LPM 2267, 1960, LP); *The Voice of Africa* (RCA Victor LSP 2845, 1964, LP); *Makeba Sings!* (RCA Victor LSP 3321, 1965, LP).

223 **got into hot water:** On the larger controversy around *Graceland*, and Paul Simon's later rapprochement with the ANC, see Joe Berlinger's documentary film *Under African Skies* (Radical Media, 2012).

225 **"proved that Americans"**: Harry Belafonte interviewed by Alex Miller in the companion book to *The Long Road to Freedom: An Anthology of Black Music* (Buddha Records/BMG, 2001), 21.

CHAPTER 21

228 **"Do you believe"**: Harry Belafonte in interview with Robert F. Kennedy, *The Tonight Show,* February 5, 1968. "Harry Belafonte Sits Down with Robert F. Kennedy" (Carson Entertainment Group), https://www.youtube.com/watch?v=3ZQnIdK7EGY.

228 **foremost lineup:** Harry Belafonte, notebook and guest list for *The Tonight Show,* 1968. Harry Belafonte Papers, Sc MG 933, Schomburg Center for Research in Black Culture, Manuscripts, Archives and Rare Books Division, New York Public Library.

229 **"give up your citizenship"**: Paul Newman, interview with Harry Belafonte, *The Tonight Show,* February 8, 1968. Audio from *The Sit-In: Harry Belafonte Hosts the Tonight Show,* directed by Yoruba Richen (Peacock/NBC 2020).

229 **"don't have faith"**: Martin Luther King Jr., interview with Harry Belafonte, *The Tonight Show,* February 8, 1968, *The Sit-In.*

230 **"most critical period"**: Footage included in *The Sit-In* and also online in "Martin Luther King, Jr.: 'The Economic Problem is the Most Serious Problem" (Carson Entertainment Group), https://www.youtube.com/watch?v=fmauhsmcY2c.

232 **weeklong "sit-in"**: Joan Walsh, "49 Years Ago, Harry Belafonte Hosted the Tonight Show—and It Was Amazing," *The Nation,* February 6, 2017, https://www.thenation.com/article/archive/49-years-ago-harry-belafonte-hosted-the-tonight-show-and-it-was-amazing/.

CHAPTER 22

236 **"head-on collision"**: "Book Gave Belafonte Idea for Harlem Spec," *New York Sunday News,* February 20, 1966, as quoted by Judith E. Smith, *Becoming Belafonte: Black Artist, Public Radical* (University of Texas Press, 2014), 221.

236 **"only become acquainted"**: Paul Gardner, "Dark Laughter in Snow White Land," *New York Times,* April 2, 1967.

237 **a historic speech:** Martin Luther King Jr., "Beyond Vietnam—A Time to Break Silence" speech at Riverside Church, New York, April 4, 1967.

Full audio and transcript: https://www.americanrhetoric.com/speeches /mlkatimetobreaksilence.htm.

239 **"institutional racism"**: Stokely Carmichael and Charles V. Hamilton, *Black Power: The Politics of Liberation* (Vintage, 1967), 2.

239 **"Belafonte is Black Power"**: Alfred Duckett, *Chicago Daily Defender*, March 2, 1968, 11.

CHAPTER 23

240 **"Television was the only thing"**: Henry Louis Gates Jr., "Belafonte's Balancing Act," *The New Yorker*, August 18, 1996, https://www.newy orker.com/magazine/1996/08/26/belafontes-balancing-act.

240 **"the best damn show"**: Alfred Duckett, *Chicago Daily Defender*, March 2, 1968, 11.

241 **"the tightest link"**: W. J. Weatherby, "Green Power—and Black—on Broadway," *The Guardian*, April 4, 1968, as quoted by Judith E. Smith, *Becoming Belafonte: Black Artist, Public Radical* (University of Texas Press, 2014), 235.

242 **"to the mountaintop"**: Martin Luther King Jr., "I've Been to the Mountaintop," address delivered at Bishop Charles Mason Temple, Memphis, April 3, 1968, in Clayborne Carson et al., eds., *A Call to Conscience: The Landmark Speeches of Dr. Martin Luther King, Jr.* (Warner Books, 2001). Audio recording from the Martin Luther King, Jr. Center for Nonviolent Social Change: https://www.youtube.com/watch?v =gC6qxf3b3FI.

244 **"going up in smoke"**: Harry Belafonte with Michael Shnayerson, *My Song: A Memoir* (Knopf, 2011), 331.

246 **"candidates, former candidates"**: Elizabeth Hardwick, "The Apotheosis of Martin Luther King," *New York Review of Books*, May 9, 1968, https://www.nybooks.com/articles/1968/05/09/the-apotheosis -of-martin-luther-king/.

249 **"the greatest terrorist"**: In January 2006 Belafonte led a delegation of American leftists to Venezuela and appeared on the weekly TV and radio broadcast of Venezuelan leader Hugo Chavez. "No matter what the greatest tyrant in the world, the greatest terrorist in the world, George W. Bush says, we're here to tell you: Not hundreds, not thousands, but millions of the American people . . . support your revolution," Belafonte told Chavez. Associated Press, "Belafonte: 'Bush Greatest Terrorist in the World," January 8, 2006, https://www.nbc news.com/id/wbna10767465.

249 **"take my family"**: Bernadette Carey, "Cats' Questions That Bug Belafonte," *Los Angeles Times*, August 25, 1968.

250 **"miracle in America"**: Nick Browne, "Would You Believe Harry Belafonte as a Jewish Angel?" *New York Times*, April 27, 1969.

CHAPTER 24

251 **"your best friend"**: Gina Belafonte, author interview, February 14, 2025.

252 **"American horror story"**: *The Sit-In: Harry Belafonte Hosts the Tonight Show*, directed by Yoruba Richen (Peacock/NBC 2020).

253 **"said the right things"**: Harry Belafonte with Michael Shnayerson,
My Song: A Memoir (Knopf, 2011), 337.

253 **"radical before it was chic"**: Henry Louis Gates Jr., "Belafonte's Balancing Act," *The New Yorker*, August 18, 1996, https://www.newyorker
.com/magazine/1996/08/26/belafontes-balancing-act.

253 **"new black militants"**: Elizabeth Hardwick, "The Apotheosis of Martin
Luther King," *New York Review of Books*, May 9, 1968, https://www.ny
books.com/articles/1968/05/09/the-apotheosis-of-martin-luther-king/.

255 **"what was celebrated"**: Hardwick, "The Apotheosis of Martin Luther
King."

255 **based on a short story**: Bernard Malamud, "Angel Levine," *Commentary*, December 1955; later published in Malamud, *The Magic Barrel*
(Farrar, Straus and Giroux, 1958).

255 **interns of color**: Donal Henehan, "A Grant Opens Door to Film Appren-
tices," *New York Times*, April 2, 1969. Belafonte's Ford Foundation-
funded apprenticeship program also received glowing attention in
Ebony, "Belafonte Plays Angel On and Off Screen," as cited by Judith E.
Smith, *Becoming Belafonte: Black Artist, Public Radical* (University of
Texas Press, 2014), 241.

255 **by Bill Gunn**: On Gunn's larger career and refractive legacies in film, see
Hilton Als et al., eds., *Till They Listen: Bill Gunn Directs America*, book
accompanying the exhibition of the same name (Artists Space, New
York, 2021). https://texts.artistsspace.org/guj6u4up.

257 **Zero Mostel walked with a limp**: On Mostel's larger life and career in
show business, see Jared Brown, (Atheneum, 1989).

257 **handled being blacklisted**: Zero and Kate Mostel Papers, Billy Rose
Theatre Division, The New York Public Library. "Transcript of Zero
Mostel's testimony before the Committee on Un-American Activities"
(1955), New York Public Library Digital Collections, https://digitalcol
lections.nypl.org/items/bbaba3c0-e53b-013c-c8e1-0242ac110002.

NOTES

257 **"at odds with itself"**: Roger Greenspun, "Screen: Kadar's 'The Angel Levine,'" *New York Times,* July 29, 1970.

258 **"advertising man's despair"**: Nick Browne, "Would You Believe Harry Belafonte as a Jewish Angel?" *New York Times,* April 27, 1969.

000 **only film produced**: Will Haygood, *Colorization: One Hundred Years of Black Films in a White World* (Knopf, 2021), 244.

259 **eulogized by Bob Marley**: Marley recorded "Buffalo Soldier" in 1978, but it wasn't released until after his death, on the posthumous album *Confrontation* (Island Records 90085-1, 1983, LP).

262 **"present to the American public"**: Sidney Poitier and Harry Belafonte on *The Dick Cavett Show* S1972E42. First aired on ABC, May 1, 1972.

262 **a firm crowd favorite**: On *Buck and the Preacher*'s popularity in Jamaica, see also Howard Campbell, "Roles that made Belafonte Popular in Jamaica," *Jamaica Observer,* August 21, 2018. https://www.jamaicao bserver.com/entertainment/roles-that-made-belafonte-popular -in-jamaica

000 **I-Roy**: I-Roy, "Buck and the Preacher" (Ackee ACK 518, 7-inch 45-rpm, 1973). https://www.youtube.com/watch?v=AiTHtAZ5ieU.

265 **series of albums**: Harry Belafonte, *Belafonte on Campus* (RCA Victor LSP-3779, 1967, LP); *Belafonte Sings of Love* (RCA Victor LSP-3938, 1968, LP); *Belafonte by Request* (RCA Victor LSP-4301, 1970, LP).

000 **final album for RCA**: Harry Belafonte, *Calypso Carnival* (RCA Victor LSP-4521, 1971, LP).

000 **Ralph McDonald**: Mel Tapley, "Ralph McDonald Is Beating His Way to the Top," *Amsterdam News,* January 29, 1977.

CHAPTER 25

269 **"the people of Grenada"**: William Drozdiak, "West German Rock Star Brings His Antimissile Message to the East," *Washington Post,* October 26, 1983. https://www.washingtonpost.com/archive/politics /1983/10/27/west-german-rock-star-brings-his-antimissile-message -to-east/a9a2745d-7848-4322-9aa4-b5acaee6a346/

269 **"a stubborn mate"**: James M. Markham, "West German Star Sings in the East," *New York Times,* October 27, 1983. https://www.nytimes.com /1983/10/27/arts/west-german-star-sings-in-the-east.html.

273 **unlicensed Hollywood IP**: *A veces miro mi vida (Sometimes I Look at My Life),* directed by Orlando Rojas (ICAIC, 1982) is in VHS form in Belafonte's archive at the Schomburg Center for Research in Black

Culture, Moving Image and Recorded Sound Division, New York Public Library. It's also now watchable online: https://www.youtube.com /watch?v=joz6da_at8U.

273 **"the most powerful impact"**: Belafonte, *A veces miro mi vida.*

273 **"History will absolve me"**: Fidel Castro, "La historia me absolverá," speech delivered by Castro in Cuban court, October 16, 1953, to defend himself against charges to the attack he led on the Moncada Barracks. Text secretly printed and distributed as a pamphlet in Cuba before Castro's took power in 1959, and thereafter by his government. See Fidel Castro, *La historia me absolverá* (Txalaparta, S.L., 1999).

000 **journalist Steve Hager**: JayQuan and Steven Hager, "The True Story Behind *Beat Street*," JayQuan.com, June 8, 2021, https://www.jay -quan.com/post/the-true-story-of-beat-street. Hager's early reporting includes a piece said to mark the first time the term "hip hop" appeared in print: Steven Hager, "Afrika Bambataa's Hip Hop," *Village Voice*, September 21, 1982.

276 **hip-hop's Cuban moment**: See Sujatha Fernandes, *Cuba Represent! Cuban Arts, State Power, and the Making of New Revolutionary Cultures* (Duke University Press, 2006), and *Inventos: Hip-Hop Cubano*, directed by Eli Jacobs-Fantauzzi (Clenched Fist Productions, 2005).

277 **"*Quién tiró la tiza?*"**: Clan 537, "Quién Tiró La Tiza?" (Cubanos en la Red Pruductions). https://www.youtube.com/watch?v=5UcG6pUhWIk.

278 **A notebook**: Harry Belafonte, Notebooks for Chatham workshop, 1975. Harry Belafonte Papers, Sc MG 933, Schomburg Center for Research in Black Culture, Manuscripts, Archives and Rare Books Division, New York Public Library.

279 **an eponymous LP**: *Turn the World Around* (CBS 86045, 1977, LP).

279 **lent his talents**: See Michael Davis, *Street Gang: The Complete History of Sesame Street* (Viking, 2008), TK.

280 **its musical numbers**: *The Muppet Show* (season 3, episode 14, orig. airdate February 19, 1979) is available in full on Disney+. Clips of "The Banana Boat Song" and "Turn the World Around" are on YouTube: https://www.youtube.com/watch?v=P-4xyg4PU-U, https://www.you tube.com/watch?v=ErhJlkdlYfw.

281 **"the ability to love"**: Jim Henson's Memorial Service, Cathedral of St. John the Divine, New York, May 21, 1990. Full video from The Jim Henson Collection: https://www.youtube.com/watch?v=mEArJX D8YFY.

CHAPTER 26

283 **A story on BBC News:** Michael Buerk, "Report on Famine in Ethiopia," BBC News, October 23, 1984, https://www.youtube.com/watch?v=XYOj_6OYuJc.

284 ***The Greatest Night in Pop:*** Directed by Bao Nguyen (Republic Pictures and MakeMake Entertainment, 2024). Distributed by Netflix: https://www.netflix.com/title/81720500.

284 **convinced Kragen:** Dennis Hunt, "The Unsung Organizers of 'We Are the World'," *Los Angeles Times*, February 13, 1985. https://www.latimes.com/archives/la-xpm-1985-02-13-ca-4769-story.html; Shari Belafonte, "What the Grammys Missed by Omitting Harry Belafonte from a Special Tribute Alongside Tina Turner and Tony Bennett," *Deadline*, February 9, 2024, https://deadline.com/2024/02/grammys-shari-belafonte-harry-belafonte-special-tribute-snub-1235817848/.

287 **"a place beset":** Moky Makura, "Live Aid Led to the Patronising 'Save Africa' Industry. We Don't Need a Musical About It," *Guardian*, October 10, 2023, https://www.theguardian.com/global-development/2023/oct/10/live-aid-led-to-the-patronising-save-africa-industry-we-dont-need-a-musical-about-it.

CHAPTER 27

291 **A massive concert:** Nelson Mandela 70th Birthday Tribute, Wembley Stadium, London, June 11, 1988. Extensive clips and documentation online including, e.g., highlights featuring remarks from Belafonte, Mandela, et al.: https://www.youtube.com/watch?v=hNpfJu1CVyc.

291 **Catherine O'Hara lip-synchs:** *Beetlejuice*, directed by Tim Burton (Warner Brothers, 1988). The "Day O" dinner scene: https://www.youtube.com/watch?v=AQXVHITd1N4.

291 ***Beetlejuice*-themed music video:** "Harry Belafonte—Day-O (Official 'Beetlejuice' Version) 1988 Music Video": https://www.youtube.com/watch?v=yfXoNKgc5c4&list=RDyfXoNKgc5c4&start_radio=1.

292 **original anti-apartheid songs:** Harry Belafonte, *Paradise in Gazankulu* (EMI-Manhattan Records 64-746971, 1988, CD, LP).

293 **entranced him on drives:** Joe Boyd, *And the Roots of Rhythm Remain* (Ze Books, 2024), 3-5.

294 **concerts featuring the living gods:** *Paul Simon, Graceland: The African Concert*, directed by Michael Lindsay-Hogg (Warner/Reprise, 1986, DVD). Clips posted online include Simon with Ladysmith Black

Mambazo, et al., "Paul Simon—Diamonds on the Soles of Her Shoes (from the African Concert, 1987)": https://www.youtube.com/watch ?v=Fmf9ZJ_YnOA&list=RDFmf9ZJ_YnOA&start_radio=1\.

294 **New York's Central Park:** *Paul Simon's Concert in the Park* (Warner Bros. Records 9 26737-2, 1991, double album on CD, cassette, LP). A concert video was also released at the time on VHS and laser disc, and in February 2025 was made available for streaming in original 4:3 aspect ratio on Apple TV+, Amazon Prime, et al.

295 **performing "Global Carnival":** Belafonte's performance at the National Sports Arena, Harare, Zimbabwe, a benefit for UNICEF, was filmed by a Kodak camera crew and edited into a film, *Harry Belafonte: Global Carnival* (directed by John Fortenberry, Kodak,1988): https://www.youtube.com/watch?v=_jXgTwMhjbU.

297 **the use of a 727:** In October 2024, Trump claimed on Fox News to have chartered a 727 for Mandela at a time when "the United States government wasn't helping him, no one was helping him," as interviewer George "Tyrus" Murdoch put it. In fact, Trump's faltering company, Trump Shuttle, which he'd put up for sale and would soon lose to his creditors, charged $130,000 for use of the plane. See Sonam Sheth, "Did Trump Let Mandela Use His Plane for Free?," *Newsweek*, October 18, 2024, https://www.newsweek.com/trump-nelson-mandela-plane -tyrus-interview-1971594.

297 **"saints become devils":** Harry Belafonte with Michael Shnayerson, *My Song: A Memoir* (Knopf, 2011), 398.

298 **"an old battery":** John Kifner, "Mandela Ends Tour of U.S. With Oakland Appearance," *New York Times*, July 1, 1990. Full transcript of Mandela's Oakland speech, from the *San Jose Mercury News*: https://www.mercurynews.com/2013/12/05/mandelas-1990-speech -in-oakland-we-cannot-turn-back/. Video: https://www.youtube.com /watch?v=SUcvjm9D2M4.

CHAPTER 28

299 **"you know you're getting old":** Harry Belafonte with Michael Shnayerson, *My Song: A Memoir* (Knopf, 2011), 395.

300 **"reversed voting rights":** John Leland, "Harry Belafonte Knows a Thing or Two About New York," *New York Times*, February 3, 2017, https://www .nytimes.com/2017/02/03/nyregion/harry-belafonte.html.

301 **controversial long-term studies:** *Three Identical Strangers*, directed by Tim Wardle (CNN Films, 2018).

NOTES

307 **stunning array of tapes:** Alex Miller, author interview, March 4, 2025.

308 **"African-matrixed":** Mari Evans, companion book to *The Long Road to Freedom: An Anthology of Black Music* (Buddha Records/BMG, 2001), 45.

309 **"beauty of this music":** Michael Eldridge, "Remains of the Day-O: A Conversation with Harry Belafonte," *Transition* 92 (2002), 130.

CHAPTER 29

311 **"the world order":** Belafonte on *Today*, interviewed by Katie Couric, September 11, 2001. Segment viewable online, as recorded and digitized by the Television Archive, on the Internet Archive, "NBC Sept. 11, 2001 8:31 am–9:12 am": https://archive.org/details/nbc200109110831-0912.

313 **"love had left the room":** Harry Belafonte with Michael Shnayerson, *My Song: A Memoir* (Knopf, 2011), 365.

315 **"love is real":** Gina Belafonte, remarks at Harry Belafonte: Celebration of Life, Riverside Church, New York, March 1, 2024, https://www.youtube.com/watch?v=Rp9X5wl1V3w.

318 **"seat of power":** Harry Belafonte, author interview, February 12, 2011; later published in edited form as Joshua Jelly-Schapiro, "Back in the Day-O: Harry Belafonte on His New Memoir, *My Song*," *New York*, October 6, 2011, https://nymag.com/arts/books/features/harry-belafonte-2011-10/.

CHAPTER 30

320 **"see the world":** Harry Belafonte with Michael Shnayerson, *My Song: A Memoir* (Knopf, 2011), 420.

320 **called him "Mr. B":** *Following Harry*, directed by Susanne Rostock (Belafonte-Nass-Zeng Productions, 2024).

320 **"anointed by the trinkets":** Harry Belafonte in conversation with Noam Chomsky and Amy Goodman for *Democracy Now!*, Riverside Church, New York, December 7, 2016, https://www.democracynow.org/2016/12/7/the_search_for_the_rebel_heart.

321 **"a shadow of need":** Charles Blow, "The Harry Belafonte Speech That Changed My Life," *New York Times*, April 25, 2023, https://www.nytimes.com/2023/04/25/opinion/harry-belafonte.html.

000 **Doug E. Fresh joined Usher:** "Doug E. Fresh and Usher Sing Happy Birthday to Harry Belafonte at the Apollo Theater": https://www.youtube.com/watch?v=VwEnT33TUnQ.

323 **"America never was"**: Langston Hughes, "Let America Be America Again" (1936), as quoted by Harry Belafonte, "What Do We Have to Lose? Everything," *New York Times*, November 7, 2016. https://www.nytimes.com/2016/11/07/opinion/campaign-stops/harry-belafonte-what-do-we-have-to-lose-everything.html.

324 **"things blown up"**: Belafonte, "What Do We Have to Lose?"

324 **"seen it all"**: Belafonte with Chomsky on *Democracy Now!*, December 7, 2016.

324 **"made a mistake"**: Mike Elk, "Harry Belafonte Tells Crowd at Likely Last Public Appearance: 'We Shall Overcome'," *Guardian*, October 21, 2017, https://www.theguardian.com/us-news/2017/oct/21/harry-belafonte-we-shall-overcome-trump.

325 **"We have learned"**: Harry Belafonte, "Trump is Standing in Our Way," *New York Times*, November 2, 2020, https://www.nytimes.com/2020/11/02/opinion/harry-belafonte-donald-trump.html.

327 **"'me' into 'we'"**: Chuck D and all other speakers—Angela Davis, Carmen Perez, Spike Lee, Kenneth Cole, Gina Belafonte, Whoopi Goldberg, et al.—remarks at Harry Belafonte: Celebration of Life, Riverside Church, New York, March 1, 2024, https://www.youtube.com/watch?v=Rp9X5w11V3w.

328 **"I look at my life"**: Belafonte in *A veces miro mi vida (Sometimes I Look at My Life)*, directed by Orlando Rojas (ICAIC, 1982).

328 **"correct thing to do"**: Belafonte in *A veces miro mi vida*.

Index

14 pages [TK]

INDEX